Re-inventing the Symptom

CONTEMPORARY THEORY SERIES

Series Editor: Frances Restuccia, Professor of English, Boston College

Re-inventing the Symptom

Essays on the Final Lacan

Edited by
Luke Thurston

OTHER

OTHER PRESS
New York

Copyright © 2002 Luke Thurston

Production Editor: Robert D. Hack

This book was set in 11 pt. Goudy by Alpha Graphics of Pittsfield, New Hampshire.

10 9 8 7 6 5 4 3 2

Library of Congress Cataloging-in-Publication Data

Re-inventing the symptom : essays on the final Lacan / edited by Luke Thurston.
    p. cm.—(Contemporary theory series ; 3)
    Includes bibliographical references and index.
    ISBN 1-59051-013-5
    1. Psychoanalysis. 2. Lacan, Jacques, 1901– I. Thurston, Luke. II. Series.

BF173 .R434 2002
150.19'5'092—dc21   2002029342

riverrun

for Parveen Adams

Contents

Foreword

We are extremely pleased to have Luke Thurston's *Re-inventing the Symptom* in the Contemporary Theory series from Other Press. This superb collection brings the appropriate sophistication to Lacan's *Le Sinthome* seminar, performing the balancing act of rendering Lacan's obscure text visible and accessible while showing admirable sensitivity to the ultimate untranslatability of Lacan's Joycean writing. A distinguished Joycean himself, Luke Thurston is in a prime position to edit a collection at such a formidable Lacanian/Joycean intersection.

We expect that this study will be regarded as necessary to maintaining a grip on what is happening in psychoanalytic theory today. Amateur Lacanians mainly acquainted with the early Lacan of the Imaginary, as well as those who have surpassed this first phase by engaging the Lacan of the Symbolic and the Real, have a great deal to gain from Thurston's collection, with its focus on the myriad implications of the *sinthome* as a tying together of the three rings (Imaginary, Symbolic, and Real) of the Borromean knot. *Re-inventing the Symptom* is not just another book in a field of study but one that expands that field.

Thurston's collection, moreover, aspires to clarify the aim of psychoanalysis, and thus to enhance the effectiveness of clincial work. Clinicians will profit as much from reading these meditations on Lacan's Joycean concept of the *sinthome* as will theorists—or literary and art critics, for that matter. This study helps to erode the already crumbling barrier between clinical and literary interpretations of Lacan's work. The untranslatable, disruptive excess that the concept of the *sinthome* italicizes clearly needs to be taken into account in both theory and practice.

The essays in this collection keep approaching the idea of the *sinthome* asymptotically from a variety of angles; the fertility of these readings of Lacan's twenty-third seminar would have impressed Lacan himself. They are written by experts freed rather than constrained by their expertise, by writers determined to allow Lacan's late work to exfoliate. It will go far in filling out the meanings of a term popping up all over the place; now the concept of *le sinthome* that was beginning to be employed promiscuously will have its weight restored.

While the Contemporary Theory series is by no means solely dedicated to Lacanian studies, *Re-inventing the Symptom* epitomizes what this series wants: smart, new theoretical work with important practical consequences, work that pushes the limits of theory as it now stands and exposes the necessary imbrication of theory with the world in which we live, day by day. This series does mean to offer a dwelling place for rich psychoanalytic work, as it welcomes all theory being done currently in, for example, feminist, queer, and other political contexts, film studies, or aesthetics—even theoretically inclined novels are invited. We want to cast an intricately woven but wide net.

Frances L. Restuccia
Series Editor

Acknowledgments

A way a lone a last a loved a long . . .

The contributors to the present volume should first of all be acknowledged: having enthusiastically climbed aboard this little vessel at its launch, they have endured its protracted journey back to Ithaca with enormous patience. My thanks also go to Richard G. Klein, who first introduced me to Roberto Harari, and especially to Frances Restuccia for bringing her exacting editorial skills to my assistance. And lastly, but not least, I thank my wife Paula for all her advice and support.

Luke Thurston

Introduction: Lacan's *pas-à-lire*

Luke Thurston

The essays collected in *Re-inventing the Symptom* explore the final period of Jacques Lacan's teaching, focusing in particular on his 1975–76 Seminar *Le sinthome*. The principal reason for choosing to address this last phase of Lacanian theory—and in the process to unravel some of its enigmas and shed light on its central questions—remains its non-accessibility, its near invisibility, to Anglo-American readers. The sheer difficulty of *reading* Lacan's last work, deriving in the first instance from the notorious restrictions that have been placed upon publication and translation, was the primary motivation that led to my assembling these essays. And, as the reader will quickly discover, this very problem of reading, in its multiple senses, is one of the major themes of the book.

The last years of the famous psychoanalyst's teaching have aroused widely divergent responses among his French interpreters. Some of Lacan's successors, indeed, have eulogized this period as his grand finale—his work on the topology of knots and his new conception of writing, inspired by Joyce, amounting to a crucial *alethia* that allows us to rethink the whole course of Lacanian theory—while others have seen in these last theoretical adventures merely signs of an old man's decline, symptoms, we might say, of terminal anecdotage (we will return to the significance of this quasi-Joycean coinage below).[1] Such arguments often hinge on the question of whether this last work entails a radical "epistemological break" from—or conversely remains strictly continuous with—the theories that Lacan had developed over the previous twenty-five years. If, for Dany Nobus, the idea of theoretical rupture and discontinuity in Lacan is ultimately implausible,[2] there remains, as several of the essays make clear, the risk that in our retrospective search for continuity and consistency, we succeed in effacing nothing so much as whatever is innovative or unexpected, whatever fails to conform to our familiar, already-understood Lacan. Of the late Seminars, *Le sinthome* in particular has been singled out as the introduction of an element radically *at odds* with the predominant emphases of Lacan's teaching—and by no less influential a critic than Slavoj Žižek.[3]

It is precisely this claim—that with *Le sinthome* Lacan introduced something radically new to his teaching—which Dominiek Hoens and Ed Pluth interrogate as the starting point for the opening article of the collection. Invoking the Freudian notion of the uncanny, Hoens and Pluth detect something strangely familiar in Lacan's invocation of an intransigent kernel immune to all interpretation, an "extimate" point at once fundamental to the Symbolic register and somehow situated beyond it. By refusing to take Lacan's rhetoric at face value, while at the same time taking seriously his "Borromean"[4] imperative to articulate anew the basic elements of psychoanalytic discourse, the authors are able to formulate some urgent questions bearing on several of Lacan's most important concepts. Supporting their argument with meticulous readings, they aim to show that the contours of Lacan's work in *Le sinthome* did not rise up suddenly from the foam of Joyce's texts, but in fact gradually took shape in the evolving theoretical landscape of the previous decades. It is especially intriguing, furthermore, that Hoens and Pluth are able to give the *sinthome* a specifically *literary* genealogy. Fifteen years before his final engagement with Joyce, Lacan had used another literary detour—into Claudel's *L'Otage*—to outline a cluster of ideas that manifestly anticipates the later problematic. By making this little-known moment of Lacan's teaching available to English readers, the authors are faithful to one of the fun-

damental aims of *Re-inventing the Symptom*: to make available new connections and new ways of reading.

If Hoens and Pluth find a knot of characteristic Lacanian preoc-
cupations behind the rhetoric of innovation in *Le sinthome*, Roberto
Harari argues that something genuinely new does emerge in Lacan's
final work, but at another level: that of thinking itself, of the specific
modality of psychoanalytic theory. For Harari, this can be best grasped
by relating the evolution of Lacan's thought to developments in contemporary physics, around so-called chaos theory. What we should not
miss in *Le sinthome*, Harari argues, beyond its elaborate engagement with
the topology of knots and Joycean writing, is its decisive break with the
"dialectical" logic that had governed the earlier phases of Lacanian
psychoanalysis. A "logic of the singular" is operating in this late work,
the author concludes, which properly belongs in the field opened up
by quantum mechanics: that is, the field of the undecidable and of paradox. If we are to absorb the lessons of this late work, Harari emphasizes,
we cannot continue to fall back on the more easily legible conceptual
foundations outlined by Lacan in the 1950s.

If, as Harari implies, contemporary interpretations of Lacan are
often unknowingly based on ideas and positions in fact adopted only
in his early work, an egregious case of such anachronistic reading would
seem to have occurred in relation to received "Lacanian" notions of
sexual difference. *Re-inventing the Symptom* aims to show how these
familiar—and often notorious—notions (The Woman, the Name-of-
the-Father, the phallus, etc.) are, precisely, reinvented in the last period
of Lacan's work.

Accordingly, Paul Verhaeghe and Frédéric Declercq set forth a
bold project: to read Lacan's Borromean work as a self-critique with
radical consequences for the entire orientation and theoretical bases of
analysis. Arguing that the *sinthome* is the concluding chapter in Lacan's
theory of the subject, they show that it at once clarifies the essential
sense of the term "subject" for Lacan, and modulates that sense signifi-
cantly by proposing a new model of the end of analysis. Indeed, the new
conception of identification entailed by the *sinthome* cannot be un-
tangled, Verhaeghe and Declercq claim, from the problematic of sexual
difference. This implies that a whole set of clinical and theoretical
questions, with directly political stakes, is to be reopened and rethought.
Thus, the Lacanian account of femininity, as famously outlined in the

seminar *Encore*, is given a new twist by the notion of the *sinthome*, which is, however, something yet to be grasped and negotiated by many analysts, for whom this late work remains encrypted, out of reach. Verhaeghe and Declercq offer a lucid and rigorous contribution to cracking the code and eliminating the distance.

A still more unorthodox attempt to articulate the *sinthome* and the question of femininity is made by Bracha Lichtenberg-Ettinger. The concept of the subject in Lacan, she argues, harbors an occult sexual politics; it is inherently bound up with a specifically phallic, masculinist version of the body, a version that would eradicate any trace of the "borderspace" where undecidable infractions of sexual difference are at work. It is precisely this liminal, unthinkable space that Lacan discovers in Joycean writing and names *sinthome*, argues Lichtenberg-Ettinger. She subsequently seeks to extend and amplify the aesthetic dimensions of that discovery by relating it in particular to the visual arts, through her concept of the "matrix." This powerful, original work is unencumbered by any sense of needing to pay fealty to conventional readings of Lacan, but with her heretical vigor, Lichtenberg-Ettinger is certainly true to the spirit of Lacan's work.

Since Lacan's work in *Le sinthome* is said to be "on Joyce" (but as Derrida has shown, Joyce's texts subvert all our traditional concepts of citation, voice, origin, and authority[5]), it is sometimes held to be a variety of the "applied" psychoanalysis invented by Freud, with his oedipal *Hamlet* and so forth. Indeed, Lacan's choice to spend a year of his famous seminar working on Joyce is often noted with interest by literary scholars, as if it immediately bespoke some special affinity between psychoanalysis and modernist writing. Jean-Michel Rabaté goes further, suggesting that by setting forth a "masterly reading" of Joyce, Lacan was paying off an intellectual debt that dated back to his youthful encounter with the great Irish writer at Adrienne Monnier's bookshop in Paris.[6] Joyce's writing is thus hailed as one of the formative influences that gave Lacan's theory its distinctive shape as an "algebra of letters," identified as simply one element to be placed alongside that theory, within the same cultural or epistemic field. What is most striking in such accounts is their complete failure even to mention Lacan's central claim about the Joycean *écrit*: that it is, precisely, something untheorizable, indeed the very *other of theory*. Joyce's texts were *pas-à-lire*, "not-to-be-read," insisted Lacan; turning to those texts offered him a way to show forth, not a confirmation of some preestablished doctrine or interpretative method, but an exemplary *resistance* to interpretation. And Lacan saw this resistance not as merely a baffling theoretical dead-end, but rather as a provocation to reconceive, to reinvent his psychoanalytic thinking.

Dany Nobus explores this psychoanalytic reinvention, first by pausing over the sheer problem of *reading* Lacan. To take Lacan's writings *à la lettre*, Nobus argues, means to attend to the shifting, ambiguous position of the text itself—between the semi-improvised speech of the seminar and the densely rewritten *écrit* that is declared to be unreadable, *pas à lire*. And our valiant readerly struggles with these textual labyrinths have *clinical* resonance, as Lacan insists; Nobus shows how that resonance comes to vary in significance over the different phases of the teaching. If Lacan's ostensibly marginal or digressive texts on writing have too seldom been articulated with the main body of his teaching, Nobus's examination of those texts—in particular "Lituraterre" of 1971—shows them to be engagements with some of the central, and still unresolved, questions of psychoanalytic thought.

Lacan's notion of the non-readerly *écrit* remains one of the major challenges of his late work. If that work is often itself considered unreadable—just as Joyce's late work was, of course—it is our task as critics to unpick the dense textual knot and trace out, rearticulate, its strands. Véronique Voruz responds to this challenge with a wide-ranging and meticulously argued piece that sets out a three-pronged analysis of how Lacan used readings of Joyce at different stages of his teaching. Voruz shows how that evolving reading was no incidental sidetrack, leading away from analysis proper, but rather the matrix for crucial advances in Lacan's thinking. By carefully explicating and examining those advances, Voruz demolishes the superficial opposition between clinical and literary interpretations, and reveals Lacan's shifting conception of the agency of the letter to have nurtured new modes of reading.

How can we relate the problematic of the unreadable *écrit* that is formulated in *Le sinthome* to wider questions of literary interpretation and cultural analysis? Philip Dravers provides an answer by situating Lacan's work on Joyce as part of a lifelong engagement with different forms of verbal and textual enjoyment. Beginning with a clear explication of the relation between language and jouissance as formulated in the late work with the notion of *lalangue*, Dravers moves on to outline a trajectory from Lacan's work on *Hamlet* to his reading of Joyce, punctuating the argu-

ment with a series of deftly worded questions. As well as giving an original account of Lacan's various literary investments, Dravers offers a clear
explication of the relation between the *sinthome* and fantasy, thought by
Lacan in terms of its "traversal" in analysis.

All of the contributors to *Re-inventing the Symptom* seek to con-
vey the peculiar weight ascribed to literary language, to writing, in
Lacan's final texts. Inevitably, the very materiality of these texts themselves—their status as partly published, partly anecdotal—comes to be
considered as part of the theoretical problem of writing. Lacan seems
to have linked the name of Joyce in particular with the question of
publication—or *poubellication*, as he liked to pun, making the book trade
a matter of the dustbin (*poubelle*), of producing litter as well as letters.
In a preface written in 1976 for his first text to be published in English
(a translation of *Séminaire XI*), Lacan declares, "I shall speak of Joyce"—
before adding hastily that his contact with Joyce's writing can only be
oblique and tangential, "in view of my embarrassment where art . . . is
concerned."[7] Three years earlier, when the same text had been published in France, Joyce was already on Lacan's mind. In a postscript to
Séminaire XI, he writes:

> . . . après tout, l'écrit comme pas-à-lire, c'est Joyce qui l'introduit, je ferais
> mieux de dire: l'intraduit, car à faire du mot traite au-delà des langues, il
> ne se traduit qu'à peine, d'être partout également peu à lire.[8]

Thus, Joyce stands for a specifically writerly or textual dimension of
language that must always remain *intraduit*, "untranslated": it cannot
be folded back into, or translated by, the discursive space of a psychoanalytic seminar. Each time Lacan publishes an *écrit*, it is Joyce who
comes to mind, as the very emblem of an irreducible, unspeakable
textuality.

In what sense, then, does the final Lacan remain partly anecdotal?
We might refer to the etymology of the latter term, the Greek *anekdotos*
meaning "unpublished" and thus secret, private, hidden. In this sense,
each of the essays in *Re-inventing the Symptom* is an effort to *reduce* the
"anecdotage" of Lacan's final period, to shed light upon its obscurities
and make accessible its supposed mysteries. At the same time, to recall
Joel Fineman's work on the anecdote—which linked it to a Real "that
can be neither specularized nor represented"[9]—might give us pause

before undertaking such a wholesale textual enlightenment. For in *Le sinthome*, Lacan struggles to place something *untranslatable* at the center of his work, a disruptive excess that no topology can finally reduce or master. As an intraduction (not yet another introduction) to the final Lacan, this book aims to engage with that irreducible excess without simply translating it.

A Note on Texts

The publication of Lacan's work is still, two decades after his death, very far from complete. The principal text discussed in this volume is Seminar XXIII (1975–76), *Le sinthome*, a version of which appeared in the journal *Ornicar?*, edited by Jacques-Alain Miller, in the following issues: 1976, 6: pp. 3–20; 7: pp. 3–18; 8: pp. 6–20; 1977, 9: pp. 32–40; 10: pp. 5–12; 11: pp. 2–9. However, there are also various pirate editions of the seminar in circulation, some of which differ markedly from the "official" versions. I have therefore allowed each contributor the freedom to choose which text to cite, without trying to impose a consistency where none exists. Where a contributor cites a version of Seminar XXIII other than the *Ornicar?* text, the reference reads simply "unpublished." In my own view, the most complete and authoritative text of Seminar XXIII is a noncommercial version produced by the Association freudienne internationale, Paris. For a full bibliography of Lacan's works, see Joël Dor, *Nouvelle bibliographie des travaux de Jacques Lacan*, Paris: E.P.E.L., 1993.

NOTES

1. See the papers collected in *Esquisses Psychanalytiques* 15, Paris: CFRP, 1991.
2. D. Nobus, "Preface," *Key Concepts of Lacanian Psychoanalysis*, ed. D. Nobus, London: Rebus Press, 1998, p. vii.
3. S. Žižek, *Looking Awry: An Introduction to Jacques Lacan through Popular Culture*, Cambridge, MA: M.I.T. Press, 1991, p. 132.
4. For this term, see L. Thurston, "Ineluctable Nodalities: On the Borromean Knot," in D. Nobus (Ed.), *Key Concepts of Lacanian Psychoanalysis*, *op. cit.*, pp. 139–163.

5. Cf. J. Derrida, "Ulysses Gramophone: Hear Say yes in Joyce," trans. T. Kendall & S. Benstock, in B. Benstock, ed., *James Joyce: The Augmented Ninth*, Syracuse, NY: Syracuse University Press, 1988, pp. 27–75.

6. J.-M. Rabaté, "Joyce the Parisian," in *The Cambridge Companion to James Joyce*, ed. D. Attridge, Cambridge, UK: Cambridge University Press, 1990, pp. 97–98.

7. J. Lacan, Preface, *Seminar XI: The Four Fundamental Concepts of Psychoanalysis*, ed. J.-A. Miller, trans. A. Sheridan, London: Hogarth Press, 1977, p. ix.

8. ". . . after all, the written as the not-to-be-read is introduced by Joyce— I'd do better to say intraduced (both introduced and not translated), because to deal with the word is to negotiate beyond languages, and he can hardly be translated being likewise little read everywhere" [my translation]. *Le Séminaire de Jacques Lacan, Livre XI, "Les quatres concepts fondamentaux de la psychanalyse,"* Paris: Seuil, 1973, p. 252.

9. J. Fineman, "The History of the Anecdote: Fiction and Fiction," *The Subjectivity Effect in Western Literary Tradition*, Cambridge, MA: M.I.T. Press, 1991, p. 71.

The *sinthome*: A New Way of Writing an Old Problem?

Dominiek Hoens and Ed Pluth

In his seminar *Le sinthome* (SXXIII, 1975–1976), Lacan adds a fourth ring to the Borromean knot he had begun discussing in 1972,[1] which had at first consisted of only three rings. He gives this fourth ring the function of holding the other three together, and labels it the *sinthome*, a term that had not appeared in Lacan's work before. It might seem that nothing had prepared Lacan's audience for the appearance of this new term. However, it is our claim here that the concept of the *sinthome* is present in all but name in Lacan's work before 1975, and that in fact it corresponds to a motif present throughout Lacan's teaching. In this article we will discuss some elements to clarify and support this claim.

Why this strange term, *sinthome*? In the first session of the seminar, Lacan explains that it is an "old way of writing what was later written *symptom*."[2] What is the purpose of reviving this old way of writing? Lacan does not state that *symptom* and *sinthome* are two different things. In fact, he suggests that the two may be used interchangeably.[3] Moreover, in French the pronunciations of "symptom" and "*sinthome*" can be difficult to tell apart. The difference between them appears only from a chronological point of view: the new way of writing the symptom is perhaps a reflection of a different understanding of what was always univocally called "symptom," and is, we shall argue, founded on a more radical way of conceiving the nature of the signifier's relation to the Symbolic.

Lacan's work is often divided into three periods: the Imaginary (1936–1952), the Symbolic (1953–1962), and the Real (1963–1981).[4] This periodization is somewhat arbitrary and thus open to debate.[5] Such problems notwithstanding, in this chapter we hope to show that throughout Lacan's work there is a recurring problematic: that is, he always conceived of a certain point where the signifying chain, or the Symbolic as such, could be said to close itself off. This would seem to be the function of the sign in his early work, and such a point is usually discussed in terms of the Imaginary in the early Lacan. For example, the sign would be Imaginary insofar as it does not depend upon a reference to other signs in the way that a signifier depends upon other signifiers. The *sinthome* represents a further development of this line of thinking; it also seems to be a point where the symbolizations of the Symbolic come to a stop, but this point is not itself Symbolic, Imaginary, or Real. This makes it possible to speak of a split in the late Lacan, which should be dated at 1975 with the introduction of the term *sinthome*.[6]

The most noteworthy aspect of the *sinthome* in the Borromean knot is that it is not, as the symptom is in the seminar *R.S.I.*, placed in the Real, but in none of the three orders or rings.[7] The consistency created for all three orders by the *sinthome* is said to be Imaginary, certainly, but this does not mean that the *sinthome* itself is Imaginary. Lacan is ultimately led to think of an element that does not fit neatly into any of the three orders involved in his teaching prior to 1975. This is why it is legitimate to speak of a split in Lacan's last period, corresponding to the thought of the *sinthome*. This split specifically concerns the Symbolic.

When Lacan first introduced the Borromean knot, such a knot implied an equivalence among the three orders; what was gained by this was an ability to think the interconnection of Real, Symbolic, and Imaginary. The problem, however, was precisely with the equivalence implied by the Borromean knot: it ruled out the possibility of making any distinction among the orders. The Symbolic had always been given a primacy in Lacan's theory, and it was on its basis that the Real and the Imaginary could be conceived. For example, in Lacan's revision of the concept of the "mirror stage," a Symbolic point is required for the identification with the mirror image;[8] likewise, the definition of the Real as something that resists symbolization is a definition that can only be understood on the basis of the Symbolic.[9] If the orders are equivalent, how can a distinction be made among them? The *sinthome* will undo the equivalence among the orders by causing a split in the very order on whose basis the other two were articulated: the Symbolic ring of the Borromean knot. The general thesis of our article is that this split resumes a problematic present throughout Lacan's teaching concerning the Symbolic order.

We shall begin by studying some of the features of the Imaginary in the early Lacan, and then discuss his early view of the function of the signifier in the symptom, which concerns the relation between the Imaginary and the Symbolic. This will introduce us to the idea of a "residue" essential to the functioning of the Symbolic. We shall then discuss Lacan's reading of Claudel's *L'Otage* in order to see how the taking up of the subject into the Symbolic presupposes an "ugly" signifier, also thought of as a sort of residue of the Symbolic that is not part of the Symbolic itself. Finally, we shall discuss the function of the *sinthome*, which emerges as a residue of all three orders, something required for their consistency.

I

It is well known that Lacan ascribes a causal role to the child's essentially premature birth. It is this prematuration that makes a child entirely dependent upon its caregivers, and without an identity of its own. The first formation of identity takes place in the mirror stage: in the mirror image, the child grasps itself as a unity, a unity at odds with its real underdeveloped motor coordination. An essential aspect of the mirror stage is that the child does not take the image to be a representation of itself, but identifies itself radically with the image. Thus, from the child's perspective, the image is not a representation, but a *presentation*: the child *is* the image. Or, to put it in terms of object-relations theory, the child *is* the object.[10] It is paradoxical, of course, that the child is at one and the same time *identical* to the image or object, and also *in relation* to the object. It is here that Lacan speaks of misrecognition (*méconnaissance*). The child misrecognizes the difference and distance that exists in fact between it and the image, or in other words, the child makes a mistake when it considers the image to be a presentation instead of a *re*presentation.[11]

A second point to be made about the mirror stage is that the child forms a unity for itself on the basis of a point lying outside it. On the basis of misrecognition, the child *is* a unity, but it receives this unity from the outside. It is only through the identification with an external point that the illusion of unity is installed and can be maintained.[12] It is as if unity can only be realized in a unity that is not *one* but in fact *two*. For this reason, the Imaginary relation is called a dual relation. There is a tension between two terms (child and image) that are at the same time one.

It is Lacan himself who ends up problematizing this schema even further. This results in a more complex version of the mirror stage, involving a third term—the Symbolic. The idea of a Symbolic point from which the child identifies can be found for the first time in the 1949 version of the mirror stage,[13] where the child is said to receive the guarantee of its image from the parent who says: "Thou art that."[14] Later in Lacan's work, this becomes the *einziger Zug*, the unary trait, a forerunner of the ego ideal: in other words, this point is thought of as some sort of signifier, and no longer only as an image.

The "two" in the Imaginary thus actually includes a third. The transition from duality to triangularity is not an easy development, however. An essential moment in this transition from the Imaginary to the Symbolic is *frustration*, which will reappear in Lacan's discussion of Claudel's *L'Otage*. Frustration introduces the child to the Symbolic via the mother, but is Imaginary to the extent that frustration misrecognizes the fact that lack in the Symbolic is structural, and thus irremediable.

According to Lacan, the misrecognition involved in frustration is overcome through the proper subjectivization of the Symbolic order. This means that the child situates itself no longer as a *signified* but as the *signifier* of the desire of the Other.[15] Roughly speaking, the signified is Imaginary and the signifier Symbolic. This transition from signified to signifier, thus from Imaginary to Symbolic, constitutes the heart of Lacan's theoretical development from 1953 to 1962. But what we can now present as a fairly simple schema actually emerges in a very complicated way in Lacan's seminars.[16] It is, for example, certainly not the case that the Imaginary is "conquered" by the Symbolic. The Imaginary remains causal for the creation of the symptom in neurosis. Yet Lacan's emphasis on the transition from the Imaginary to the Symbolic is what leads many people to maintain that the goal of analysis is to definitively cut out the Imaginary through a symbolization of the symptom.

There is a problem with this, however. The problem is that a bit of the Imaginary remains as a persistent point that resists interpretation in terms of signifiers. This resistance to interpretation also appears in Lacan's theory of the symptom, and is the gateway that leads to his formulation of the *sinthome*. In his Rome Discourse, Lacan claimed that "the symptom resolves itself entirely into an analysis of language, because the symptom is itself structured like a language."[17] But as his teaching continues, he develops the idea of a resistant kernel that cannot be simply dissolved by interpretation. We turn now to a study of this kernel of the symptom resistant to interpretation.

II

In "The Agency of the Letter" of 1957, we get an idea of how Lacan sees the metaphorical structure of the symptom:

> The double-triggered mechanism of metaphor is the very mechanism by which the symptom, in the analytic sense, is determined. Between the enigmatic signifier of the sexual trauma and the term that is substituted for it in an actual signifying chain there passes the spark that fixes in a symptom the signification inaccessible to the conscious subject.[18]

In any metaphor, there are two signifiers at work: for example, in the poem "Booz Endormi" by Victor Hugo, often cited by Lacan, the metaphorization occurs between the proper name "Booz" and "sheaf" in the line "His sheaf was neither miserly nor spiteful."[19] In terms of the symptom, the two signifiers involved are the "enigmatic signifier of the sexual trauma" and any signifier put in its place, presumably. A meaning is produced for a sexual trauma by putting one signifier in place of another. Is the "repressed" signifier, then, the meaning of the symptom? No: no more than "Booz" is the meaning of the signifier "sheaf." "Booz" is not the meaning at stake in Hugo's metaphor, but simply one of the signifiers involved in the meaning-effect of the metaphor. The meaning produced by this metaphor occurs between the two signifiers, and does not settle down in either one of them. Similarly, the signifier of the sexual trauma should not be seen as the meaning at stake in the symptom: the meaning produced by the symptom is not localizable in this signifier, but in the "spark" between this signifier and the one that is put in its place. The signifier of the sexual trauma should be seen as the nonsensical kernel of the metaphor, a non-meaning that can only be taken up into meaning by a substitution, and thus in a relation to another signifier.

The question for us now is: What is the status of this nonsensical signifier? Is it Symbolic? Imaginary? In the passage above, we can say that there is a traumatic signifier stuck to the Real, and as such is not really a signifier since it is a *one*. A signifier normally involves a lack insofar as it refers to other signifiers. This signifier, however, would be a strange one that defies Lacan's definition of the signifier (in Seminar XIV) as something that cannot signify itself, that does not fall under the principle of identity, a = a.[20] This (non)signifier only takes on a meaning by being replaced by another signifier, by being, precisely, taken up into symbolization. It would seem, by elimination, that one could speak of this nonsensical signifier as Imaginary: it is a point where the signifying chain comes to a halt and stumbles, a place where a substitution is necessary for any meaning to be produced out of it. Analysis would consist, then, of making further symbolizations of this point possible, by dissolving the resistance of this point into a signifying chain, an interpretation. In other words, analysis interprets the symptom, it symbolizes the Imaginary.

But there may also be reason to think that this point, this core signifier of the symptom, is not Imaginary but Real. In Seminar X, Lacan says that the symptom "in its nature is jouissance."[21] What is important for our purposes here is the connection of jouissance to the Real. Both present us with an "impasse in formalisation."[22] The symptom as jouissance involves signifiers that are bound together, but not in a meaningful way. In the '70s, Lacan will call this a *jouis-sens*, a knot of

signifiers that is itself a type of enjoyment, and not primarily a signification. The first major clue that the core signifier in the symptom is
shifting to the *Real* can be found in Lacan's reading of Claudel's *L'Otage*.

III

The Lacanian subject is always said to be a subject of signifiers, but
the question is: How is the point where the chain of signifiers comes to
a stop or closes itself off to be characterized? Is this point Imaginary or
Real? What is clear at least is that Lacan wants to indicate that the point
where the subject is interpellated into the signifying chain is not a signifier like any other, but a sign.[23] The phantasm, as a perverse formation—
a perverse scene, for example—includes the subject as a *pure sign*:

> There is here [in the perverse phantasm] something like a Symbolic re-
> duction, which has progressively eliminated the entire subjective struc-
> ture of the situation, only allowing a residue to subsist that is entirely
> desubjectivated and ultimately enigmatic, because it preserves the whole
> charge—but the charge as unrevealed, unconstituted, and not assumed
> by the subject. . . . At the level of the perverse phantasm all the elements
> are there, but everything concerning signification, namely, the inter-
> subjective relation, is lost. What one can call signifiers in a pure state
> are maintained without intersubjective relation, emptied of their subject.
> We have here a sort of objectivation of the signifiers of the situation.
> What is indicated here, in the sense of a fundamental structuring rela-
> tion of the subject's history at the level of perversion, is at the same time
> maintained, contained, but it is so in the form of *a pure sign*.[24]

The subject is able to take its place in the Symbolic order by means
of an element heterogeneous to that order. Yet this element is also included in the Symbolic in some way. This order is, then, ultimately
grounded in something that is not of the order itself. From the point
of view of the subject, one can say that the condition of the possibility
of being a subject implies that it must stick to a certain *sign* that cannot be integrated into the Symbolic order, even though it is not completely alien to the Symbolic. This pure sign, referred to above, cannot
be taken to be a signifier, even though Lacan made no sharp distinction between sign and signifier until Seminar IX, *L'identification*. From

the way Lacan describes the *pure sign*, it is clear that signifiers in a "pure state" are not entirely like signifiers in what would be their normal state, functioning within the Symbolic.[25]

It is precisely at this point that it is useful to consider Lacan's discussion of frustration as *Versagung*. To put it briefly: the dimension of the Symbolic order presupposes a sacrifice. This implies that the subject does not situate itself in relation to a radical lack of being, but in relation to the lack that is constitutive of the Symbolic order as such. This is the point of transition from the Imaginary to the Symbolic. *Versagung* implies a discontent with the order in which the subject is constituted, but "The more the subject affirms itself as wanting to leave the signifying chain with the help of the signifier, and the more it enters and integrates itself into it, the more it itself becomes a sign of this chain."[26] *Versagung* is primarily a Symbolic act within the Symbolic but it indicates a radical discontent with any Symbolic *Bejahung* (affirmation). Essentially, it is a gesture that negates any inclusion of the subject in the Symbolic, and it can only appear as an *isolated* signifier/sign taken out of the Symbolic order. *Versagung*, then, emerges in a signifier that does not refer to other signifiers (as signifiers included within the symbolic order usually do), but to the Symbolic order as such.

This is illustrated well in the first part of Claudel's trilogy about the Coûfontaine family, *L'Otage*, which Lacan discusses in his seminar *Le transfert*.[27] In the first part we are introduced to Sygne[28] de Coûfontaine and her cousin, Georges de Coûfontaine. They meet one another after the French revolution and make a pact against the new post-revolutionary order: they get engaged, thereby hoping to preserve what is left of the family name. The hostage (*l'otage*) in this play is the Pope; he is in a precarious situation, and in order to save him from betrayal, Sygne is asked to give up everything that binds her to her family and tradition. She can do this only by marrying the enemy of the family, Toussaint Turelure. After a few developments, her cousin Georges challenges Turelure to a fight, they exchange gunfire, and Sygne is the one hit by the bullet her cousin fires at his enemy. On her deathbed, Sygne is asked by Turelure for a last forgiveness, and also if she wishes to see their child, who was to be baptized that day. Sygne makes no answer, or rather, it is her body that performs an answer in the form of a tic, a sign of "no." Sygne, who sacrificed everything in order to preserve a past order of things, who broke off her engagement with her cousin in order to save the Pope, cannot and will not tolerate this last and ultimate sacrifice to Turelure. As Claudel's stage directions put it, she "signs No" (*Signe que non*).[29]

Lacan interprets Sygne's sacrifice as a *Versagung*. A *Versagung* is a promise and at the same time a breaking of the promise.[30] Sygne gives up everything in order to bind herself to an enemy, Turelure, and ultimately saves his life from her cousin's gunshot, but, when asked to confess that she did this out of marital love, only answers with a negating *trait*. The place where Sygne gives up everything in order to enter into a Symbolic universe that is not hers appears later on as a negation of this order. Is this not the endpoint of the Symbolic order, where an ugly, obscene feature puts the whole order into question and is thus a pure negation of what the order stands for? Sygne herself ultimately becomes a sign incarnate, saying "No" to the very point where the subject's introduction to or assumption of the Symbolic order begins (with a primordial sacrifice).[31] The *Ver* of *Versagung* indicates an irresolvable dilemma: the Symbolic order finds here its closure in its opening. Lacan connects this with the *me phunai* of Oedipus, "it would have been better never to have lived," which implies a desire that does not concern "life" but lies radically beyond it.[32] The *me* of *me phunai* and the *Ver*[33] of *Versagung* are signifiers that permit the subject to refuse the Symbolic order within the Symbolic order, or, what amounts to the same thing, to refuse him- or herself.[34] But where the Symbolic order is radically refused, there remains only a *sign*: a *Sygne/signe que non*.

To return to our question: Is this point Imaginary or Real? Lacan seems to hesitate a while between the two. He will ultimately think it as neither of the two, but as the *sinthome*. The ground is prepared for this by Lacan's growing emphasis on the symptom as enjoyment.

IV

Perhaps it is useful to begin with some brief comments on Lacan's idea of *jouissance*. This term means satisfaction, or enjoyment, but it also has the more restricted meaning of orgasm. In most English-language works on Lacan, including this collection, it is left untranslated. This is in fact helpful, because jouissance as Lacan conceives it is not simply a satisfaction or enjoyment in the normal sense of the terms. It is not a

kind of end-point or goal that is reached on the path of pursuing pleasure. Jouissance is for Lacan the term for a kind of pleasure in pain,
or painful pleasure. Freud already noted that the work of psychoanalysis
often runs up against a certain *Schmerzlust* on the part of the analysand.[35]
The analysand often seems to be enjoying the very conditions that he
or she is complaining about. Is it not appropriate to speak of this
"enjoyment" in terms of a pleasure in pain, or a sort of painful pleasure to which the analysand is perhaps quite attached, despite him-
or herself?

Such an enjoyment could easily be characterized as something
beyond language. The analysand may go on and on about his or her situation, but the fact that there is some kind of enjoyment in it is never
explicitly said, and is not taken (by the analysand) to be the object of
analytic work. And what is not spoken about cannot be analyzed: psychoanalysis is, after all, the "talking cure." This idea of a "beyond of
language" is often used to correct a common misinterpretation of Lacan:
that his theory was too intellectualist, neglecting affects or emotions,
and only focusing on signifiers and linguistic formations. Certainly,
jouissance is on the side of the classical Freudian ideas of drive, affect,
and energy. Thus, it is something other than language. But does this
mean that it is actually beyond language? This is a difficult question,
and its answer often depends upon which period of Lacan's teaching
we are discussing. What interests us most here is the link between the
sinthome and what Lacan calls *jouis-sens*. This is a play on words: it
sounds just like the word jouissance in French, but the hyphenation and
altered spelling make it also mean an enjoyment in sense or meaning.
Finally, it can be taken to mean "I hear sense" ("*J'ouïs sens*"). This latter refers to a kind of superego voice commanding one to enjoy: in response to the command to enjoy, one can only say, "I hear."[36] With the
idea of *jouis-sens*, it is more accurate to say that jouissance insists in language, and is not exactly "beyond" it. Or, that it is *within* language, but
with a very specific status.

The *sinthome* is an example of just such an enjoyment-in-meaning,
an enjoyment insisting "within" language. But it is here that a further
question must be asked. What is the status of the term "meaning" in "*jouis-
sens*"? Is the enjoyment involved here actually the enjoyment of a meaning? The problem is that this would contradict what was said earlier about
the nature of the symptom. Our investigation showed that what is cru-

cial about the symptom is not meaning, although in Lacan's earlier work he did see it that way. Does he return to his earlier view in 1975? Not exactly. That the *sinthome* is a *jouis-sens* does not mean that the *sinthome* communicates a meaning to someone, or even that it has a meaning that could be communicated. The *sinthome* is not itself a meaning—it has no "truth"—but it does produce meanings. In what sense? In the sense of an enigma.[37] An enigma confronts you with one or more signifiers that evoke many meanings. It is poetic. For example, after a certain number of readings of a poem you do not necessarily grasp the poem's ultimate meaning; rather, it is as if the poem has read you: it remains opaque and produces whole chains of signifiers within you. The *sinthome* could also be considered as a poem, or as an object that is very familiar to you but at the same time absolutely unknown in that you do not quite know what to make of it. The whole idea here is that the *sinthome* produces meanings out of nothing, again and again. It should be noted that meaning here does not imply any end point in some ultimate signification. What is at stake, rather, are inventions of meaning where there is nothing but the *sinthome* as a pure, evocatory thing.

In the light of this, we can see the *sinthome* as a thing that makes meaning possible. On the other hand, is the *sinthome* itself not a meaning? Is this not what the idea of *jouis-sens* is getting at? This is the paradox: the *sinthome* is meaningless, but at the same time it is enjoyment-in-meaning. The solution to the paradox centers on a difference in the use of meaning or *sens* in the two cases. The *sinthome* is meaningless, in the sense that it does not have any particular signification. It is a pure signifier, and in that respect, it is meaningless. For Lacan, meaning is always produced through the connection of signifiers, in what he called a signifying chain. The *sinthome* is an enjoyment-in-meaning, however, in the following sense: as a production of meaning, the *sinthome* is not concerned with the meanings produced, but with the activity of production itself. The unconscious produces meaningless symptoms, symptoms that are on the one hand enigmatic to you, but with which on the other hand you are completely involved.[38] It is this unconscious production that Lacan is aiming at with his conception of jouissance.

Earlier, we explained jouissance in terms of how an analysand might be enjoying the very situation he or she is complaining about. What *jouis-sens* evokes is this situation in terms of how it is enjoyed, in terms of a grounding scenario or framework by means of which the analysand orients him- or herself in relation to others. The *sinthome* is precisely a structure, and this structure is in itself an enjoyment. Clearly, it is difficult to conceive of such a structure as a meaning; it does not really mean anything. The *sinthome* as *jouis-sens* can be seen, then, as the ultimate support of the subject,[39] and at the same time the source of the subject's openness to or production of meanings. In relation to this openness, the *sinthome* as *jouis-sens* could be construed as the meaning of meaning, a kind of tautological point presupposed for the development of a chain of differentiated, open-ended significations. One can only be open to meanings because one is always-already enjoying the structure within which meaning occurs. Your ultimate identity, the ultimate support of your being, is the particular way in which you enjoy meaning: your *sinthome*.

The *sinthome* can thus be taken as the foundation of the Symbolic; yet this foundation introduces a split in the Symbolic, as Lacan had always conceived of it. We have already spoken of the paradoxical grounding point of the Symbolic, and Lacan's preoccupation with it. With the idea of the *sinthome*, this preoccupation is seen from a different point of view. In the early view of the Symbolic, its guiding principle is a split between two signifiers. It is because of the split or gap between signifiers that there is a Symbolic order: this order is constituted on the basis of primordial lack. This implies an indefinite process of the development of meaning, and leads to the unsettling conclusion that analysis might be endless. The *sinthome* corrects this, by pointing out how the Symbolic itself is split in two, a split Lacan characterizes as being between symptom and symbol.[40]

What this means is that there is a difference between signifiers insofar as they are related to each other in the production of meaning—

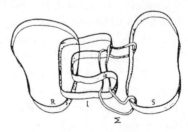

Figure 1–1. The Borromean knot with four rings

the symbol—and signifiers insofar as they are related to a One, a signifier that resists any linking. This split, Lacan says, is a "false hole." We take this to mean that the Symbolic order and the symptom could be seen as being radically distinct. That is, there might appear to be a "hole" separating them. Thus, according to this view, symbols would be aiming at a symptom that remains elusive, and the symptom itself would be trying to achieve symbolization. But this is not the case: so, it is only a false hole. The Symbolic is grounded in the symptom and the symptom is a signifier. Or we could say that the Symbolic is not without the symptom. To put this in terms of signifiers, one could say that the referential aspect of any signifier is capable of becoming *auto*-referential, taking on the function of the symptom that closes off the signifying system. This explains why there is a false hole between the symptom and the symbol. The Symbolic itself is a symptomatic structure, in the sense that any element within it is capable of becoming a symptom.

We have shown that the *sinthome* is a concept with a history in Lacan's thought. In the margins of his early work, one can find a preoccupation with what one could call an impasse or interruption point of the Symbolic. Lacan arrives at this point in his discussions of the perverse phantasm and Sygne's tragic act. It is only later that he thinks this point in terms of an enjoyment "outside" of the Symbolic, as Real. In a final phase, this enjoyment comes to be reflected back into or diffused throughout the Symbolic, or, the Symbolic is what it is on the basis of an enjoyment-in-meaning, and enjoyment is no longer really outside the Symbolic, or beyond language. There are actually many concepts in Lacan's work that play a role similar to the *sinthome* as a grounding of the Symbolic. For example, in the seminar *R.S.I.*, it is the Name of the Father that occupies the place of the fourth ring that holds the three other rings together.[41] Likewise, object *a* arguably plays a similar role earlier on in Lacan's theory. An obvious question arises here: Is there a difference between all these concepts? And if there is a difference, are the concepts still related in some way, or do they replace each other? Finally, if they are not different but identical, from what perspective are they identical? From what point of view can the Name of the Father be seen as identical to the *sinthome*?[42]

What is clear, at any rate, is the way in which the *sinthome* is an innovation in that it allows us to conceive of the grounding principle of the Symbolic as an enjoyment not outside of but inherent to the Symbolic; its function can potentially be taken on by any signifier in the system. This leads us to say that the *sinthome* is not so much an ultimate ground of the Symbolic—as one could conclude from Lacan's early analyses of the perverse phantasm and the tragedy of Sygne de Coûfontaine—but something more along the lines of a principle, a category that allows one to see the Symbolic in its connection to the Real and the Imaginary. This is why it is a fourth ring in the Borromean knot. Lacan was already able to think the connections between the Imaginary and the Symbolic in his revision of the mirror stage, but it was the category of the *sinthome* that allowed him to think the Symbolic as permeated by the Real, instead of as radically distinct from it.

NOTES

1. See J. Lacan, *Le Séminaire XIX: . . . ou pire* (1971–1972), unpublished, lesson of 2/9/72.

2. J. Lacan, *Le Séminaire XXIII: Le sinthome* (1975–1976), texte établi par J.-A. Miller, *Ornicar?*, 1976, 6: pp. 3–20; 7: pp. 3–18; 8: pp. 6–20; 1977; 9: pp. 32–40; 10: pp. 5–12; 11: pp. 2–9; here 6: p. 3.

3. J. Lacan, *Ibid.*, 6: p. 9.

4. As Lacan himself says: "I began with the Imaginary, I then had to chew on the story of the Symbolic, with this linguistic reference for which I did not find everything that would have suited me, and I finished by putting out for you this famous Real in the very form of the knot." J. Lacan, *Le Séminaire XXII: R.S.I.* (1974–1975), texte établi par J.-A. Miller, *Ornicar?*, 1975, 2: pp. 88–105; 3: pp. 96–110; 4: pp. 92–106; 5: pp. 16–66; here 3: p. 102.

5. See the periodization by J. Allouch, "Tel 36 53 75," *Esquisses psychanalytiques*, 15, 1991, pp. 9–30.

6. One could on this basis say that the notion of the Real was a solution to a theoretical problem connected to the Symbolic, and that the *sinthome* is a reopening of the problem and at the same time a new answer to it.

7. J. Lacan, *R.S.I.*, *op. cit.*, 2: p. 99.

8. Cf. J. Lacan, "Remarque sur le rapport de Daniel Lagache: 'Psychanalyse et structure de la personnalité'" (1961), *Écrits*, Paris, Seuil, 1966, pp. 647–684.

9. For an early version of this idea, see J. Lacan, *Le Séminaire, Livre I. Les écrits techniques de Freud* (1953–1954), texte établi par J.-A. Miller, Paris, Seuil, 1975, p. 80.

10. Cf. S. Freud, "Findings, Ideas, Problems" (1941 [1938]), *SE* XXIII, pp. 299–300: "Having" and "being" in children. Children like expressing an object-relation by an identification: "I am the object." . . . "The breast is a part of me, I am the breast" (p. 299).

11. The problem of presentation and representation is also inherent to knot theory: Is it a scheme, an image of something beyond the knot itself? Lacan refers explicitly to S. Agacinski's article, "Découpages du Tractatus," in S. Agacinski, J. Derrida, S. Kofman et al., *Mimesis: des articulations*, Paris, Aubier/Flammarion, 1975, pp. 17–53, in which the notion of *Vorstellung* ((re)presentation) in the young Wittgenstein is discussed. See J. Lacan, *Le sinthome, op. cit.*, 7, p. 4.

12. Gertrudis Van de Vijver, inspired by biosemiotics, comes to a similar conclusion when she claims that the organism becomes a body at the moment that it closes (!) itself off in an exterior point. Cf. G. Van de Vijver, "Psychic Closure: A Prerequisite for the Recognition of the Sign Function?" in *Semiotica*, 1999, vol. 126 (1/2). Going further with this, one can posit that the closure decenters itself; the closure closes in its dis-closing.

13. A more completely worked out version of this idea of a Symbolic point involved in the mirror stage is to be found in Lacan's eighth seminar and in his commentary on an essay by D. Lagache. See J. Lacan, *Le Séminaire, Livre VIII. Le transfert* (1960–1961), texte établi par J.-A. Miller, Paris, Seuil, 1991, pp. 401–418 and footnote 8 above.

14. J. Lacan, "The Mirror Stage as Formative of the Function of the I as Revealed in Psychoanalytic Experience" (1949), *Ecrits: A Selection*, trans. A. Sheridan, New York, Norton, 1977, p. 7.

15. J. Lacan, *Le Séminaire, Livre V. Les formations de l'inconscient* (1957–1958), texte établi par J.-A. Miller, Paris, Seuil, 1994, pp. 173–176.

16. We should also mention that it is only in December 1961 that the distinction between signifier and sign is made unambiguously: "The signifier, in contrast to the sign, is not what represents something for someone, it is precisely what represents the subject for another signifier." J. Lacan, *Le Séminaire IX: L'identification* (1961–1962), unpublished, lesson of 12/6/61. It is thus noteworthy that the "Lacan of the Symbolic" (1953–1962) ends with what is often presumed to be the beginning! Before 1962, Lacan generally tends to mix up signifier and sign. Still, it is remarkable that the notion of sign is used to refer to a problematic point of the Symbolic. This will be seen in our discussion of Lacan's treatment of Claudel's *L'Otage*. We agree with Jacques-Alain Miller when he argues that Lacan exchanges the dichotomy of signifier and signified for sense and sign (see e.g., J. Lacan, *Télévision*, Paris, Seuil, 1974, pp. 19, 21); we would just add that this new dichotomy is already apparent in earlier works. See J.-A. Miller, "Le

sinthome, un mixte de symptôme et fantasme," *La Cause freudienne*, 1998, 39: pp. 7–17.

17. J. Lacan, "The Function and Field of Speech and Language in Psychoanalysis" (1953), *Ecrits: A Selection*, *op. cit.*, p. 59.

18. J. Lacan, "The Agency of the Letter in the Unconscious: or Reason since Freud" (1957). *Écrits: A Selection*, *op. cit.*, p. 166.

19. *Ibid.*, p. 156.

20. J. Lacan, *Le Séminaire XIV: Logique du fantasme* (1966–1967), unpublished, lesson of 11/16/66.

21. J. Lacan. *Le Séminaire X: L'angoisse* (1962–1963), unpublished, lesson of 1/23/63.

22. J. Lacan. *Le Séminaire, Livre XX. Encore* (1972–1973), texte établi par J.-A. Miller, Paris, Seuil, 1975, p. 85.

23. This is never quite clear in Lacan's texts prior to Seminar IX. As we said in note 16 above, the radical difference between signifier and sign is only made in 1961.

24. J. Lacan, *Le Séminaire, Livre IV. La relation d'objet* (1956–1957), texte établi par J.-A. Miller, Paris, Seuil, 1994, p. 119. Later on Lacan will explicitly identify *signe* and *sinthome*. See: J. Lacan, *Le Séminaire XXIV: L'insu que sait de l'une-bévue s'aile à mourre* (1976–1977), texte établi par J.-A. Miller, *Ornicar?*, 1977, n° 12/13, pp. 4–16; 1978, n° 14, pp. 4–9; n° 15, pp. 5–9; n° 16, pp. 7–13; 1979, n° 17/18, pp. 7–23; here 17/18: p. 17.

25. This is parallel to the distinction Lacan later makes between letter and signifier. See J. Lacan, "Lituraterre," *Ornicar?*, 1984, 41: 5–13.

26. J. Lacan, *Le Séminaire, Livre V. Les formations de l'inconscient* (1957–1958), *op. cit.*, p. 245. Here we have an example of Lacan using sign and signifier as interchangeable terms.

27. J. Lacan, *Le Séminaire, Livre VIII. Le transfert* (1960–1961), *op. cit.*, pp. 311–381.

28. "The word begins with an S, and it is really there as a hint to recognize in the word a sign. Moreover, there is this imperceptible change, the substitution of the *i* for the *y*," *Ibid.*, p. 352.

29. P. Claudel, *L'Otage* suivi de *Le pain dur* et de *Le père humilié*, Paris, Gallimard, 1993, p. 151. A foreshadowing of this ultimate "no" appears in the very first scene (p. 19) when she receives the news about the death of Georges's wife and children. At that moment, Claudel gives the following stage directions: "Sygne remains for a moment without movement, eyes closed and distant, then she moves her head slowly like someone saying 'no.'"

30. See J. Lacan, *Le Séminaire, Livre IV. La relation d'objet* (1956–1957), *op. cit.*, p. 180; J. Lacan, *Le Séminaire, Livre V. Les formations de l'inconscient*

(1957–1958), *op. cit.*, p. 463; J. Lacan, *Le Séminaire, Livre VIII. Le transfert* (1960–1961), *op. cit.*, p. 353.

31. Lacan links Sygne to Sade, which hints at a possibly perverse structure. This encourages us to make a link between her "no" and the quasi-imaginary sign of the perverse fantasm.

32. Philippe Julien, in his work *L'étrange jouissance du prochain* (Paris, Seuil, 1994), makes it clear where the difference lies between an ancient tragic heroine like Antigone and a modern one like Sygne de Coûfontaine. One of the differences is that Antigone can act as if an inhuman, divine law exists. Sygne, by contrast, can only bear this moment of negation within herself.

33. The concepts with the *Ver*-prefixes that Freud uses in his theory, such as *Verdrängung* and *Verneinung*, have a similar ambiguity: *Verdrängung* (repression) as such is always a failed *Verdrängung*; *Verneinung* (negation) always includes an affirmation.

34. J. Lacan, *Le Séminaire, Livre VIII. Le transfert* (1960–1961), *op. cit.*, p. 377.

35. S. Freud, "The Economic Problem of Masochism" (1924), SE XIX, pp. 155–170; here pp. 161–163.

36. J. Lacan, "The Subversion of the Subject and the Dialectic of Desire in the Freudian Unconscious" (1960), *Ecrits: A Selection, op. cit.*, p. 319.

37. Lacan claims that the enigma is an enunciation in which one does not find a statement. See J. Lacan, *Le sinthome, op. cit.*, 7: p. 13. Earlier, he spoke of the enigma in the context of analytic interpretation. There, it was used to characterize the analyst's interventions. These interventions are effective precisely to the extent that they are enigmatic: they do not force the subject to understand anything in particular, but produce a signifying work on the part of the analysand around the enigma, permitting him or her to "look awry" at his or her own symptomatic structure, catching a glimpse of how there is an enjoyment underlying his or her productions of meaning. See J. Lacan, *Le Séminaire, Livre XVII. L'envers de la psychanalyse* (1969–1970), texte établi par J.-A. Miller, Paris, Seuil, 1991, p. 41.

38. The site where you are involved with the symptom is of course *Eine andere Schauplatz*, another scene, the unconscious.

39. See J. Lacan, "Conférences et entretiens dans des universités nord-américains" (1975), *Scilicet*, 6/7, 1976, p. 58.

40. The figure is taken from *Scilicet* 6/7, p. 59.

41. As far as we know, Lacan first uses the notion of the *nom du père* in his "Le mythe individuel du névrosé," where it is already connected to what he calls a fourth element, death, and is also thought as the point of a subject's inscription in a symbolic system. See J. Lacan, "Le mythe individuel du

névrosé" (1953), *Ornicar?*, 17/18: 1979, pp. 289–307. Here, p. 305. He also refers to the *nom du père* in his Rome discourse: J. Lacan, "The Function and Field of Speech and Language in Psychoanalysis" (1953), *Écrits: A Selection*, *op. cit.*, p. 67.

42. The name of the father was construed throughout Lacan's work as the point of a necessary inscription into the Symbolic. The *sinthome* is also the site of one's inscription in the Symbolic, if we recall that the *sinthome* is the grounding of the Symbolic in an enjoyment. In *Le sinthome*, Lacan performs an analysis of James Joyce, in which he argues that Joyce's *sinthome* is precisely the name of the father, the patronym "Joyce," which Joyce sought to eternalize and honor by means of his writings. Yet there may be grounds for saying that there is a difference between the name of the father and the *sinthome*. It may be the case that *sinthome* and the name of the father are connected on a formal level insofar as both have to do with naming. But not every naming would be *à la* name of the father, and some *sinthomes* might not work in terms of the name of the father either.

2

Illiterature

Dany Nobus

READING LITERATE AND ILLITERATE

In a rare discussion of the analyst's recommended code of conduct during the treatment, Freud disapproved of the fairly common practice of note taking. He believed that analysands might find the analyst's scribbling offensive, criticized the selectiveness it imposes, but scorned above all the fact that it was likely to distract the analyst's attention from the interpretation of what was being said. Freud even went so far as to state that whenever he found something of interest in the text of a patient's dream he would ask his patient to repeat it to him, so that he could record it more accurately in his mind.[1] Whereas according to Freud, then, analysts need not be deterred from taking notes once the session has finished, they should refrain from writing during the analytic process, because it prevents them from reading their patients' words. Here, the analyst appears not only as a listener, the analysand not merely as somebody who speaks, but the former functions as a listener-reader for a speaker-writer. Instead of transcribing what they hear, analysts are urged to ensure that the text remains on the side of the analysand, restricting their own interventions to translation, interpretation, or deciphering.

Situating the analyst and the analysand in the dimensions of listening-speaking and writing-reading elicits a number of challenging questions, which have both clinical and theoretical relevance. If the analysand is the one who engages in writing, manipulating letters in such a way that they give rise to a textual narrative, how does this take place and how does it relate to the production of spoken words? Isn't writing of lesser importance, given the traditional emphasis on speech within psychoanalytic treatment? And to what extent is psychoanalysis also a writing-cure? What value are we to accord to the numerous websites offering "psychodynamic counseling" over the Internet? Is it possible to conduct analytic sessions via e-mail or, away from cyberspace, on the basis of an exchange of traditional letters? How should analysts read their analysands' writing? Should they read everything according to the rebus principle Freud adduced in *The Interpretation of Dreams* as a guideline for decoding the text of a dream?[2]

Reading the analysand's writing in line with the latter principle would entail a complete disregard for the logographic meaning of linguistic elements in favor of their phonetic value. Yet if this were an appropriate procedure, the script would probably become questionable in its very status as a writing system, since every fully developed writing incorporates a combination of logographic and phonetic symbols. In other words, if the analysand's formations of the unconscious indeed operate as complete writing systems, the analyst should not rely solely on the phonetic quality of the symbols. Are we entitled to expect, then, that analysts can read the analysand's writing in the same way as they would read any old text? May we reasonably assume that the analysand writes in a language known to the analyst, and that the analyst simply has to read, either literally or figuratively, what has been written? Isn't the analyst also supposed to know how to read between the lines? Isn't he or she also supposed to be literate in the repressed representations that have been deleted from the text?

Although Freud intermittently discussed the psychical significance of reading and writing until the end of his career, the issue figures much more prominently in Lacan's contributions to psychoanalysis. Apart from its significance as a conceptual crux within Lacan's oeuvre, the contentious relationship between listening-reading and speaking-writing governs the way in which his works came about and it presides over the circumstances of each and every encounter with them. Long before he decided to collate his most important texts in a single volume of *Écrits*, Lacan already enjoyed the dubious reputation of being illegible. Of course the latter notion should not be taken literally here, but rather as denoting a singular challenge to knowledge that confronts every reader of the Lacanian text. Lacan's writings appear unreadable to many readers because of the enormous demands they put on one's general familiarity with the history of ideas, in the broadest sense of the term, and one's specific acquaintance with psychoanalytic literature. The reader might imagine that it is his or her illiteracy that prevents an understanding of the pleiad of allusions pervading Lacan's writing, a painful lack of knowledge that stymies the reading of the text. It is as if our reading is made impossible by Lacan's superabundant knowledge and his refusal to share it with others.

Somewhat ironically, the frustrated reader's solution to this epistemological impasse, assuming that he does not give way in his desire to read the unreadable text, is often to widen his reading in order to enhance his literacy. And it may seem at first that Lacan himself entertained such a strategy during the late 1950s as the requisite procedure for interpreting the unconscious within a Freudian paradigm:

> In order to interpret the unconscious as Freud did, one would have to be, as he was, an encyclopaedia of the arts and muses, as well as an assiduous reader of the *Fliegende Blätter*. And the task would not be made easier for us by putting us at the mercy of a thread woven with allusions, quotations, puns, and equivocations.[3]

Yet how are we to read this passage? How can we be sure that this sentence conveys an opinion fully endorsed by Lacan and not his ironic denunciation of a totally inappropriate conception of the unconscious fueling the analyst's accumulation of knowledge? In the latter case, the implication would be that gathering knowledge assists neither the analyst nor the reader of Lacan's own texts in unearthing the meaning of what is written; on the contrary, this intellectualist enterprise would only drive the reader-analyst further and further away from the writer-analysand. And the paradoxical result would be that the reader's literacy stands in inverse proportion to his capacity to read a text, unreadability finding its resolution in the evacuation rather than the inflation of knowledge. Or, to put it in yet another way, the access to the text would be barred less by the reader's ignorance than by what she (thinks she) already knows.

Turning the tables, one could argue that the difficulty of Lacan's writing does not so much stem from the subjective burden of our own illiteracy as from the writer's implicit supposition of an active body of knowledge on our part. The text does not clarify what it presumes to be common knowledge among the readers; each omission on the level of the writing coincides with an assumed representation in the space of reading. The reader's acknowledgment of this condition does not normally incite further reading; if anything, it sparks off speech and writing in its own right, which can take the form of a complaint ("He does not even realize I am ignorant"), a series of questions ("Why am I unaware of the knowledge he attributes to me, and why does he think I possess it?"), or a declaration of knowledge ("If I am knowledgeable, then this is what I know").

If the content of Lacan's oeuvre reflects a continuous preoccupation with the processes of reading and writing, and its written form stretches the boundaries of reading, then the Lacanian text itself occupies an extraordinary position on the spectrum of speech and writing. It is well known that his contributions divide into a series of annual seminars (Le Séminaire) and an impressive collection of writings (Écrits), some of which were bundled together in the eponymous 1966 volume.[4] Faced with Lacan's seminars, the reader needs to bear in mind that they derive from a spoken discourse and were therefore addressed to a group of listeners, rather than a readership. As Jacques-Alain Miller notes in an addendum to his transcription of Lacan's Seminar XI, the transition from a spoken discourse to a written text entailed the invention of a writing, to which Lacan adds in his own afterword to the transcription that the writing is not to be read.[5] That "there is a mountain between saying and writing," as Lacan put it in 1975, can be confirmed by scanning the alternative, unauthorized versions of the seminars, or (if one is fortunate enough to have them) by listening to tape recordings of Lacan's presentations.[6] A similar ambiguity characterizes Lacan's actual "writings," whether those included in Écrits or those featuring in other collections. "It is rather well known that those Écrits cannot be read easily," Lacan quips in (the transcription of) his *Seminar XX, Encore*, ". . . that is exactly what I thought. I thought, perhaps it goes that far, I thought they were not meant to be read (*pas à lire*)."[7] But the question is: Not meant to be read by whom? For there is hardly a text in the *Écrits*, and in the voluminous body of writings outside the *Écrits*, that was not (re)read, in one way or another, by Lacan himself. Some texts, like the (in)famous "Seminar on 'The Purloined Letter'" were read aloud before they were put into writing, whereas others, such as the equally (in)famous "Lituraterre"—to which I shall return below—were read aloud after having been written. In both cases, there is a conspicuous difference between the written text and (the transcription of) Lacan's reading of it at his seminar. The status of the *Écrits* is therefore highly ambiguous or, as Lacan himself phrased it in "Lituraterre": "*Écrits*, a title more ironic than one might think: when it concerns either reports, a function of Conferences, or let's say 'open letters' where I raise the matter of a swatch of my teaching."[8]

Despite having been declared *pas à lire* by their author, the *Écrits* attracted a panoply of readers, and some of these readers even read the texts with the utmost care and determination. This was, for example, the case with Jean-Luc Nancy and Philippe Lacoue-Labarthe, who read Lacan's "The Agency of the Letter" and published the results of their reading in *Le titre de la lettre*, a book that constitutes yet again the transcription of an oral presentation at a seminar.[9] In (the transcription of) his own seminar, Lacan congratulates the authors on their work: "I can say in a certain way that, if it is a question of reading, I have never been so well read—with so much love . . . Let us simply say that it is a model of good reading, such good reading that I can safely say that I regret never having obtained anything like it from my closest associates."[10]

The threefold stratification of the conflictual relation between reading and writing in Lacan's works—from the content of his texts and the way in which they were composed to their function for the reader— makes it extremely difficult to evaluate their precise status and significance. Moreover, each of these interlocking strata changes over time, so that the synchronic interaction among the three levels also differs at each moment according to the diachrony of Lacan's intellectual itinerary. Lacan continuously rewrites his own writings in a dialectical spiral of rectification and (often implicit) self-criticism, through which their meaning is endlessly reassessed retroactively from the perspective of a specific historical scansion. To grasp this process, it is enough to compare and contrast the 1966 introduction to the French volume of *Écrits* and Lacan's "Introduction to the German Edition of a First Volume of the *Écrits*," written in 1973.[11] It is as if these two small texts, composed within an interval of barely seven years, introduce the reader to two completely different collections of papers, so divergent is their conception and so irreconcilable their frame of reference.

THE CUTTING EDGE

Taking account of these disparities in Lacan's work, I have decided to develop my argument about the function of reading and writing in psychoanalysis through a reading of some of Lacan's digressions on the problem of writing from the early 1970s, in particular those included in the essay entitled "Lituraterre."[12] This choice was mainly inspired by the observation that in this text Lacan advances a new interpretation of writing that overthrows many of his previous arguments, while setting the tone for most of his subsequent theoretical developments on the themes of the Real, the Symbolic, and the Imaginary. In addition, my decision was bolstered by the fact that "Lituraterre" has received relatively little critical attention within Anglo-American as well as French circles.[13]

A quick glance at Lacan's bibliography suffices to reveal a long-standing interest in the value of the letter and the importance of literary style for making judgments about the structure of the human psyche. During the early 1930s, while completing his doctorate, Lacan devoted a series of papers to the issue of writing and psychosis, and when he retraces his own milestones at Yale University in 1975, he divulges that his principal motive for choosing the case of Aimée as the *pièce de résistance* of his dissertation was the fact that "the person in question had produced numerous . . . writings [*écrits*]."[14] During the 1950s, Lacan resumed his discussion of the letter in his notorious "Seminar on 'The Purloined Letter,'" the equally illustrious text on "The Agency of the Letter in the Unconscious," and a less well-known essay on the youth of André Gide.[15] He pursued his exploration of writing in the seminar on *Identification* of 1961–62, eventually deciding upon the publication of his *Écrits* some five years later.[16] When the question of writing became the prime topic of investigation for a plethora of French intellectuals during the second half of the 1960s, Lacan did not respond to the criticisms of his contemporaries without simultaneously espousing some of their ideas.[17] Indeed, Lacan's assertions about writing in the early 1970s in many ways epitomized an engagement with this new wave of critique on the letter, which subsequently paved the way for a return to the question of writing in psychosis during his groundbreaking seminar on Joyce of 1975–76.[18]

Lacan's minute unraveling of Poe's story in the "Seminar on 'The Purloined Letter,'" his detailed reflections on Gide's novels and letters to Madeleine, and his readings of Joyce's *Ulysses* and *Finnegans Wake* may give the impression that he was especially devoted to works of literature (*les belles lettres* in French) because they enabled him to substantiate his psychoanalytic theory of the letter. Yet Lacan himself repudiated the view that literary works can function as objects for illustrating and justifying the knowledge set forth by psychoanalytic theory, violently criticizing those scholars who believed it was *de rigueur* to use psychoanalytic knowledge as an instrument for revealing the true, hidden meaning of a text. In his essay on Gide, he proclaims that "Psychoanalysis can only be applied, in the proper sense of the term, as treatment and thus to a subject who speaks and hears/understands."[19] And while commenting on his own dissection of "The Purloined Letter," he states in "Lituraterre":

> In any case, far from compromising myself in this literary smoochy-woochy [*frotti-frotta*] with which the psychoanalyst who is short of ingenuity denotes himself, I bear witness there [in the *Écrits*] to the inevitable attempt at demonstrating the unevenness of his [the psychoanalyst's] practice to motivate the least of literary judgements . . . My critique, if it can deservedly be taken for literary, could only bear, I try my hand at it, on what Poe does in being a writer forming such a message about the letter. It is clear that in not saying it [the message] as such therein, it is not insufficiently, but all the more rigorously that he confesses it. Nonetheless, the elision [of the message] could not be elucidated by means of some trait of his psychobiography: it [this elision] would rather be occluded by it.[20]

What purpose could possibly be served, then, by the dozens of literary texts that permeate Lacan's discourse, a series running from *Athalie* to Claudel's Coûfontaine trilogy, and from *Hamlet* to Duras's *Le ravisse-*

ment de Lol V. Stein?[21] What function could still be reserved for the letter of literature in Lacan's psychoanalytic readings, within and outside the theoretical context of writing? In "Lituraterre," Lacan offers the following answer:

> It is certain that, as usual, psychoanalysis receives here, from literature, if it takes from it a less psychobiographical idea about repression in its mainspring. As for me, if I propose to psychoanalysis the letter as in abeyance [*en souffrance*], it is because it [psychoanalysis] shows its failure there. And it is through this that I illuminate it [psychoanalysis]: when I invoke in this way the Enlightenment [on the back-cover of the French *Écrits*] it is to demonstrate where it [psychoanalysis] constitutes a *hole* . . . Method through which psychoanalysis justifies better its intrusion: for if literary criticism could effectively renew itself, it would be because psychoanalysis is there for the texts to measure themselves against it, the enigma being on its side.[22]

In other words, literature is an appropriate bedfellow for psychoanalysis because it shows where the wealth of accumulated psychoanalytic knowledge fails. Rather than enlightening a body of literary texts through an application of solid psychoanalytic knowledge, Lacan sought to enlighten the persistent enigmas of psychoanalysis by applying to them the knowledge embedded in literature.

Proceeding from this reevaluation of his own reading, Lacan subsequently deploys a completely new psychoanalytic theory of the letter, in which it no longer operates as an "insistence" or "agency" (*instance*) but as a shoreline, a littoral between knowledge and jouissance. At this stage, it is worth recalling that during the mid-1950s Lacan put the letter on a par with the signifier, the two units circulating strictly within the register of the Symbolic. Stopping short of actually identifying the letter with the signifier, he argued that the letter is the material support of the signifier, the "essentially localised structure of the signifier" and, in his "Seminar on 'The Purloined Letter,'" a pure signifier inasmuch as its connection with signification is radically severed.[23] From a different angle, Lacan's alignment of the letter and the signifier during the 1950s may also be gauged from his claim that the trajectory of the letter in Poe's story governs the characters' roles, that is to say that the "displacement of the signifier determines the subjects in their acts," propositions that precipitated in the formula that the signifier represents the subject for another signifier.[24]

During the early 1970s, the picture changes dramatically and irreversibly. From being a companion of the signifier, an associate equal in status and power(lessness), the letter becomes the signifier's traumatic offspring. The gist of this crucial theoretical move is summarized in the mysterious title of Lacan's 1971 contribution to the debate on literature and psychoanalysis. In the first sentence of "Lituraterre," Lacan comments briefly on the origin of his peculiar title:

> This word [lituraterre] is legitimised by the Ernout and Meillet: *lino, litura, liturarius*. It nonetheless occurred to me through this word-game with which one happens to make a witticism: the spoonerism appearing on the lips, the reversal at the ear.[25]

The "Ernout and Meillet" from which Lacan draws legitimacy is a French etymological and historical dictionary of Latin.[26] According to this reference work, the Latin *littera*, from which both the French *littérature* and the English "literature" derive, refers to a letter of the alphabet, a writing character, all kinds of written work, literature, culture, and instruction. The authors also point out that the spelling of the word with one "t" (*litera-*) is due to a mistaken association of *littera* with *lino* and *litum*. Under the latter entries one finds that *lino* means "to coat" (*enduire*), *litum* and *litura* referring to a "coating" (*enduit*), hence the subsidiary meanings of deletion (*rature*), correction, erasure, and spot/stain (*tâche*). *Liturarius* means "that which shows deletions."[27] This term is homophonic with *litorarius* (from *litus* and *litoris*), which means shore, coast, littoral.[28] Considering the meanings of *litura* (coating, deletion) and *terre* (ground), Lacan's neologism *lituraterre* might thus be translated literally as "deletion on the ground," "erasureland," or "stainearth." Yet, the central significance of Lacan's substitution of *litura* for *littera*, on the basis of his own play on words and an inappropriate etymological connection, is that the letter (writing and culture) is replaced with the notions of erasure, deletion, and correction.

Having explained the linguistic backdrop of his title, Lacan subsequently refers to "A litter to Mr James Joyce," the title of a letter of protest ostensibly written by one Vladimir Dixon in response to Joyce's

"Work in Progress," and published in the 1929 apologia for some of Joyce's published fragments.[29] Whereas some literary scholars have emphasized that Lacan failed to take account of the diversity of meanings the word "litter" can have here—from rubbish to bedding, and the entire brood of offspring produced along the way—Lacan was clearly thinking of the expression "to make litter of" (*faire litière de*), which means "to sacrifice heavily," "to relinquish," "to erase completely."[30] So much is confirmed by another paragraph in "Lituraterre," in which Lacan wonders where Joyce's littering of the letter could have come from: "In making litter of the letter, is it still Saint Thomas who comes back to him, as the work bears witness to through its entire length?"[31]

But if the letter can be a litter, and culture (one of the other meanings of *littera*) and civilization something like a sewer, as Lacan stated provocatively, what is left then of their association with the signifier, language, and the Symbolic order?[32] Nuancing his own previous formulations, Lacan argues during the early 1970s that the letter (writing) and the signifier (speech and language) belong to completely different registers. Whereas the signifier is situated within the Symbolic, the letter belongs to the Real.[33] For Lacan, this did not imply that the letter should be regarded as a primary element, the signifier emerging at a (chrono)logically later stage of development, as Derrida had suggested in "Freud and the Scene of Writing" and *Of Grammatology* through a deconstructive reading of Freud's *Project for a Scientific Psychology* and "A Note upon the 'Mystic Writing-Pad.'"[34] As Lacan contends in "Lituraterre":

> What I have inscribed, by means of letters, of the formations of the unconscious in order to recuperate them from that with which Freud formulates them, for being what they are, effects of the signifier, does not authorise making the letter into a signifier, nor to affect it, what is even more, with primacy in relation to the signifier. Such a confused discourse could only have arisen from that [the discourse] which imports me [*celui qui m'importe*].[35]

In opposition to Derrida, Lacan postulates that the letter (writing) cannot exist without the signifier or, similarly, that the signifier is a necessary and sufficient precondition for the birth of the letter. In terms of Lacan's registers, this entails that the Real (the realm of the letter) cannot emerge separately and independently from the Symbolic (the country of the signifier). Of course, this does not mean that the signifier and its offspring coexist peacefully within the same boundaries. After having been produced by the Symbolic order, the letter breaks away from it, keen to lead a life outside the laws of the signifier and resisting all attempts at recuperation within the bosom of language.

Lacan's thesis is relatively easy to understand when thinking of the way in which writing systems relate to spoken language. Although all fully developed scripts reflect articulated sounds (and, if one agrees to follow Lacan, would not exist without those sounds), no script whatsoever constitutes a perfect, element-by-element phonetic representation of spoken language. Some writing systems are phonetically more adequate than others, but certain forms of logography (complete word semantic symbols, such as "&" and "£" in English) cannot be avoided. The more efficiently the letters or characters of a writing system represent single sounds, the more phonographic, the less intrinsically meaningful, and the more alien they are to the semantic dimension of speech.[36] When Lacan claimed that letters belong to the Real, he intimated that as phonograms they are completely stripped of all meaning; it is impossible to say what the letter "X" means, because as a phonogram it does not have any meaning whatsoever.[37]

This idea was foreshadowed in the reading of "The Purloined Letter," a tale in which the content of the vexed missive is never revealed; yet at that point Lacan was still designating the letter as a pure signifier. Now, some fifteen years later, Lacan surmises that the letter cannot sustain itself as such within the Symbolic order when it is radically deprived of meaning. Formerly the signifier *par excellence*, an essentially meaningless unit, the letter now presents itself as a radical antisignifier, an excrement that has turned against its own progenitor. This separation of letter from signifier was not without its effects on the status of the signifier itself; having given birth to the letter, and seen it enter the arena of the Real, the signifier is no longer the same. Having acknowledged that the signifier is always already polluted with meaning, Lacan progressively emphasizes its aspect of semblance. Indeed, the theme traversing Lacan's Seminar XVIII, "On a Discourse that Would not be of Semblance," is that there is no such thing as a discourse that has *not* been erected on the grounds of semblance, not even the discourse of the analyst.

Lacan's claim that the body of psychoanalytic knowledge is re-vealed wanting or "holed" (*fait trou*) in its confrontation with the let-ter thus corresponds to a more general theory about the relationship between writing and the Symbolic order. Leaving behind a hole in the body of the signifier, which Lacan also designated as the body of knowl-edge (S_2), the letter can be said to initiate a process of excavation, an act of digging and drilling, which challenges the integrity of the Sym-bolic order. Or, to put it more provocatively, literature evokes the il-literacy of the Symbolic. As a result of the letter, the Symbolic body of knowledge falls into illiterature.[38]

In a renewed critique of Derrida, Lacan also explained that the letter does not delete any primordial object. To Derrida's assertion that "the trace is the erasure of selfhood, of one's own presence, and is con-stituted by the threat of its irremediable disappearance, of the disap-pearance of its disappearance," Lacan retorts (in equally convoluted language): "Erasure of no trace whatsoever that is prior, this is what constitutes the land [*terre*] of the littoral. Pure *litura*, that is the literal. To produce it [this erasure], is reproducing this half without comple-ment of which the subject subsists."[39] In leaving behind a hole in the Symbolic, the letter could be compared to a violent intruder who takes something precious away from his own ancestry, like the ruthless ex-cavators who removed the Elgin marbles from their rightful place. Yet for Lacan the erasure in question does *not* have an object; although it definitely induces a gap in knowledge, there has never been any pri-mordial fullness. The rupture in knowledge effectuated by the letter does not annihilate an original experience of complete harmony.

This dynamic conjures up the schema of frustration, privation, and castration, which Lacan had constructed during his seminar of 1956–57, and in which the object of castration (a Symbolic cut) is strictly imaginary.[40] Developmental theorists such as Mahler had argued that the child, under ideal circumstances, progresses from a dual unity with the mother to separation (triangulation) and individuation. By contrast, and even before Mahler's theory had gained momentum, Lacan empha-sized that castration cuts away neither the penis, nor the mother, nor anything else for that matter.[41] It does not cut off, away, or through; it simply *cuts*, as one would say about a sharp knife or, indeed, a thought-provoking text, a mind-blowing performance, or an innovative creation (one "at the cutting edge"). Instead of removing something, the erasure limits and delineates the signifier—as the shore does in relation to a stretch of land—and it is this imposed restriction on the radius of the Symbolic order (knowledge) that Lacan dubs the split subject ($\$$). To put it more explicitly, the erasure induced by the letter is identical with the split subject, which in turn is but another way of designating the absent center of control at the level of the unconscious.

Because the letter is a deletion without an object, trying to retrieve what is lost can evidently only take place on an Imaginary level. How else would one describe a quest for the recuperation of something that has never been there in the first place? The objects that come to occupy the empty space in the Symbolic are thus by definition inadequate, which does not preclude their providing enjoyment (*jouissance*). In compensating for the Imaginary lost object, which Lacan formalizes as $-\phi$, these objects (the famous objects *a*), remedy the hole ($\$$) hewn by the letter in the Symbolic order (the Other) and this is what endows them with the power of jouissance. In "Lituraterre," Lacan puts it as follows:

> The edge of the hole in knowledge, isn't this what it [the letter] outlines. And how could psychoanalysis, if, precisely what the letter says 'literally', through its mouth, one must not fail to acknowledge that in it, how could it [psychoanalysis] deny that it is, this hole—that it is by filling it that it [psychoanalysis] has recourse to evoking jouissance there?[42]

Apart from confirming the idea that any artificial stuffing of the hole in the Symbolic coincides with the production of jouissance, this paragraph of course also raises questions as to the course and finality of psychoanalytic treatment, which I shall explore in the last section of this chapter.

First, let me return briefly to Lacan's proposition that the letter, as fallout of the Symbolic order, delineates the field of knowledge, thereby producing an erasure. If the letter is the edge of knowledge, how are we to grasp the other side? If the letter is a shore demarcating a Symbolic Landsend, what does this coastline reveal beyond its own boundaries? In "Lituraterre," Lacan explicitly defines the other side of knowledge as jouissance, that is to say as that which is derived from the (inevitably inadequate) filling of its constitutive holes: "Between centre and absence, between knowledge and jouissance, there is littoral. . . ."[43]

But on other occasions, he intimates that the "absence" could equally well be defined in terms of truth, which he had already dubbed "the sister of jouissance" in *Seminar XVII*.[44] Hence, the epistemological distinction between truth and knowledge acquires a new dimension in Lacan's later works, insofar as the relationship between the two is theorized from the perspective of writing. The dividing line installed by the letter also now triggers the contention that the two separated territories are by no means equivalent. Indeed, Lacan is at great pains to maintain that the two areas (of knowledge and jouissance/truth) have nothing in common anymore:

> The frontier certainly, in separating two territories, symbolises for them that they are the same for who crosses it, that they have a common measure. It is the principle of the *Umwelt*, which reflects the *Innenwelt* . . . The letter, isn't it more appropriately . . . littoral, that is to say figuring that an entire domain is frontier for the other, in that they are foreign, to the point of not being reciprocal.[45]

In other words, the letter is not a dividing line that one would be able to cross, leaving one country behind in order to enter another (similar) country. Knowledge and jouissance/truth are incommensurable, and this is reconfirmed time and again in the experience of writing, as what traces the boundary between the Symbolic and what lies beyond it.

WRITING THE *SINTHOME*

For the final part of my chapter, I will endeavor to draw some conclusions from my reading of Lacan's writings on the letter from the early 1970s as regards the clinical practice of psychoanalysis. This will provide me with an opportunity to readdress some of the questions formulated at the outset. Two passages from "Lituraterre" deserve a closer reading here. At the beginning of the text, Lacan observes that in transforming letters into litter, Joyce had achieved through his writing what can be ideally expected from an actual analysis:

> One will recall that a "Maecenas" [*messe-haine*], in wishing him [Joyce] well, offered him a psychoanalysis, as one would offer a shower. And with Jung even . . . In the game we evoke [a letter, a litter], he would

have won nothing there, going straight in it to the best of what one may expect from psychoanalysis at its end.[46]

Later in his article, Lacan reflects upon the peculiarities of the Japanese language, and more specifically the two separate readings of the *kanji* (the Japanese characters) known as *on-yomi* (the Sino-Japanese reading) and *kun-yomi* (the native Japanese reading). Which of these two completely different readings applies to a certain character depends on the context in which it appears, yet it is in principle perfectly possible to read the same series of characters according to each of the two sound systems.[47] Having just returned from his second trip to Japan, Lacan claims in "Lituraterre" that this peculiarity of the Japanese language has important consequences for the status of the subject: "That it [the subject] takes support from a constellated sky, and not merely from the unary trait, for its fundamental identification, explains why it can only take support from the You."[48] Five years later, in his seminar on Joyce, Lacan himself found enough support in these lines to be able to argue that Japanese people are not qualified to be analysands.[49]

When taken together, these two fragments evoke questions about the importance of writing for entering into and reaching the end of a psychoanalytic process. On the one hand, Joyce is purportedly capable of obtaining the best possible psychoanalytic result through his writing, without ever having entered any form of psychoanalytic treatment. On the other, Japanese people are regarded as incapable of entering a psychoanalytic process as a result of their singular writing system, despite the history of Japanese interest in Freudian theory and practice.

If we concentrate on Joyce's relationship with the letter, we may very well ask ourselves what it means to "make a litter" of the letter, and how this operation is related to the end of analysis. In the unpublished transcription of his seminar *Ce qui fait insigne*, Miller has pointed out that the words "destitution," "evacuation," "waste," and "refuse" almost always appear when Lacan discusses the end of the psychoanalytic treatment.[50] For example, in his "Proposition of 9 October 1967 on the Psychoanalyst of the School," Lacan launches the notion of "subjective destitution" to typify the most advanced of psychoanalytic outcomes.[51] And some two years later, in the seminar "The Other Side of Psychoanalysis," Lacan introduces the discourse of the analyst as one of four structures in a comprehensive theory of social bonds, in which the master signifier (S_1) occupies the place of the product, the inevitable remainder that cannot be accommodated within the system.[52] The littering of the letter can thus easily be included in the series of terms Lacan had already adduced to describe the end of analysis. Yet this still begs the question as to the exact nature of the operation and its significance for the psychoanalytic endgame.

What happens when Joyce makes a litter of the letter in *Ulysses* and, more radically, in *Finnegans Wake*? Lacan formulates an answer to this question in his seminar of 1975–76, in which he argues that with his writing Joyce created a new name for himself, a name that can be termed *sinthome*.[53] At the very beginning of this seminar, Lacan divulges that *sinthome* is an ancient spelling of *symptôme*, but it rapidly emerges that he does not intend to use the two words interchangeably.[54] It seems to me possible to argue here that the *sinthome* is what becomes of the symptom after the letter presiding over its structure has been "littered."

To clarify this point, and because a detailed exposition of the nature and function of the symptom within Lacanian theory falls beyond the scope of this chapter, I shall restrict myself to the idea that the symptom always results from the subjective inadequacy of ignorance. To put it differently, the symptom originates in the fact that the absent subject ($\$$) of the unconscious (S_2, a body of knowledge) is compensated for by all kinds of substitute satisfactions. As we noted above, the letter is simultaneously responsible for the installation of the divided subject, the cut that constitutes the limit of knowledge, and the separation between knowledge and truth/jouissance. Making a litter of the letter does not therefore entail a restoration of the fullness of subjective knowledge, for this would be equivalent to the annihilation of the unconscious. Rather, it signals that the endless repetition of symptomatic compensations for the lack in knowledge is halted and replaced by an acknowledgment of ignorance. Whereas the symptom originates in a desperate attempt to know and control oneself, the *sinthome* is—literally—a locus of illiterature.[55]

Analysts as listener-readers are thus not supposed to do away with the holes in their analysands' knowledge by telling them what they, as qualified and literate analysts, know about the workings of the mind. However strongly analysands may invest their analysts with the function of the supposed subject of knowing (*sujet supposé savoir*), that "pivot on which everything to do with the transference is hinged," analysts should refrain from incarnating this supposed subject of knowing, because it involves a closure—even the abolishment—of the unconscious.[56] As well as avoiding this kind of reparative therapy or, *sit venia verbo*, this epistemological stuffing, analysts are even less supposed to drain away the jouissance from their analysands' bodies. For all the enjoyment it may bring to the analyst, this castrating role is a recipe for analytic disaster, because the analysand has never possessed and will never own this jouissance. Rather, analysts are urged to interpret what their analysands are saying in such a way that the shoreline that delineates the territory of their knowledge becomes accessible. Through the analyst's interpretations, which operate as punctuations rather than explanations, the meanings with which the signifier (as semblance) is equipped are gradually traced back and reduced to the erasure of the letter. When reading an analysand's letters, the analyst should not try to understand what they mean, for they are intrinsically meaningless, but rather facilitate their transformation into bits of debris. Neither fostered, nor interdicted, jouissance and truth consequently rejoin the realm of the Symbolic, an integration which Lacan conveyed in *Television* with the idea that psychoanalysis should espouse an ethics of well-saying (as opposed to one of well-being).[57]

Of course, the possible coincidence of truth/jouissance and knowledge does not mean that knowledge becomes truthful, but that knowledge is able to function in the place of truth, that one's ignorance no longer poses a problem, or that one is able to seek it actively and unreservedly. If it is true that the analytical process on the side of the analysand follows a logical course from speech (the signifier) to writing (the letter), and from writing back to speech, the effectiveness of psychoanalytic treatments that rely exclusively on writing must necessarily be limited.

According to Lacan, similar limitations hold for subjects whose first language is Japanese, because their writing system does not make room for the installation of a primordial identification. Without deciding in favor of or against Lacan's contention, I merely wish to underline that the universality of psychoanalytic knowledge is as much at stake in it as the mental health of the Japanese subject. The Japanese letter carves out its own hole in the imperialist ambitions of a Western body of psychoanalytic knowledge, as Freud had already experienced with Dr Heisaku Kosawa during the 1930s. After a training analysis with

Richard Sterba and supervision with Paul Federn, Kosawa decided that he would only be capable of becoming a successful analyst in his homeland by exchanging the Oedipus for the Ajase complex.[58] What the story of Kosawa reveals is not so much the "unanalysable" quality of the Japanese subject as the cultural limits of the psychoanalytic theories and practices deployed in the wake of Freud's original discoveries. While Joyce may have accessed a point of illiterature (a *sinthome*) with the composition of *Finnegans Wake*, I wish to propose here that psychoanalysis reaches its own shoreline of illiterature in confrontation with non-Western cultures, as exemplified in the Japanese "resistance" to the Freudian Oedipus complex. The erasure epitomized by the Japanese *kanji* not only constitutes a singular linguistic feature; it delineates the edge of psychoanalytic knowledge, beyond which there lies but the jouissance of interpretative imperialism.

NOTES

1. S. Freud, "Recommendations to Physicians Practising Psycho-Analysis" (1912), *SE* XII, p. 113.
2. S. Freud, *The Interpretation of Dreams* (1900), *SE* IV, pp. 252–253.
3. J. Lacan, "The Agency of the Letter in the Unconscious or Reason since Freud" (1957), *Écrits: A Selection*, trans. Alan Sheridan, London: Tavistock, 1977, pp. 170–171 (translation modified).
4. J. Lacan, *Écrits*, Paris: Seuil, 1966.
5. J. Lacan, *Le Séminaire, Livre XI. Les quatre concepts fondamentaux de la psychanalyse* (1964), texte établi par J.-A. Miller, Paris: Seuil, 1973, pp. 249–251. All translations from French source materials for which no English translation is currently available are mine.
6. J. Lacan, "Conférences et entretiens dans des universités nord-américaines," Columbia University/Auditorium School of International Affairs, *Scilicet* 6/7, 1976, p. 43.
7. J. Lacan, *The Seminar, Book XX. On Feminine Sexuality, the Limits of Love and Knowledge* (1972–73), trans. with notes by B. Fink, edited by J.-A. Miller, New York and London: Norton, 1998, p. 26.
8. J. Lacan, "Lituraterre," *Littérature*, 1971, 3, p. 4 (my translation).
9. J.-L. Nancy and P. Lacoue-Labarthe, *The Title of the Letter: A Reading of Lacan* (1973), trans. François Raffoul and David Pettigrew, Albany, NY: State University of New York Press, 1992.

10. J. Lacan, *The Seminar, Book XX. op. cit.*, p. 65. It should be noted that Nancy and Lacoue-Labarthe's reading crystalized in a ruthless exposure of the surreptitious metaphysical stakes of Lacan's text, conclusions Lacan called "inconsiderate," without insisting on the point any further.

11. J. Lacan, "Ouverture de ce recueil," *Écrits, op. cit.*, pp. 9–10; J. Lacan, "Introduction à l'édition allemande d'un premier volume des *Écrits*" (1973), *Scilicet* 5, 1975, pp. 11–17.

12. The article was commissioned for a special issue of the journal *Littérature* on literature and psychoanalysis, and Lacan read the text during his seminar "On a Discourse that Would not be of Semblance" on May 12, 1971, some five months before it was published. See J. Lacan, "Litturaterre," *op. cit.*; J. Lacan, *Le Séminaire XVIII, D'un discours qui ne serait pas du semblant* (unpublished), session of May 12, 1971.

13. My reading of "Lituraterre" benefited from the following source materials: J. Allouch, "La 'conjecture de Lacan' sur l'origine de l'écriture," *Littoral* 7/8, 1983, pp. 5–26; P. Julien, "Le nom propre et la lettre," *Littoral*, 1983, 7/8, pp. 33–45; J.-A. Miller, *Ce qui fait insigne*, seminar of 1986–87, Department of Psychoanalysis, University of Paris VIII. Unpublished; J.-A. Miller, "Remarques et questions," *Analytica*, 55 (Lacan et la chose japonaise), Paris: Navarin, 1988, pp. 95–112; N. Bousseyroux, *Pratiques de la lettre et usage de l'inconscient*, Toulouse: Presses Universitaires du Mirail, 1993; E. Laurent, "La lettre volée et le vol sur la lettre," *La cause freudienne*, 1999, 43, pp. 31–46.

14. See J. Lacan, "Écrits 'inspirés': Schizographie" (1931), in *De la psychose paranoïaque dans ses rapports avec la personnalité, suivi de Premiers écrits sur la paranoïa*, Paris: Seuil, 1975, pp. 365–382; J. Lacan, "The Problem of Style and the Psychiatric Conception of Paranoiac Forms of Experience" (1933), trans. Jon Anderson, *Critical Texts*, 1988, 5(3), pp. 4–6; J. Lacan, "Conférences et entretiens dans des universités nordaméricaines": Yale University, Kanzer Seminar, *Scilicet* 6/7, 1976, p. 9.

15. J. Lacan, Seminar on "The Purloined Letter" (1956), trans. Jeffrey Mehlman, in John P. Muller and William J. Richardson (Eds.), *The Purloined Poe: Lacan, Derrida and Psychoanalytic Reading*, Baltimore, MD and London: Johns Hopkins University Press, 1988, pp. 28–54; J. Lacan, "The Agency of the Letter in the Unconscious or Reason since Freud" (1957), *Écrits: A Selection*, trans. Alan Sheridan, London: Tavistock, 1977, pp. 146–178; J. Lacan, "Jeunesse de Gide ou la lettre et le désir" (1958), *Écrits, op. cit.*, pp. 739–764.

16. J. Lacan, *Le Séminaire IX, L'identification* (1961–62), unpublished.

17. See J. Derrida, *Writing and Difference* (1967), trans. Alan Bass, New York and London: Routledge, 1978; J. Derrida, *Of Grammatology* (1967), trans. Gayatri Chakravorty Spivak, Baltimore, MD and London: Johns Hopkins University Press, 1997; P. Sollers, *L'écriture et l'experience des limites*, Paris: Seuil,

1971; R. Barthes, *S/Z* (1970), trans. Richard Miller, preface by Richard Howard, Oxford: Blackwell, 1990; R. Barthes, *Empire of Signs* (1970), trans. Richard Howard, London: Cape, 1983.

18. J. Lacan, *Le Séminaire XXIII, Le sinthome* (1975–76), *Ornicar?* 1976, 6, pp. 3–20; 7, pp. 3–18; 8, pp. 6–20; 1977, 9, pp. 32–40; 10, pp. 5–12; 11, pp. 2–9.

19. J. Lacan, "Jeunesse de Gide ou la lettre et le désir," *op. cit.*, p. 747.

20. J. Lacan, "Lituraterre," *op. cit.*, p. 4 (my translation). Let me remind the reader here that in Poe's story the actual content of the incriminating letter is never revealed.

21. See J. Lacan, *The Seminar, Book III. The Psychoses* (1955–56), ed. J.-A. Miller, trans. with notes R. Grigg, London: Routledge, 1993; J. Lacan, *Le Séminaire, Livre VIII. Le transfert* (1960–61), texte établi par J.-A. Miller, Paris: Seuil, 1991; J. Lacan, "Desire and the Interpretation of Desire in *Hamlet*" (1959), ed. J.-A. Miller, trans. J. Hulbert, in S. Felman (Ed.), *Literature and Psychoanalysis—The Question of Reading: Otherwise*, Baltimore, MD and London: Johns Hopkins University Press, 1982, pp. 11–52; J. Lacan, "Homage to Marguerite Duras, in *Le ravissement de Lol V. Stein*," trans. P. Connor, in Marguerite Duras, *Marguerite Duras* (1987), San Francisco, CA: City Lights Books, pp. 122–129.

22. J. Lacan, "Lituraterre," *op. cit*, pp. 4–5. In his "Seminar on 'The Purloined Letter,'" Lacan had adduced "The Letter in Abeyance" (*la lettre en souffrance*) as an alternative title for Poe's story. See J. Lacan, "Seminar on 'The Purloined Letter'" (1956) in J. P. Muller and W. J. Richardson (Eds.), *The Purloined Poe: Lacan, Derrida and Psychoanalytic Reading*, Baltimore, MD and London: Johns Hopkins University Press, 1988, p. 43. The reader should note that in this translation of Lacan's "Seminar on 'The Purloined Letter,'" *lettre en souffrance* has been rendered as "letter in suffering."

23. J. Lacan, "The Agency of the Letter in the Unconscious, or Reason since Freud," *op. cit.*, pp. 147, 153; J. Lacan, "The Seminar on 'The Purloined Letter,'" *op. cit.*, p. 32.

24. J. Lacan, "The Seminar on 'The Purloined Letter,'" *op. cit.*, pp. 43–44; J. Lacan, "Position of the Unconscious" (1964), trans. B. Fink, in R. Feldstein, B. Fink, and M. Jaanus (Eds.), *Reading Seminar XI: Lacan's Four Fundamental Concepts of Psychoanalysis*, Albany, NY: State University of New York Press, 1995, pp. 259–282.

25. J. Lacan, "Lituraterre," *op. cit.*, p. 3.

26. A. Ernout and A. Meillet, *Dictionnaire étymologique de la langue latine. Histoire des mots*, 4ème édition, Paris: Librairie Klincksieck, 1959. Lacan gives the full reference in his Seminar "On a Discourse that Would not be of Semblance" during the session of May 12, 1971, when he read the text of

"Lituraterre." He had already referred to the same dictionary ten years earlier in his Seminar *Identification*. See J. Lacan, *Le Séminaire XVIII, D'un discours qui ne serait pas du semblant*, session of May 12, 1971. Unpublished. J. Lacan, *Le Séminaire IX, L'identification*, session of February 21, 1962, unpublished.

27. A. Ernout and A. Meillet, *Dictionnaire étymologique de la langue latine. Histoire des mots, op. cit.*, pp. 360–363. The meaning of *litura* (deletion) can still be found in the obsolete English verb of "to liturate," i.e., to blot out, to erase.

28. *Ibid.*, p. 364.

29. See *Our Exagmination Round his Factification for Incamination of Work in Progress* (1929), London: Faber & Faber, 1961, pp. 193–194. The entire text of Vladimir Dixon's "litter" is a parody of Joyce's constant twisting and turning of the English language, and some scholars have argued that Vladimir Dixon was in reality the master himself. Lacan had already used the play on a letter, a litter in his 1956 "Seminar on 'The Purloined Letter.'" See J. Lacan, "The Seminar on 'The Purloined Letter,'" *op. cit.*, p. 40. In his note to the text, Lacan "erased" (accidentally or intentionally) the letter "g" from the second word of the book's title, writing "examination" instead of "exagmination." Nearly twenty years later, in the transcription of Lacan's Seminar *Encore*, the event somehow repeated itself when Lacan referred (at least in writing) to *Finnegan's Wake* instead of *Finnegans Wake*. See J. Lacan, *Le Séminaire, Livre XX. Encore* (1972–73), texte établi par J.-A. Miller, Paris: Seuil, p. 37. Whereas the first erasure was faithfully copied in the English translation of Lacan's text, the second one was corrected for the English edition. On these and other aspects of Lacan's bungled engagement with the Joycean letter, see L. Thurston, "Proteiform Graphs: From Lacan's *Écrit* to Modernist Writing," *PS: Journal of the Universities Association for Psychoanalytic Studies*, 1999, 2(1), pp. 73–80.

30. See G. Lernout, *The French Joyce*, Ann Arbor, MI: University of Michigan Press, 1990, p. 72.

31. J. Lacan, "Lituraterre," *op. cit.* p. 3. Why would Joyce's "littering of the letter" be indebted to Thomas Aquinas, as is indeed the case for his theory of aesthetics? In December 1273, Aquinas had a mystical experience that prompted him to cancel all his work on the third part of the *Summa Theologica*. Aquinas explained the decision to his secretary with the famous words: "All the things I have written are like chaff (*sicut palea*) to me, compared with what I have seen and what has been revealed to me." After this event, Aquinas did not put a single word on paper anymore and he died three months later. For Joyce's espousal of Aquinas's doctrine of aesthetics, see W.T. Noon, *Joyce and Aquinas*, New Haven, CT and London: Yale University Press, 1957; U. Eco, *The Aesthetics of Chaosmos: The Middle Ages of James Joyce* (1962), Cambridge, MA and London: Harvard University Press, 1989. The anecdote of Aquinas's

final revelation is recounted in almost every scholarly study of the Church father's (uneventful) life and (massive body of) works. See, for example, F. Copleston, *Thomas Aquinas*, London: Search Press, 1955.

32. In 1971, Lacan divulged that he had already been dwelling on the idea of culture as pollution shortly before the student revolts of May 1968, when traveling to Bordeaux "so as to take nothing away from the frenzy of the affluences I move wherever I pay a visit nowadays." At the time Lacan had indeed been invited to Bordeaux by the staff members of the Charles Perrin hospital, at the initiative of Michel Demangeat. The text of his lecture, insofar as it exists, was (to the best of my knowledge) never released and/or published, but according to Demangeat Lacan discussed with eloquent enthusiasm "the great anal circuit of culture." Lacan liked the idea so much that he continued to use it throughout the 1970s. When lecturing at the prestigious Massachusetts Institute of Technology in December 1975, for instance, he reminded the honorable Willard von Orman Quine: "Civilization is refuse [*déchet*], *cloaca maxima.*" See J. Lacan, "Lituraterre," *op. cit.*, p. 3; J. Lacan, "Conférences et entretiens dans des universités nord-américaines": Massachusetts Institute of Technology, *Scilicet* 6/7, 1976, p. 61.

33. J. Lacan, *Le Séminaire XVIII, D'un discours qui ne serait pas du semblant*, *op. cit.*, session of May 12, 1971. For a similar point, see J. Lacan, *The Seminar, Book XX. On Feminine Sexuality, The Limits of Love and Knowledge* (1972–73), *op. cit.*, p. 29.

34. J. Derrida, "Freud and the Scene of Writing" (1966), in *Writing and Difference*, trans., A. Bass, London and New York: Routledge, 1978, pp. 196–231; J. Derrida, *Of Grammatology*, *op. cit.*, pp. 3–93; S. Freud, *Project for a Scientific Psychology* (1895), SE I, pp. 281–397; S. Freud, "A Note upon the 'Mystic Writing-Pad,'" SE XIX, pp. 227–232.

35. J. Lacan, "Lituraterre," *op. cit.*, p. 5 (my translation). The French *celui qui m'importe* is highly ambiguous and could also be rendered as "the one who is important to me." However, when Lacan read the text of "Lituraterre" during his seminar, he clarified that the word *celui* referred to "a discourse" and further in his text he indicated that he had used the verb *importer* in a very specific sense. Therefore, I have opted for the translation "that which imports me." Of course, it was Derrida's discourse that Lacan was accusing of importing his own work.

36. The relation between writing and speech is evidently more complicated than what my brief exposition suggests, if only because different letters can represent the same sound (and should thus be read in the same way) depending on the words in which they appear. For example, the letter "j" in the word "joke" is pronounced in the same way as the letter "g" in the word "germane." Conversely, one and the same letter can represent two or more differ-

ent sounds, as the "g" in the words "germane" and "gangrene." For an excellent discussion of these and other related issues, see J. DeFrancis, *Visible Speech: The Diverse Oneness of Writing Systems*, Honolulu, HI: University of Hawaii Press, 1989.

37. In his Seminar XXIII, *Le sinthome*, Lacan stated very clearly: "The Real is devoid of meaning." See J. Lacan, *Le Séminaire XXIII, Le sinthome* (1975–76), *Ornicar?*, 1977, 10, p. 9. When "X" is employed in words such as "X-rated" or "X-files," it acquires the status of a logogram because it refers to a specific idea, pornography and top-secret respectively.

38. Unlike Lacan's legitimized spoonerism, my "illiterature" has a less contrived origin. Although unusual, the word exists in English and refers to "want of learning," "lack of knowledge."

39. J. Derrida, "Freud and the Scene of Writing," *op. cit.*, p. 230; J. Lacan, "Lituraterre," *op. cit.*, p. 7. In his seminar "On a Discourse that Would not Be of Semblance," Lacan reminded his audience of the children's story of the half chicken (*Histoire d'une moitié de poulet*), which he had recounted the year before as an allegory for the condition of the divided subject. See J. Lacan, *Le Séminaire, Livre XVII. L'envers de la psychanalyse* (1969–70), texte établi par J.-A. Miller, Paris: Seuil, p. 63.

40. J. Lacan, *Le Séminaire, Livre IV, La relation d'objet* (1956–57), texte établi par J.-A. Miller, Paris: Seuil, 1994. Lacan did not use the schema in "Lituraterre," but he did refer to it in "A Man and a Woman," the second text he read during the seminar "On a Discourse that Would not Be of Semblance," which was not published until 1993. See J. Lacan, "Un homme et une femme" (1971), *Bulletin de l'Association freudienne internationale*, 1993, 54, pp. 13–21. For a (rather poor) English translation of Lacan's text, see J. Lacan, "A Man and a Woman," trans. C. J. Henshaw, *Papers of the Freudian School of Melbourne*, 1996, 17, pp. 79–97.

41. See M. S. Mahler, *On Human Symbiosis and the Vicissitudes of Individuation: Infantile Psychosis*, New York: International Universities Press, 1968; M. S. Mahler, F. Pine, and A. Bergman, *The Psychological Birth of the Human Infant: Symbiosis and Individuation*, London: Hutchinson, 1975.

42. J. Lacan, "Lituraterre," *op. cit.*, p. 5 (my translation).

43. *Ibid.*, p. 7.

44. See J. Lacan, "A Man and a Woman," *op. cit.*, pp. 80–81; J. Lacan, *Le Séminaire, Livre XVII. L'envers de la psychanalyse* (1969–70), texte établi par J.-A. Miller, Paris: Seuil, 1991, pp. 61–77.

45. J. Lacan, "Lituraterre," *op. cit.*, p. 5 (my translation).

46. *Ibid.*, p. 3. Lacan's neologism *messe-haine* is homophonic with the French word *mécène* (Maecenas, benefactor). In 1918 Mrs. Harold McCormick (Edith Rockefeller), a wealthy American who had been supporting Joyce fi-

nancially since his arrival in Zurich, advised him to start an analysis at her expense with Jung, who had been her own analyst and whose work she found profoundly interesting. When Joyce refused, McCormick ceased paying immediately. See R. Ellmann, *James Joyce*, Oxford and New York: Oxford University Press, 1959, pp. 466–467.

47. Perhaps the easiest way to understand how *on-yomi* and *kun-yomi* work is to imagine, for example, that in English the word "ghost" would sometimes have to be read as "ghost" and at other times as "fist" (because "gh" is "f" in "tough," and "o" is "i" in "women"), so that the same phonogram can have two completely different sounds and meanings. For an accessible explanation of the history and practice of *on-yomi* and *kun-yomi* within the wider social context of Japanese language politics, see N. Gottlieb, *Kanji Politics: Language Policy and Japanese Script*, London and New York: Kegan Paul International, 1995.

48. J. Lacan, "Lituraterre," *op. cit.*, p. 9 (my translation).

49. J. Lacan, *Le Séminaire XXIII, Le sinthome, op. cit.*

50. J.-A. Miller, *Ce qui fait insigne, op. cit.*, session of March 4, 1987, unpublished.

51. J. Lacan, "Proposition of 9 October 1967 on the Psychoanalyst of the School," trans. Russell Grigg, *Analysis*, 1995, 6, p. 8.

52. J. Lacan, *Le Séminaire, Livre XVII. L'envers de la psychanalyse, op. cit.*, p. 205.

53. J. Lacan, *Le Séminaire XXIII, Le sinthome, op. cit.*

54. Exactly fifty years after having discarded his voluminous writings as a load of chaff, Thomas Aquinas was canonized, through which he too in a sense gained access to the *sinthome*. Indeed, in French the word *sinthome* is homophonic with *saint homme* (holy man), which emboldened Lacan to talk about *sinthomadaquin* (*Saint Thomas d'Aquin*).

55. The fact that Lacan introduced the *sinthome* to account for the stabilization of Joyce's psychosis does not invalidate the generality of my claim. It merely invites further reflection upon the differential status of the *sinthome* (and writing) in neurosis, psychosis, and perversion.

56. J. Lacan, "Proposition of 9 October 1967 on the Psychoanalyst of the School," *op. cit.*, p. 5. On the analyst's mandatory refusal to identify with the supposed subject of knowing, see J. Lacan, *Le Séminaire IX, L'identification* (1961–62), session of November 22, 1961, unpublished; J. Lacan, *Le Séminaire XIV, La logique du fantasme* (1966–67), session of June 21, 1967, unpublished. On transference and the supposed subject of knowing as a closure of the unconscious, see J. Lacan, *The Four Fundamental Concepts of Psychoanalysis* (1964), trans. Alan Sheridan, Harmondsworth, UK: Penguin, 1994, pp. 130–133. On the supposed subject of knowing as the abolition of the unconscious,

see J. Lacan, "De Rome 53 à Rome 67: La psychanalyse—Raison d'un échec," *Scilicet*, 1, p. 46.

57. J. Lacan, *Television* (1973), trans. D. Hollier, R. Krauss, and A. Michelson, in J. Copjec (Ed.), *Television/A Challenge to the Psychoanalytic Establishment*, New York: Norton, 1990, pp. 1–46.

58. For Heisaku Kosawa's role in the history of psychoanalysis see, for example: K. Okonogi, "Japan," in P. Kutter (Ed.), *Psychoanalysis International: A Guide to Psychoanalysis throughout the World*, Vol. 2, Stuttgart-Bad-Canstatt, Germany: Frommann-Holzboog, 1995, pp. 123–141.

3

The *sinthome*:
Turbulence and Dissipation

Roberto Harari

Translated by Luke Thurston

We might say that we were looking for global schemas, symmetries, universal and unchanging laws—and what we have discovered is the mutable, the ephemeral, the complex.

—*Ilya Prigogine*

What is the sign that we have achieved freedom? No longer being ashamed of ourselves.

—*Friedrich Nietzsche*

We should not forget that a language game is, so to speak, something unpredictable. I mean: it has no foundations on which it could be based. It is not rational (or it is non-rational). It is there—just like our life.

—*Ludwig Wittgenstein*

INTRODUCTION

In this paper, I aim to clarify certain points made in previous texts,[1] as well as to extend the scope of a conceptual apparatus that will allow us to give a productive account of what I have termed the third break (*coupure*) in Lacan's work. In the course of my writing, I have brought to light the way in which Lacan distanced himself, self-critically, from a dialectical conception in order to adopt that of the vortex (*tourbillon*).[2] Even when barely sketched out, this point immediately connected up with something I had outlined in another paper,[3] namely, that the theory of the vortex or turbulence (taken from physics and mathematics) could provide us with invaluable concepts and methods for defining the third break in question. One of the characteristics of this break, of course, was the invention of the *sinthome*. Now, in referring beyond that theory itself, and in abstracting a series of Lacanian categories of the same order, we clearly risk giving the *sinthome*—which in truth is crucial—the rank of a mere transient doctrinal feature, something ephemeral and anecdotal, of little interest. The elaboration that follows will therefore seek to concentrate on the basis of the psychoanalytic significance of theories deriving from the vortex, and on a brief outline of the conceptual articulation we have mentioned, which must be elaborated in other contexts more carefully.

ON THE VORTEX IN LACAN: SOME ARTICULATIONS

There are three related moments that allow us to see how Lacan begins, little by little, to take up the question of the vortex. First, at the Grande-Motte Conference in 1973, he acknowledges having himself been "sucked into" (*aspiré*) the discourse founded by Freud, insofar as that discourse was able to create a hole (*faire trou*) and thus to catch up every analyst in its maelstrom.[4] Thus, the discourse forms a "cone of suction"; in this sense, each analyst has to struggle to avoid being swallowed up by it. In what way, though? By managing, as Lacan puts it, to hang on to an edge. It is thus already clear that the edge of this hole has features unlike those of the hard edges of Euclidian geometry, and equally unlike those produced by continuous deformation, the governing principle of topology. The edges of the maelstrom appear fractured, unstable, mobile; they tend to disappear rapidly, ostensibly governed by an unfeasible order. Nevertheless, Lacan declares, one of the edges of this vortical hole is *logic*. The hole, once again, does not consist of a line closed in upon itself in space; it is not what Lacan refers

to in his classical example of the potter molding his vase around a defined, stable hole, one that can be circumscribed.[5] Regarding the vortex, he insists that we need to find a "handhold" or a "point of lever-
age" to avoid being swallowed up.

Lacan introduces logic, then—but what kind of logic? As his
critical remarks about dialectic make clear,[6] such a logic cannot—
must not—be dialectical. Since dialectical logic is substantialist, pre-
dicative, and antinomial, it could only fill out a system, making it
more than complete—tautological, overflowing with meaning. This
is why Lacan adds another statement affirming that, regarding this
fundamental category of understanding, "there is something undecidable" (and not "something undecidable exists").[7] In this crucial quali-
fication, Lacan implicitly relies on Gödel's theorem, which shows
formal mathematical systems to be incomplete, insofar as they are
governed at a certain level by axioms whose truth-value is unverifi-
able, which are neither true nor false; Lacan's "undecidable" stems
from this. The result is a precise, crucial clinical point for analysts.
Instead of complementing a psychical trait of the analysand with its
opposite—like conflicting substances—the *paradox*, as an articulation
of the undecidable, no longer produces meaning but in fact, as we
observe, fragments it, obliterates it, does away with it. And if meaning disappears, there can be space for something to be invented, which
connects back to the *sinthome*.[8] In what way? By moving, now, from
the analysand to the theory of our discipline: due to the rupture of
the reproductive circuit after the discovery elsewhere of what will
ultimately lead to the renewal of ideas devalued by feverish over-
inflation. In more simple terms, if the same thing comes around more
and more frequently, this will result each time in a decreasing conceptual exchange value. Thus Lacan's warning, his demand: "It would
seem more reliable for us to refer to other categories."[9]

The third stage comes in some brilliant and highly significant
statements made in Seminar XXII, *R.S.I.* Effectively, we can see this
seminar as marking Lacan's definitive break with his notion of the
Name-of-the-Father as agency of the Law and vector of the Symbolic,
its place determined as secondary in relation to the Desire of the
Mother. Thus, concerning the disclosure of the paternal metaphor, we
often hear constructions such as "the mother did not accord the father
his place," or "she—and not he—was the one who imposed the Law,"

and so on. Such banal psychologizing has been a great help to those who wish to criticize a psychoanalytic "three easy steps to Oedipus." Now, in R.S.I. this position of the Name-of-the-Father as S_2, as secondary, is shattered: we now understand it as the Father-of-the-Name, in other words, the Father as the one who names. And this "giving names" to things must be distinguished from "so-called divine creation,"[10] because the latter is an effect of the signifier God; in other words it creates from and with the signifier. The act of giving names bears on a thing already created, but by means of chit-chat. In other words, we are dealing not with the proper name but with the common noun. This is called *nomination*, and it can be Real, Symbolic, or Imaginary. Such nomination calls for the fourth ring in the Borromean chain, and thus it relates to the *sinthome*, the paradigmatic fourth element.[11]

Now this fourth element, the *sinthome* as Symbolic nomination, marks the limits of metaphor, a theme Lacan announces at the beginning of the same Seminar in the following terms: "What is the maximum gap allowed between the two (in the substitution of one signifier for another)?"[12] For it turns out that nomination, the act of the naming Father, is no longer bound up with metaphor—which is, fundamentally, paternal—but invokes another chapter of Lacanian theory: that of suppletions (*suppléances*). A suppletion is not, in this sense, a substitution; it does not comprise "one word for another"[13] but is what Lacan calls in Seminar XXIV a "new signifier,"[14] one that does not replace but attaches, not a complement but a supplement. This signifier does not, of course, "enter" into the habitual recourse to the triple Borromean chain, where the trajectory of many a Lacanian has run aground. If we remain stalled at Real, Symbolic, and Imaginary, the signifiers of the treatment will be obtained by the lifting of censorship; that is, the treatment is conceptually oriented toward a historicist analysis of Imaginary infancy, foreclosing any possibility of invention. In short, we do not go beyond the unconscious, as is proposed conversely by Lacan with his notion of *l'une-bévue*.[15]

If we return to the Father-as-Name, we can now see its close relation to the vortex. In one session of R.S.I., Lacan argues as follows: "A hole, if you believe my little schemas, is what engulfs things (like a vortex), and then there are moments when it spits things out. What does it spit out? The name, the Father as name."[16] We can therefore see how the inflection of the Name-of-the-Father requires a different disciplinary bond; in such a texture, the vortex arises as a decisive gauge.

THE "STRANGE ATTRACTOR"
OF PSYCHOANALYSIS

In the vortex, then, Lacan encounters an object that had for centuries given sleepless nights to anyone with some idea of its importance. Not only did it allow the immeasurable Leonardo to explain the apparently inexplicable but, much closer to our own time, the quantum theorist Werner Heisenberg was to murmur on his deathbed that "he will have two questions for God: why relativity and why turbulence? Heisenberg says, 'I really think He may have an answer to the first question.'"[17]

With turbulence, it is also a matter of how physics came to give overwhelming importance to a "minor" field of study—which we can link directly to Freud's interest in things considered insignificant or trivial—so that it took priority over the great theses dating back to Newton, for instance those concerning the movement of the planets. What, then, is turbulence, this close relative of the vortex (*tourbillon*)? It occurs when a "smooth flow breaks up into whorls and eddies . . . [it is] a mess of disorder at all scales, with small eddies within large ones."[18] Astonishing forms, like the eddying plume of smoke drifting up from a cigarette in the ashtray, or the spiraling motion of a leaf caught by the wind as it falls, or even the way water flows from a tap into the basin: all of these offer support to a *physics of everyday life* as full of riddles as the psychopathology thus designated by Freud.

If we pause over these phenomena, what seems in any event hardest to determine is the point when the initial uniformity of the dynamic systems breaks up, becomes turbulent. It is a question of grasping the possibility of ascribing a certain lawfulness to a movement that appears, phenomenologically speaking, to be chaotic. And this is precisely what the name entails: chaos theory today comprises, not something to do with complete disorder or confusion, but "Stochastic behaviour occurring in a deterministic system."[19] "Stochastic" means random or aleatory. Its definition was established in 1986 at an international conference in London, and distinguishes between phenomenon and structure: the stochastic, it was said, concerns conduct or behavior; while the system, as structure, is deterministic. In other words, there is an order in the chaos.

Did Lacan not state that within the vortex there are moments of something spewing forth after being engulfed? If that is the case, then there is intermittence, discontinuity, periodicity. Might we be able to say that the act of naming is chaotic? Is it unpredictable and risky? Can it be programmed? Let us say, with Ian Stewart, that from the moment when chaos was first studied, "[n]o longer was order synonymous with law, and disorder with lawlessness. Both order and disorder had laws. . . . One law for the ordered, another for the disordered."[20] For Lacan, the Real is without law or order[21] because it comes "in little bits," it cannot be totalized. Now, what is remarkable in morphogenetic theories—which include the theory of chaos—is that they consider that the local does not respond to global laws.[22] Neither deductive nor inductive, it is a *logic of the singular* that consequently, in contrast to positivist science, does not aim "for–all" (*pour-tout*),[23] to invoke Lacan's notion of law.[24]

But what sort of order are we dealing with here? In order to elucidate it, it is indispensable to go back to the notion of the *attractor* in its different guises. What is an attractor? According to Hayles, it is "any point in an orbit which seems to attract the system towards it."[25] For example, the movement of an oscillating pendulum that finally stops in the center of the period indicates the action of a fixed-point attractor (Figure 3–1). If, on the other hand, the pendulum was driven by a motor that canceled the friction of the air, its movement would always follow the same pattern, its attractor being known as a *limit* cycle (Figure 3–2). Other system are governed by a trajectory important in the developments triggered by the second shift in Lacan's work. Effectively, they move according to turns that can be mapped onto a torus, as for example in the air chamber of a car (Figure 3–3). (The torus, we should recall, is what for Lacan writes the structure of neurosis.)[26]

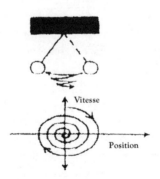

Figure 3–1

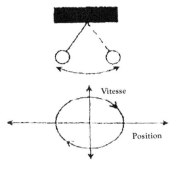

Figure 3–2

Up to this point, the movements of the system have been rhythmic, predictable, whether they are periodic or quasi-periodic. But, as Lacan points out, in order to approach the vortex it is necessary for the hole to be made "multiple," for it to be a "conjunction." Consequently, "at least three are needed for it to become a hole with a vortex."[27] Three, which we may understand as the three "jumps" between the different types of attractors: first, from the fixed point to the limit cycle, and second, from the limit cycle to the torus. In the first two alterations, the system can, as Stewart puts it, only "sit still" or "go round and round."[28]

Here we should ask ourselves how many psychoanalytic ideas are used wrongly in a clinical setting by remaining at the level of these two kinds of attractor. More straightforwardly, we could point to the frequent references to repetition, regression, fixation, identification, the Nirvana principle, the death drive, to name only those concepts that

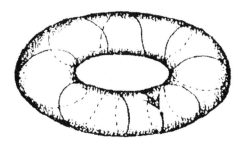

Figure 3–3

are subsequently absorbed by a "dialectic." What *episteme* underlies this kind of interpretation? Something known as Freudian determinism. Is there thus no margin for any freedom, any effect of separation?[29]

It is not the first two kinds of attractor that should concern us in psychoanalysis, but the kind that allows us to move to the third modification, the *strange attractor*, which can be located, among other sites, in turbulence. What characterizes this type of attractor? A trajectory that is absolutely strange, in the sense that its lines, its orbits, remain always within a certain volume, resulting in a form—not a dialectical substance—that is fairly clear. What, then, is its definitive outline? We can see this, for example, in the Lorenz attractor (Figure 3–4), which strikingly resembles a butterfly with opened wings. We move back and forth along the edges, but there are not two orbits that cross or coincide, so that the structure never repeats the same movement. As Hayles comments, it is a strange—and complex—combination of chance and order, determinism and unpredictability.[30] This *turbulent episteme*, with multiple implications that we are unable to explore fully here, constitutes the support of Lacan's *sinthome* as Symbolic nomination: it concerns the site of the third transformation that allows the *sinthome* to emerge as the vehicle for a creative unbalancing, able to disrupt the sterile symmetry of the triple Borromean chain.

Thus, the "disinvestment" of the unconscious[31]—there was an investment, a site fixed through repetition, but no longer—marks the limit

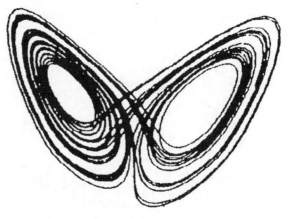

Figure 3–4

of the dependence on metaphor, supporting with no regrets the *ab-sense* of the sexual relation.[32] Instead of any regret, addressed to the Other as a demand for sense, resulting in the "moral cowardice" known as sadness, the *ab-sense* of the *sinthome* embodies what Lacan terms a *gay sçavoir*.[33] This last phrase, punning on *savoir*, could be read as *ça à voir*, "it/id to see." This, in contrast to sadness, constitutes a "virtue" to the extent that it seeks not to understand or chew over meaning, but to "crush it as much as is possible."[34] Thus, for the Lacan of the third period, there is no knowledge (*savoir*) but in non-sense, opening onto a space of the scopic and an undefined future, far from the closed circuits and anticipations of the Imaginary. For this reason, *gay sçavoir*—the Nietzschean root of which is patent—is the corollary of the stochastic, the unpredictable. *Gay sçavoir* is the affect that authorizes the invention of the *sinthome*.

SOME THOUGHTS ON DISSIPATION
IN PSYCHOANALYSIS

So far, we have passed several beacons on the way to an inquiry into the order in chaos. There is another branch of the science of chaos that is harder to outline, which demonstrates that once a system moves beyond a condition of equilibrium into a state of extreme or chaotic oscillation, it gives rise to a surprising new structure that Prigogine names *dissipative*. Isolated during attempts to prove the second law of thermodynamics, this notion seeks to deal with the effects produced by entropy, or the loss of caloric energy, and it is here that we come across the dissipative. However, in a magnificent oxymoron, dissipation is able to produce a structure that is stable but that suffers unpredictable transformations when stimulated from the outside. That stimulation, moreover, may be absolutely minimal, such as the speech of the analyst; despite this, its effects are often far-reaching. There is a nonlinearity, an ultrasensitive dependence on the initial conditions, because of which we formulate dissipation as irreversible. Far from the structure moving backward toward its initial state, its fluctuations expand in a turbulent way, giving rise to the dissipative formations in question. Hence, the structure appears "historical," as its state is the result of unpredictable "choices," whereas if it had no history, it would simply remain in the same state.

Thus it emerges that the *sinthome* corresponds, in my view, to the "disinvestment" of the unconscious discussed above, as a truly dissipative structure. In this sense, the disinvested *sinthome* tends toward the side of a new signifier, going beyond the substantification of the unconscious. Its principle feature is to set forth its self-organization,[35] a "unary" point that Lacan formualtes as "the identification of the Other with the One."[36] It thus follows that *gay sçavoir* does not resemble a dynamics for which "the past and the future play the same role—that is, none."[37] Rather, *there is* the arrow of time, or, as Prigogine puts it, "the order of fluctuations refuses the static universe of dynamics in favour of an open world in which activity creates something new, evolution is innovation, creation is destruction, birth is death."[38] Such is the context of the vortex; it is far removed from any dialectic of equilibrium.

These ideas also allow us to reformulate a crucial clinical question concerning the fact that the classical reference to the Freudian conception of object-choice proves inadequate. I refer to the dichotomy between an anaclitic or oedipal object and a narcissistic one, from which ensue various "lists," stereotypes, or copies.[39] Whether in relation to the subject's own self or to the nurturing woman/protective man, this conception cannot take account of the surging up before the speaking being of an object that I propose to call *dissipative*. Following Lacan, we would isolate this object in its characteristic as *sinthome*. There is invention, there is oneness, and not only various "elective" series. Although in the Seminar *Le sinthome* Lacan states that the woman may be the man's *sinthome* but not vice versa,[40] he relativizes this position at the Congrès de l'École freudienne de Paris in July 1978. Let us read the relevant passage, which follows Lacan's claim that the *sinthome* seems to evoke the fall of something, but

[a] *sinthome* is not a fall, even if it seems to be. To the extent that I consider that you, in so far as you exist, have every man his woman as *sinthome*. There is a his and a her *sinthome*. That is all that is left of the so-called sexual relation. The sexual *rapport* is a relation between *sinthomes*.[41]

Thus for analysts, the question does not lie in the bland repetition of the phrase "there is no sexual relation," but rather in isolating whether the analysand chooses his object in terms of the Freudian series that are governed by non-strange attractors—that is, rest, turning round and round, or neurosis—or is situated in the *turbulence of the dissipative object or sinthome*. Even though, of course, this opposition is of an ideal kind, it does not in my view prevent the distinction harboring an incalculable value in the direction of the treatment.

CONCLUSION

In this brief synthesis, I wished to set out some new conceptual points that mark the distinct orientation brought in by the third shift in Lacan's work, encapsulated in the opposition dialectic/vortex. Pausing over Lacan's implied references to the morphogenetic theories of chaos and dissipative structures, I highlighted the importance of this trajectory for the interrogation of a group of fundamental concepts in our discipline. This was, of course, to draw attention to the opening of an almost completely unexplored field in clinical psychoanalysis: that of *suppletions*. In approaching this field, we should authorize ourselves, as analysts, to deploy Lacan's advice-demand: "One can very easily do without (the Name-of-the-Father), on condition that one makes use of it."[42] In other words, we can make use of the Name-of-the-Father as a way of naming on the path of inventing new signifiers.

NOTES

1. Cf. in particular R. Harari, "No hay desenlace sin reanudación" in *¿De qué trata la clinica lacaniana?*, Catálogos, Buenos Aires, 1994, pp. 191–211.
2. Cf. J. Lacan, "Discours de clôture des Journées de l'École freudienne de Paris," *Lettres de l'École freudienne* 18, 4/13/1975, p. 267.
3. *Del sujeto dividido finalmente puesto en cuestión* (presented at the Reunión Lacanoamericana de Psicoanálisis, Porto Alegre, August 1993).
4. J. Lacan, "Intervention à la séance de travail sur l'École freudienne en Italie," Congrès de l'École freudienne de Paris de la Grande-Motte, *Lettres de l'École freudienne*, 15, 11/1–4/1973, pp. 241–244.
5. [Harari is referring to an example given by Lacan in his seminar of January 27, 1960; cf. *Seminar VII, The Ethics of Psychoanalysis*, ed. J.-A. Miller, Trans. D. Porter, London: Routledge, 1992, pp. 120–121. Editor].
6. Cf. Lacan's intervention in the 1975 *Journées sur les cartels*.
7. [The distinction is between the phrase *il y a de l'indécidable* and the

use of the verb *être* (i.e., *il est indécidable*). Arguably, Lacan's use of this alternative can be mapped onto the opposition he develops in the 1970s between (symbolic) "existence," and (real) "ex-sistence"; cf. Bruce Fink, *The Lacanian Subject*, Princeton, NJ: Princeton University Press, 1995, p. 122. Editor].

8. Cf. J. Lacan, *Le sinthome*, SXXIII, April 13, 1976, unpublished.

9. J. Lacan, "Discours de clôture . . . ," *op cit.*, p. 267.

10. J. Lacan, *Le sinthome* (SXXIII), 11/18/1975, unpublished.

11. J. Lacan, *R.S.I.* (SXXII), 5/13/1975, unpublished.

12. *Ibid.*, 12/17/75, unpublished.

13. J. Lacan, "The Agency of the Letter in the Unconscious or Reason since Freud," *Écrits: A Selection, op. cit.*, p. 157.

14. J. Lacan, *L'insu que sait de l'une-bévue s'aile à mourre* (SXXIV), 5/17/1977, unpublished.

15. *Ibid.*, 11/16/1976, unpublished.

16. J. Lacan, *R.S.I.* (SXXII), 4/15/1975, unpublished.

17. J. Gleick, *Chaos: Making a New Science*, London: Heinemann, 1988, p. 121.

18. *Ibid.*, pp. 121–122.

19. J. Stewart, *Does God Play Dice? The Mathematics of Chaos*, Oxford, UK: Blackwell, 1989, p. 17.

20. J. Stewart, *op. cit.*, p. 54.

21. J. Lacan, *Le sinthome* (SXXIII), 4/13/1976, unpublished.

22. M. Serres, *Le passage due Nordeste*, Madrid: Débat, 1991, p. 70.

23. J. Lacan, *Encore* (SXX), *op. cit.*, p. 74.

24. Cf. J. Lacan, "Discours de clôture . . . ," *op. cit.*, p. 266.

25. N. K. Hayles, *Chaos Bound: Orderly Disorder in Contemporary Literature and Science*, Ithaca, NY: Cornell University Press, 1990, p. 28.

26. J. Lacan, "L'Etourdit," *Scilicet* 4, Paris: Seuil, 1973, p. 42.

27. J. Lacan, "Discours de clôture . . . ," *op. cit.*, p. 265.

28. J. Stewart, *op. cit.*, p. 110.

29. J. Lacan, "Position de l'inconscient," *Écrits, op. cit.*, pp. 829–850.

30. N. K. Hayles, *op. cit.*, pp. 191–192.

31. J. Lacan, "Joyce le symptôme I," in J. Aubert (Ed.), *Joyce Avec Lacan*, Paris: Navarin, 1987, p. 21.

32. J. Lacan, "L'Etourdit," *op. cit.*, p. 47.

33. [*gay sçavoir*: Lacan's untranslatable visual pun makes Nietzsche's "Joyful Wisdom" (the title of his 1887 work) include the French version of Freud's *Es* or "id," *le ça*. Editor].

34. J. Lacan, *Télévision*, Paris: Seuil, 1973, p. 40.

35. J. Prigogine, *El naciemento del tiempo*, Barcelona: Tusquets, 1991, p. 83.

36. J. Lacan, *Télévision, op. cit.*, p. 41.

37. J. Prigogine and I. Stengers, *Order Out of Chaos: Man's New Dialogue with Nature*, New York: Bantam, 1984, p. 189.

38. *Ibid.*

39. S. Freud, *On Narcissism: An Introduction* (1914), SE XIV.

40. J. Lacan, *Le sinthome* (SXXIII), 2/17/1976, unpublished.

41. J. Lacan, "Discours de clôture . . . ," *op. cit.*, p. 176.

42. J. Lacan, *Le sinthome* (SXXII), 4/13/1976, unpublished.

4

Lacan's Analytic Goal: *Le sinthome* or the Feminine Way

Paul Verhaeghe and Frédéric Declercq

INTRODUCTION

Freudian psychoanalysis started as a therapeutic treatment meant to remove pathological symptoms. Moreover, it was Freud's ambition to install a causal treatment, by which the symptoms would be removed in a permanent way. His initial enthusiasm about psychoanalysis as psychotherapy gave way to a more pessimistic view at the end of his career. Finally, he considered the analytic process to be "interminable," thus turning psychoanalysis into an impossible profession. In the mean-time, he had elaborated a whole new theory of psychopathology.

Since Freud's discovery of the unconscious, pathological pro-cesses are explained on the basis of defense, in which repression takes the prominent place. After Freud, it was more or less forgotten that repression in itself is already a *secondary* moment within the dynam-ics of the pathogenesis. Indeed, repression is an elaboration of the defense process against the drive. Right from the beginning of his theory, Freud recognized a twofold structure within the symptom: on the one hand, the drive, on the other, the psyche. In Lacanian terms: the Real and the Symbolic. This is clearly present in Freud's first case study, that of Dora. In this study, Freud does not add to his theory of defense, which had already been elaborated in his two papers on the psychoneuroses of defense (Freud, 1894, 1896). It can be said that the core of this case study resides precisely in this twofold structure, as he focuses on the Real, drive-related element, what he terms the "*Somatisches Entgegenkommen*."[1] Later, in the *Three Essays*, this will be called the fixation of the drive.[2] From this point of view, Dora's conversion symptoms can be studied from two perspectives: a Symbolic one, that is, the signifiers or psychical representations that are repressed, and a Real one, related to the drive, in this case the oral drive.

Freud will confirm this hybrid composition of the symptom in all his later case studies. Little Hans's phobia is built upon and against oral, anal, and scopic drives; the obsessions of the Rat-man go back to the scopic and the anal drive; and the same holds for the Wolf-man's phobia and conversion symptoms (Freud, 1909a, 1909b, 1918b).

In the light of this twofold structure, every symptom has to be studied in a double way. For Lacan, both phobia and conversion symptoms come down to the formal envelope of the symptom, that is, they are what gives Symbolic form to the Real of the drive.[3] Thus considered, the symptom is a Symbolic construction built around a Real kernel of jouissance. In Freud's words, it is "like the grain of sand around which an oyster forms its pearl."[4] The Real of the jouissance is the ground or the root of the symptom, while the Symbolic concerns the upper structure.

Both Freud and Lacan discovered that it is precisely this root of the symptom in the Real that obstructs therapeutic effectiveness. They had to acknowledge the fact that the resistance of certain symptoms to interpretation and the relapse of symptoms after or during the analysis have everything to do with this drive root. We can demonstrate this by referring to the two Freudian case studies that have been followed up.

Six years after his analysis with Freud, the Wolf-man was seen by another psychoanalyst, Ruth Mack Brunswick. She noted a change in the Wolf-man's character, analogous to one during his early childhood: "In this contemporary change of character, one finds the same regression to the anal sadistic and masochistic phase."[5] Translated into

Lacanian terminology, we can understand this regression as the "*refente*," the splitting of the subject by the Real of anal jouissance. At least, this is what Brunswick's next remark suggests: "I invite the reader here to refresh his memory by rereading Freud's case study. All the infantile material is already there, nothing new was revealed during the analysis he did with me."[6] This remark endorses the idea that the character change is caused by the Real of the drive, and has nothing to do with any Symbolic material that might not have been analyzed during the analysis with Freud. Indeed, Brunswick's affirmation that her further analysis of the Wolf-man revealed no new material leads to the conclusion that the two analyses with Freud had exhausted all the Symbolic aspects of the symptom. The repressions had obviously been overcome but the drive root, on the other hand, had not been rendered inactive. Moreover, it is clear that the analysis with Brunswick, and all the others that followed, did not succeed in this respect; at the age of 77, the Wolf-man was still haunted by the anal drive.

Concerning Dora, the same kind of reasoning can be applied. The postscript published by Felix Deutsch fifty years after Dora's analysis with Freud reveals that the original symptoms—the catarrh, the tussis nervosa and the aphonia—had returned in their original form.[7] Obviously, the limited analysis that Freud undertook with her was enough to remove the Symbolic material of her symptoms, but it did not touch on the relationship between the subject and the oral drive. Consequently, this oral drive reinserted itself into the chain of signifiers.[8]

Thus it is no surprise that Lacan considers the drive to be central to what he terms Freud's legacy. Indeed, Freud's conclusion, after fifty years of clinical practice, can be summarized as follows: it is the drive that determines the lasting success of the treatment.[9] The same evolution is to be found in Lacan's work: the early Lacan will focus on the Symbolic and the Imaginary, but from seminar XI (1964) onward, the Real and the drive come to be given the most attention.

THERAPEUTIC EFFECTIVENESS: INSIGHT OR CHANGE?

In the second period of Lacan's teaching, after 1964, he systematically demonstrated the twofold character of the symptom—Real and

Symbolic—thus continuing a central theme of Freud's work.[10] The reason for this is clear: traditionally, analysis tackles the Symbolic component of the symptom, but it is the Real part that jeopardizes the effectiveness of therapy. All the well-known problems—the partial resistance of certain symptoms to analytic treatment, the symptom relapse after a certain period, the negative therapeutic reaction—can be understood as expressions of the Real, that is, the drive component of the symptom. That is why the overcoming of repression—the Symbolic component of the symptom—does not lead automatically to the expected results. Lacan will summarize these problems in his theory of the object *a*, thus echoing Freud's conclusion in *Analysis Terminable and Interminable*: "There are nearly always residual phenomena."[11]

We can draw up a balance sheet for the therapeutic results of psychoanalysis. Let us remember that Freud aimed at a causal treatment, rather than a superficial management of symptoms. It is clear that the overcoming of repression leads to insight and to the disappearance of symptoms. But even when the same or different symptoms stay away for months after the conclusion of an analysis, this clarification of the unconscious contents does not lead automatically to what we might consider to be a change in the subject. A "hysteria without symptoms," or character-neurosis, refers to a subject *that is still determined by its drives*. Even if the subject is freed from its symptoms, it can still function in a specific, repetitive manner. In Freudian terms, this reads as the particular instances of repression having been undone, but not the *process* of repression itself. For example, in his paper on "Negation," Freud stresses the relativity of the effects of overcoming repression: "In the course of analytic work we often produce a further, very important and somewhat strange variant of this situation. We succeed in conquering the negation as well, and in bringing about a full intellectual acceptance of the repressed; but the repressive process itself is not yet removed by this."[12] Ergo, even if the subject knows and accepts (*"Bejahung"*) the repressed contents, there is still a *status quo ante* on the level of subjective functioning. According to the Wolf-man, Freud expressed this as follows: "Freud said that one could get cured by analysis, on condition that one wanted to be cured. He compared it to a railway ticket. The ticket gives me the possibility to travel, but does not oblige me to. The decision is mine."[13] With this metaphor, Freud makes it obvious that the change at the end of the treatment, or a general recovery, does not depend solely on the revelation or decoding of the unconscious, but to a far greater extent on a decision of the Ego. And this decision has everything to do with the drive.

A psychoanalytic cure removes repressions and lays bare drive-fixations. These fixations can no longer be changed as such; the decisions of the body are irreversible.[14] This is not the case for the positions of the subject toward the drive processes; these can be revised. There are two possibilities: either the subject now accepts a form of jouissance that he earlier refused, or he confirms this refusal.

> All repressions take place in early childhood; they are primitive defensive measures taken by the immature, feeble ego. In later years, no fresh repressions are carried out; but the old ones persist, and their services continue to be made use of by the ego for mastering the instincts. New conflicts are disposed of by what we call "after repression." . . . Analysis, however, enables the ego, which has attained greater maturity and strength, to undertake a revision of these old repressions; a few are demolished [the drive is accepted by the subject], while others are recognised but constructed afresh out of more solid material [the drive is refused in a more conclusive way].[15]

This process entails a refusal that does not belong any more to the process of repression and symptom-formation. "In a word, *analysis replaces repression by condemnation.*"[16]

We must stress the fact that this decision of the subject concerns solely the drives in their pure form; in order to be able to take such a decision, the subject has to be connected in a direct way to the object *a*, which means that the analytic process has to have run its course and fulfilled its task of clarification. This implies that, first, the repressions have to be lifted, that is, the symptom has to be cleared of its Symbolic components. Thus, it is not possible to save oneself the trouble of an analysis and go directly for the underlying cause, the drive root. Freud's answer to this idea can be found in his response to Rank's suggestion that we should directly tackle the primal trauma of birth. It would be of no more use than if the fire brigade contented themselves with removing the overturned lamp that set fire to the whole house—the building keeps burning.[17]

Lacan's theory of the relationship between the Real and the Symbolic presents us with a more consistent view. His metaphor of the jar is a better illustration of the reasons one can't save oneself the trouble of an analysis.[18] According to Lacan, the essence of making pottery does not reside in shaping the sides of the jar, but in the emptiness, the hollow space that these sides precisely create. The jar elaborates and localizes a hole in the Real; eventually, this elaboration and localization amounts to an authentic creation. The similarity of this to the genesis of psychopathological symptoms is due to the fact that *it is only through the elaboration of the Symbolic constellation that the Real of the drive appears.* In other words, one is obliged to pass through the Symbolic if one wants to approach the Real, because it is the Symbolic that delineates this Real. That is why psychoanalysis creates a new subject:[19] "Is it not precisely the claim of our theory that analysis produces a state which never does arise spontaneously in the ego and that this newly created state constitutes the essential difference between a person who has been analysed and a person who has not?"[20]

Let us conclude our discussion of Freudian theory. With regard to the fixation of the drive (and thus the fixation of a jouissance), Freud evokes the free will of the patient. For instance, concerning moral masochism—jouissance in humiliation—Freud states: "It must be honestly confessed that here we have another limitation to the effectiveness of analysis; after all, analysis does not set out to make pathological reactions impossible, but to give the patient's ego freedom to decide one way or the other."[21] He repeats the same idea when he discusses character-neuroses (Lacan's "hysteria without symptoms"):

> [In character-neurosis] it is not easy to foresee a natural end, even if one avoids any exaggerated expectations and sets the analysis no excessive tasks. Our aim will not be to rub off every peculiarity of human character for the sake of a schematic "normality," nor yet to demand that the person who has been "thoroughly analysed" shall feel no passions and develop no internal conflicts. The business of the analysis is to secure the best possible psychological conditions for the functions of the ego; with that it has discharged its task.[22]

It is important to see that Freud does not consider it the task of psychoanalysis to intervene in the way the patient handles his drives; its task is to provide the analysand with all the necessary information to be able to assess his stance toward this drive-fixation and eventually either change or keep that stance. What Freud abhors most of all, and refuses in a categorical way, is any identification of the patient with the therapist as a "therapeutic solution," an end point of the analysis.[23]

IDENTIFICATION WITH THE SYMPTOM

In this respect, Lacan will present us with an identification of another kind, with which he specifies the decision-making process of the subject. Lacan coins the new subject, or the finally analyzed subject, as the subject that has made a choice to identify with (the Real kernel of) his symptom or object *a*:

> In what does this sounding that is an analysis consist? Would it, or would it not be to identify with the symptom, albeit with every guarantee of a kind of distance? To know how to handle, to take care of, to manipulate . . . *to know what to do with the symptom, that is the end of analysis.*[24]

Before we explore this formula, we have to stress the fact that Lacan not only elaborated this kind of decision-making process, but also radicalized it. Freud's liberalism concerning the subject's position toward the acceptance of a drive-fixation sometimes seems inspired by a sense of powerlessness, of failure to do any better. Several of his papers leave us with the impression that the acceptance of a fixation comes down to an ersatz for some unattainable ideal. Such an ideal would be the exhaustive genitalization or phallicization of the pregenital drives.[25] Thus, Balint's idea of "genital love" as the criterion for psychological health and normality, and hence as the end point of the treatment, can be very easily endorsed by Freudian theory.

By contrast, Lacan always took a clear stance against this idea of a supposedly normal genital-sexual life and a corresponding goal of analytic treatment.[26] According to Lacan, the pre- and extra-genital objects constitute the essence of human sexuality, because the genital-sexual relationship does not exist. The sexual partner always takes the place of the fixated drive or object *a*:

> This $ never deals with anything by way of a partner but object *a* inscribed on the other side of the bar. He is unable to attain his sexual partner, who is the other, except inasmuch as his partner is the cause of his desire. In this respect, as is indicated elsewhere in my graphs by the oriented conjunction of $ and *a*, this is nothing other than fantasy.[27]

The phallus is a kind of prosthesis, and even an incomplete prosthesis. The residues Freud is talking about are for Lacan not accidental: phallicization is structurally incomplete, the lack in the Other cannot be completely remedied. These ideas belong to the late Lacan, but they are already present in his fourth seminar (1956–57), with its major thesis: the phallus is not an object, but an instance symbolizing the drives. Indeed, Lacan will systematically repeat that the phallus is not the genital organ, but a signifier. Hence the phallus does not concern a drive such as the oral, anal, scopic, or invocatory: "a genital drive, which no-one would be capable of defining as such."[28] The phallus is not an object, but an instance that regulates the jouissance coming from other sources, that is, the objects *a*. Their jouissance is regulated through being interpreted by the phallic signifier, and thus turned into phallic pleasure. Structurally, this symbolization remains incomplete. The object *a* is that part of the Real that resists symbolization.[29]

Fixations, which Freud considered to be primal symptoms, are of a general nature, in Lacan's view. The symptom is what defines mankind, and as such it cannot be rectified or cured. This is Lacan's final conclusion: *there is no subject without a symptom.*[30] In his last conceptualizations, the concept of symptom receives a new meaning. It is a question of a purified symptom, that is, one stripped of its symbolic components—of what ex-sists outside the unconscious structured as a language: object *a* or the drive in its pure form.[31] The Real of the symptom or object *a* demonstrates the particular jouissance of the Real body of this particular subject: "I define the symptom as the way everyone enjoys the unconscious insofar as they are determined by the unconscious."[32] Lacan prefers the idea of symptom to that of object *a*, in accordance with his thesis that there is no sexual relationship. If there is no normal sexual relationship as such, every relationship between sexual partners is a symptomatic one.

BELIEVING IN ONE'S SYMPTOM

The meaning of the formula—to identify with one's symptom— is to be understood by comparing it with its opposite: to believe in one's symptom. Both formulas—identification with and belief in—fit into a certain conceptual logic of Lacan's teaching. This logic can be reconstructed as follows. In his seminar *R.S.I.* (1974–75), Lacan designates the Real part of the symptom or object *a* through the concept of the "Letter."[33] The letter is the drive-related kernel of the signifier, the substance fixating the Real jouissance. The signifier, by contrast, is a letter that has acquired a linguistic value. In the case of the signifier, the Real of the drive is already absorbed by the Symbolic, it is semiotized. Within this reasoning, Lacan identifies the "letter" or object *a* with the master signifier, S_1, on condition that this S_1 is understood as disconnected from S_2, the battery of other signifiers. The "letter" S_1 is only turned into a signifier when connected to S_2.[34]

With this idea of the letter, Lacan wants to highlight the fact that the border between the Real and the Symbolic is a weak one; it is always possible for the Real to be colonized by the Symbolic. The chain of signifiers absorbs, for example, Dora's oral jouissance; the Real of the drive has been semiotized through the symptoms of tussis nervosa and hoarseness. All of the symptoms analyzed by Freud, that is, the Symbolic, representational part of them, returned later almost unchanged.[35]

It is within this field of tension between letter and signifier that Lacan situates the decision of the subject. A subject can choose either an *identification with* or a *belief in* his symptom. As a matter of fact, this choice concerns two radically different forms of identification.

To believe in one's symptom (or "letter") consists in adding three dots (. . .) to the letter: S_1 . . . To believe in the symptom is to believe in the existence of a final signifier, S_2, to reveal the ultimate signification and sense of the S_1. The condition for this is the existence of a guarantee that the Other has no lack. Hence, such a belief in the symptom implies a belief in the Other. It is not difficult to see that such a belief in the symptom or the S_2 amounts to a belief in the existence of a sexual relationship: "The three dots of the symptom are as a matter of fact, if I can put it this way, question marks within the non-rapport. This justifies the definition that I gave you already: that what constitutes the symptom, what sucks the unconscious, is that one believes in it."[36]

This belief in the symptom or the letter is typical of the beginning of an analysis, not its final phase. The patient comes to the analyst because he is convinced—and rightly so—that his symptom has a meaning. Thereby the analyst is put in the position of the one who knows, the one who will reveal this hidden signification, the Other without any lack. To put it differently: the patient lets his symptom be followed by (. . .), hoping that these will receive a meaning during the analysis, based on the interpretations of the analyst. This is the element of insight and clarification within analysis. It works only up to a certain point, the point when the signifying chain S_2 is used up; this is the point of the inconsistency of the Other. At this crossroads between S_2 and the lack in the Other, the analysand has two possible choices: either he chooses a new solution and identifies with the Real of the symptom, or he sticks to the previous solution and looks for yet another meaning by way of another hysterical identification: $\$ \rightarrow S_1 \rightarrow S_2$.

The formula "identification" applies to both subjective positions, because both entail a different identity. With the belief in the symptom, the subject connects itself to the signifying chain $S_1 \rightarrow S_2$, which Lacan considers "a whole-hearted preference for the unconscious."[37] This Symbolic identity is accompanied by a lack of being (*manque-à-être*). It can barely be considered an identity because it shifts continuously through the chain of signifiers—hence the typical hysterical question: "Who am I?" On the other hand, through identification with the letter, fixating the jouissance, the subject acquires a Real identity, connecting it to the Real of its being. This is the identity which defines the subject, that is, his particular, privileged way of enjoying. "Well, similarly, the reciprocity between the subject and object *a* is total."[38]

We have to stress the fact that this identification with the symptom does not come down to surrendering. On the contrary, to surrender is an expression of impotence and thus characterizes the attitude of belief in the symptom. The personal failure is considered to be isolated and individual, while the conviction still exists that other people, the Other, succeed in realizing The Relationship. This is not the case for a subject who has identified with his symptom and who has verified, during his analysis, that the failure of the sexual relationship is not a matter of individual impotence, but of a structural impossibility. The analysis has made clear that the essence of the subject—*son être du sujet*—is situated at the place of the lack of the Other, the place where the Other does not provide us with an answer. The analysand has experienced the fact that the subject is "an answer of the Real" and not "an answer of the Other."[39]

This change implies a change in the subject's position vis-à-vis jouissance. Before, the subject situated all jouissance on the side of the Other and took a stance against this (a position that was particular to this particular subject, i.e., its fundamental phantasm); after this change, the subject situates jouissance in the body, in the Real body.[40] Hence, there is no longer a jouissance prescribed by the Other, but a jouissance entailed in the particular drives of the subject. Lacan coins the *sinthome* to designate the idiosyncratic jouissance of a particular subject.[41] The identification with the symptom is in this respect not a Symbolic or an Imaginary one, but a Real identification, functioning as a suppletion (*suppléance*) for the lack of the Other.

On the other hand, the subject who believes in his symptom, believes in a sacred prescription of the Other . . . that will never arrive. Meanwhile, this subject has to fall back on suppletions for this nonexistent Other, the most commonly practiced suppletion being the institution of marriage, regulating the relations between the two genders in conformity with contemporary law and religion. Which, of course, does not prevent such a believing subject from complaining about these suppletions. The belief in the symptom is the Symbolic suppletion for the lack of the Other.

A NEW SUBJECT AS A RESULT OF THE TREATMENT?

Lacan's final theory of the end of the cure is not without its internal difficulties; the two main ones concern the status of the subject and the significance of the function of the father.

The notion of the "subject" has a long history in Lacan's theory, which can be understood as his attempt to take his distance from ego psychology in general and from the autonomous ego in particular. The Lacanian subject lacks all substance, and comes down to a liminal process of opening and closing that never reaches any final stage. The underlying "being" is always lost, at the very moment it is supposed to appear in the signifiers of the Other. That is why it is condemned to a structurally determined form of never-being-there. Hence the paradoxical fact that the essence of the Lacanian subject comes down to its lacking any kind of essence whatever, and that the whole accent has to be put on its divided character.[42]

Nevertheless, with this final theory, Lacan introduces another subject, one that has, after all, a kind of substantiality. It is tempting to consider this, in the light of what we inherit from the Sixties, as a Lacanian version of the "authentic self." Beyond the ever-present fascination of such a temptation, it is interesting to note what differentiates the Lacanian neosubject: it is not an authentic subject; on the contrary, it no longer focuses on the (lack of the) Other, that is, the Symbolic and the Imaginary. Rather, this neosubject tries to come and go with the Real of the jouissance dictated by its own drive, without falling back into the previous trap of stuffing it full of signification. This is how the decision, the choice of the subject, is to be understood. If there is anything original or authentically present, it has to be looked for in the Real of the body and the drive.

As a consequence, there is no such thing as a "liberation" of the subject from the desire of the alienating Other, setting free "the original, authentic subject." On the contrary, there has never been an authentic subject, so there can be no return to it. This neosubject is a creation of the analytic process: it becomes a possibility once the analysand has reached the point where the interpretations have revealed the final non-sense of his symptoms.[43] The condition for this is that both the analyst and the analysand "fall" from their belief in the Other. It is this process that Lacan constantly tries to grasp from Seminar XI onward, with expressions such as "separation," the "traversal" of the phantasm, or "subjective destitution."[44] As a creation, it is indeed a creation *ex nihilo*, that is, one not based on any previous identity, which in one way or another would be tributary to the Other. Hence the implicit, but very important, meaning of separation in Seminar XI: *se parer*: to give birth to oneself.[45]

The trouble is that such a decision or choice by the subject implies the existence of a decision-making instance, *independent* of the Other. This hardly tallies with the constitutive process of becoming a subject, that is, the alienation, which makes the subject dependent on the Other —hence the necessity of the ideas of separation and destitution. Beyond this, the instance acquires *substantiality* through its decision. After all, we are talking about identification with the *Real* of the symptom. This hardly tallies with the idea, mentioned above, that the subject lacks any kind of essence whatever. Concerning this first difficulty, it is obvious that in this context Freud always refers to the ego, and with the post-Freudians this becomes the autonomous ego. It is quite clear that here Lacan is close to a revised version of the autonomous ego.

The second problem is bound up with the first: it concerns the role of the father in the becoming of the subject. With the early Lacan, the whole emphasis was put on the metaphor of the Name-of-the-Father, whose function was to free the subject from the desire of the mother, and so on. The continuing popularity of this theoretical motif in contemporary Lacanian thinking contrasts sharply with Lacan's decision not only to abandon it, but even to replace it with the opposite idea: that there is no Other of the Other. The belief in the father is a typically neurotic symptom, a fourth ring within the Borromean structure. Lacan takes his leave from it, and starts looking for a new signifier to fulfill the required function, to bind together the three rings.

In this context, it is important to differentiate between the father and his function. The function relates to the separation of mother and child, entailing the liberation of the latter from the jouissance of the Other. If this separation ends up as an alienation, with the father as a second Other, then there is structurally no difference between it and the previous alienation. It was Lacan's intention to get beyond this point, and that is why he focused on the function—separation—and its Symbolic character, meaning that the operative factor is a signifier. In Freud's time, this signifier was linked to the real father, but this is a mere historical contingency. The very same function can be installed through a totem name-giving within a clan structure. There, separation is also attained through name-giving, and likewise there a first, externally determined identity—member of the mother group—is also replaced by a second, externally determined identity—member of the brother and uncle group. In both cases, the process of name-giving is the central one, and it is precisely this process that Lacan privileges in his later theory.[46] Nevertheless, the fact remains that in both cases the subject still has to believe in this name-giving and what it stands for— and these are determined by the Other.

In other words, Lacan does not escape the very same problem that Freud had to cope with, and even in the same context; the separation function of the signifier is only operative on condition that one believes in it. Hence the whole thing remains in the realm of the Imaginary, and one has to fall back on the "Credo quia absurdum." Freud quoted this expression of Tertullian's precisely in questioning the whys and wherefores of paternal authority, thus expressing its arbitrary character.[47]

This deadlock is all the more important because a Lacanian analysis precisely demands of the analyst that he take his leave from the position of the father.

THE BELIEF OF THE ANALYST

So far, we can summarize our findings as follows. Both Freud and Lacan agree that the success of an analysis depends on a decision—that of the ego (Freud) or of the subject (Lacan). Lacan tried to elaborate this decision-making process. The identification with the symptom promises a positive prognosis, a sufficient neutralization of the pathogenesis. This identification implies that the subject has reached a certain conclusion through his analysis, that the pathological process is ultimately an effect of the general trauma of the nonexistence of a sexual rapport, and that its signification always comes down to an alienation in the signifiers of the Other.[48] Based on this conclusion, the subject chooses a certain modality of jouissance and takes his leave of the three dots that used to follow his symptom. With this conclusion, the analysand testifies to a kind of positive not-wanting-to-know, through which he detaches himself from the linguistically structured unconscious.

Of course, it is possible that the analyst himself has never reached this conclusion, and that he still believes in the ultimate S_2 . . . in which case *he* continues to push the analysand's "letter" back into the chain of signifiers with his interpretations. This turns the analysis into an interminable process; indeed, one can always find yet another S_2 to add to the S_1. In this way, psychoanalysis is turned into a fraud (*escroquerie*).[49] The belief of the analyst in the existence of a sexual relationship and the guaranteeing father does not make it easier for the analysand. In this respect, Colette Soler has criticized Freud for the position he took in his analytic practice. One of her pertinent remarks is that Freud's interpretation of the deadlocks of castration and penis envy in terms of *transference* resistances says a lot about his own position in these matters.[50] It is Soler's thesis that the structural deadlock does not consist of castration and penis envy, but of Freud's relationship to both of these. On several occasions, Lacan commented on Freud's taking this father position during his analytic practice: "We know that we cannot operate anymore in our position of analyst as Freud did, who took in analysis the position of the father. . . . And that is why we don't know any more where to go to—because we have not learned to rearticulate which position should be ours starting from there."[51]

Privately, Freud admitted that he took the position of the father during the transference, and he even added that this made him a bad analyst.[52] At the end of the day, Freud placed the father in the place of the lack of the Other:

> The lack referred to here is indeed that which I have already formulated: that there is no Other of the Other. But is this mark made by the Unbeliever of the truth really the last word that is worth giving in reply to the question, "What does the Other want of me?" when we, the analysts, are its mouthpiece? Surely not, and precisely because there is nothing doctrinal about our office. We are answerable to no ultimate truth; we are neither for nor against any particular religion. *It is already quite enough that at this point I had to situate the dead Father in the Freudian myth.*[53] [italics added]

If the analyst believes in the existence of the sexual relationship, it is understandable that his analysands, and especially the ones who have to take the position of the spiritual son, demand an account of this. And on this point, the "father" of psychoanalysis reveals himself to be impotent as well. The discussion between Freud and Ferenczi is paradigmatic in this respect.

Again, we meet here with the difficulty we discussed above. The function of separation that liberates the subject from the first alienation with the first Other is indispensable, but introduces inevitably a new alienation, this time with the liberator, *in casu* the father, who thereby receives the status of symptom. The proper cause of desire and jouissance—the object *a*—is left aside. In other words, the function of the father is the regulating factor, but not the Real cause of desire. The Real is the root of the drive; the function of the father stands for the Symbolic shaping of the symptom. Therefore psychoanalysis should not be turned into the ritual of the father: "and psychoanalysis is not the rite of the Oedipus complex."[54] On the contrary, it should create the possibility for the subject to get to the heart of the matter, the object *a*. Its precondition is the insight that the function of the father is a Symbolic suppletion.

CREATIO EX NIHILO: LE SINTHOME

The identification of the subject with the object *a* not only replaces this Symbolic suppletion with a more stable, Real one, but has in addition creative effects: the jouissance of one's own drives creates the "Other gender." To be sure, this Other is a fiction, but it is a fiction that does not turn the subject into a dupe because he has created it by himself, based on his particular way of jouissance. Lacan calls this self-created fiction a *sinthome*: a particular signifier that knots the three registers of the Real, the Symbolic and the Imaginary into a particular sexual rapport. "That which I have defined for the first time as a *sinthome*, is what permits the Symbolic, the Real and the Imaginary to be kept together. . . . On the level of the *sinthome*, there is a relationship. . . . There is only a relationship where there is a *sinthome*."[55]

The condition for such a creation is that the subject has become free of the Other, of the language of the Other. "In any case, what I am saying is that the invention of a signifier is something different from memory. *It is not that the child invents—he receives the signifier*, and it is even this that makes it worthwhile to do it more. *Our signifiers are always received.* Why shouldn't we invent a new signifier? For instance, a signifier that would have no sense at all, just like the Real?"[56] [italics added]

At the end of the *Encore* seminar, Lacan had already evoked this idea—the creation of a new signifier—in talking about poetry. A new knowledge can be created only at the place of the lack of the Other. As long as one stays under the umbrella of the Other, there is no new knowledge possible. In this sense, it is no coincidence that Lacan's continuation and crossing of Freud's theory coincides with his expulsion from the IPA.[57]

In the context of the creation of a new signifier or *sinthome*, creation is only creation insofar as it builds upon the lack of the Other; that is, insofar as it is a *creatio ex nihilo*: "It is by this [the lack] that I try to meet the function of art, what is implied by what is left blank as fourth term, when I say that art can even reach the symptom."[58]

This is the lesson learned by Lacan from Joyce's "savoir faire." Joyce's *sinthome* comes down to his literary productions, built on the lack of the Other, which for Lacan is hardly surprising, because he allots Joyce a psychotic structure. And based on these creations, based on this *sinthome*, he knots the three registers of the Real, the Imaginary, and the Symbolic into a particular "sexual rapport:" "I have said of Joyce that he is the symptom. His entire work testifies to it. *Exiles* touches his central symptom, the symptom made of the lacking as such of the sexual rapport."[59]

What is there to be deduced from this concerning neurosis, especially concerning the conclusion of a psychoanalytic cure? We have already stated that normally, that is, neurotically, the signifier of the Name-of-the-Father is expected to take the place of the lack in the Other and to knot the registers of the Real, the Symbolic, and the Imaginary in such a way that the jouissance is forbidden. The seminar on Joyce demonstrates that it is possible for a *sinthome* to take the role of the signifier of the Name-of-the-Father. Lacan invites everyone to follow Joyce's example and to create their own *sinthome* at the place of the lack of the Other; the aim of this creative act is to be able to function without the signifier of the Name-of-the-Father, that is, the Other.

Lacan specifies that this new signifier, just like the Real, has no sense (*sens*), which implies that it cannot be exchanged with other subjects. Not only would it not "fit" another subject, worse still, this new signifier cannot be formalized. It belongs to the field of the orthodox: it is a particular way of handling a particular jouissance. In our reading, this explains why Lacan in his last seminars repeatedly returns to the idea of creation and the act. In this, the accent is not so much on the result of the creation as on the fact that creation is highly individual, particular.

To conclude on the creative effect of identifying with the symptom, we have to return to the specific character of this identification. We have already said that this identification belongs to a specific context. The idea of "identification with the real of the drives" may not be taken literally, because the Real of the drives remains heterogeneous to the subject, the object *a* maintaining its traumatic character. Lacan emphatically recommends taking a distance from the symptom: "to identify, *while assuring oneself of a kind of distance towards one's symptom.*"[60] This is the function of the new signifier: it creates a band around the lack in the Symbolic, although this band is completely different from the phobic one. The castration phobia marks out the Real as impenetrable, while the new signifier—the *sinthome*—on the contrary provides a con-

nection to the jouissance, creating a particular sexual relationship: "On the level of the *sinthome*, . . . there is a rapport. . . . there is only a rapport where there is a *sinthome*."[61]

Last but not least, this theory permits a completely new approach to the question of gender. The Woman does not exist in the Symbolic, the Man exists far too much there. Just like a man, a woman has to alienate herself in the ever-phallic signifiers of the Other. The man, due to his relationship to the phallic signifier and the S_1, is taken "naturally" in the direction of identification with the signifier; he sticks to alienation. Woman knows this alienating relationship as well, but at the same time, she entertains a special relationship to the object *a* and jouissance. Due to this double relationship, a woman is "naturally" invited to create something of herself, in the very process of becoming a woman.

In this sense, the Lacanian conclusion of the treatment—the identification with the Real of the symptom, the choice of jouissance, and the creation of a neosubject—is a particular process that is situated entirely in the line of femininity.

NOTES

1. S. Freud, *Fragment of an Analysis of a Case of Hysteria* (1905), SE VII, pp. 40-41.
2. S. Freud, *Three Essays on the Theory of Sexuality* (1905), SE VII, *passim*.
3. J. Lacan, "De nos antécédents," in *Écrits*, Paris: Seuil, 1966, p. 66.
4. S. Freud, 1905, *op. cit.*, p. 83.
5. Ruth Mack Brunswick, "A Supplement to Freud's *History of an Infantile Neurosis*," in M. Gardiner, *The Wolf-man by the Wolf-man*, New York: Basic Books, 1971.
6. *Ibid.*
7. F. Deutsch, "A Footnote to Freud's *Fragment of an Analysis of a Case of Hysteria*," in C. Bernheimer & C. Kahane (Eds.), *In Dora's Case: Freud—Hysteria—Feminism*, New York: Columbia University Press, 1985, pp. 35–44.
8. For a related discussion of the transition from letter to signifier, see above, p. 67.
9. S. Freud, *Analysis Terminable and Interminable* (1937), SE XXIII, p. 224 ff.; J. Lacan, *The Seminar, Book I. Freud's Papers on Technique, 1953–1954*, ed. J.-A. Miller, trans. J. Forrester, Cambridge: U.K., Cambridge University Press, 1988.

10. The very same twofold structure can be found in every key Freudian concept. Each time, Freud makes a differentiation between a "primal" form and a secondary version: primal repression—"after-repression," primal father—oedipal father, primal phantasm—phantasm. In the context of our paper, the idea of primal repression is the most interesting one because we can situate there the drive root of the symptom, that is, the Real. It is only with the after-repression that the Symbolic component comes into being. For Freud, there is always a "faulty connection" (*falsche Verknüpfung*) between a drive component and a representation. For an elaboration of this idea cf. P. Verhaeghe, *Does the Woman Exist? From Freud's Hysteric to Lacan's Feminine*, New York and London: Other Press—Rebus, 1999, pp. 149–205.

11. S. Freud, 1937, SE XXIII, p. 228.

12. S. Freud, "Negation" (1925) SE XIX, p. 236.

13. Freud's metaphor is all the more interesting when one knows about his train phobia. K. Obholzer, *The Wolfman: Conversations with Freud's Patient—Sixty Years Later*, trans. M. Shaw, New York: Continuum Books, 1982, p. 77.

14. This irreversibility can be understood from a Freudian point of view concerning primal repression, which is first of all a primal fixation. In his descriptions of primal repression, Freud makes it clear that this primal fixation concerns the drive (see S. Freud, *Psycho-analytic Notes on an Autobiographical Account of a Case of Paranoia (Dementia Paranoides)*, 1911, SE XII, pp. 66–67, and *Inhibitions, Symptoms and Anxiety*, 1926, SE XX, p. 94). Freud's idea of fixation is the precursor and the precondition of repression. Lacan made it clear that Freud's fixation implies the idea of a choice-making instance. For Lacan, this instance is the Real of the body, that is, the Real of the drive. This Real of the bodily drive is independent of the subject; it is an instance that judges and chooses independently: "Ce qui pense, calcule et juge, c'est la jouissance" ("What thinks, computes and judges, is the Enjoyment," J. Lacan, ". . . Ou pire," *Scilicet*, 5, Paris: Du Seuil, 1975, p. 9). Subsequently, the subject has to take a position vis à vis these choices of the body. If the subject does not accept a certain choice of the drive, this constitutes repression. From the etiological point of view, repression is simply a mechanism, which will be stressed by Lacan when he states that "l'inconscient travaille sans y penser, ni calculer, juger non plus." ("the unconscious operates without thinking, computing or judging," J. Lacan, Introduction à l'édition allemande d'un premier volume des *Écrits*, *Scilicet*, 5, *op. cit.*, p. 14). It is in this context that one has to understand another Lacanian statement: that the subject is not condemned to his consciousness, but to his body ("Ce n'est pas à sa conscience que le sujet est condamné, mais à son corps," J. Lacan, Réponses à des étudiants en philosophie sur l'objet de la psychanalyse, *Cahiers pour l'analyse*, 3, 1966, p. 8). For a more detailed elaboration of these ideas, see F. Declercq, *Het Reële bij Lacan*, forthcoming.

15. S. Freud, 1937, *op. cit.*, p. 227.

16. S. Freud, *Analysis of a Phobia in a Five-Year-Old Boy* (1909), SE X, p. 145.

17. S. Freud, 1937, *op. cit.*, pp. 216–217.

18. J. Lacan, *The Ethics of Psychoanalysis: Seminar VII, 1959–60*, ed. J.-A. Miller, trans. D. Porter, London: Routledge, 1992, pp. 120–123.

19. It's important to note that while Freud is talking about the ego, we are talking about the subject. We'll have to come back to this, especially because it entails an ontological problem. Moreover, in contemporary literature, the concept of "subject" is used in a very careless way, often almost as a synonym of "person" or "ego." The specific Lacanian meaning of the term is different, and makes it very hard to consider the subject an instance that chooses or decides. According to Lacan's "pre-ontology" of Seminar XI, the subject is not a decision-making instance, but an ever-failing realization of one's identity. If the treatment ends with a subject that can make decisions, then this indeed has to be a completely different kind of subject. This tallies with Lacan's ideas in Seminar XI about the effect of "se parer" in the process of separation, which means: to "dress" oneself, to defend oneself, but also to give birth to oneself (J. Lacan, *The Four Fundamental Concepts of Psycho-Analysis*, Seminar XI, ed. J.-A. Miller, trans. A. Sheridan, London: Hogarth Press 1977, p. 214; the original French version can be found at the end of chapter XVI of the seminar). See also P. Verhaeghe, "Causation and Destitution of a Pre-Ontological Non-Identity: On the Lacanian Subject," in D. Nobus (Ed.), *Key Concepts of Lacanian Psycho-Analysis*, Rebus Press, 1998, pp. 164–189.

20. S. Freud, 1937, *op. cit.*, p. 227.

21. S. Freud, *The Ego and the Id* (1923), SE XIX, p. 50, n.1.

22. *Ibid.*, p. 250.

23. Freud understood quite early on that the "natural" end of a psychotherapy consisted in the identification of the patient with the therapist in the position of the Ego-Ideal, and refused this immediately for his psychoanalysis: ". . . but otherwise the outcome of one's efforts is by no means certain. It depends principally on the intensity of the sense of guilt; . . . Perhaps it may depend, too, on whether the personality of the analyst allows of the patient's putting him in the place of his ego ideal, and this involves a temptation for the analyst to play the part of prophet, saviour and redeemer to the patient. Since the rules of analysis are diametrically opposed to the physician's making use of his personality in any such manner, it must be honestly confessed that here we have another limitation to the effectiveness of analysis; after all, analysis does not set out to make pathological reactions impossible, but to give the patient's ego *freedom* to decide one way or the other." (S. Freud, 1923, SE XIX, p. 50, n.1, italics in original).

24. "En quoi consiste ce repérage qu'est l'analyse? Est-ce que ce serait, ou non, s'identifier, tout en prenant ses garanties d'une espèce de distance, à son symptôme? savoir faire avec, savoir le débrouiller, le manipuler . . . *savoir y faire avec son symptôme, c'est là la fin de l'analyse.*" J. Lacan, *Le Séminaire XXIV, L'insu que sait de l'une bévue, s'aile a mourre, Ornicar?*, 12/13, 1977, pp. 6–7 (our translation, italics added).

25. If Freud equates the subjective acceptance of a pregenital fixation with infantilism or perversion, he indirectly implies that a fixation is by definition abnormal, that is, it does not tally with the genital norm. This can be read in his papers on the drive. In his Introductory Lecture 21 on "The Development of the Libido," he states clearly that during the genital phase, the drive has to submit itself to the genital. The very idea of development implies in itself the idea of a "normal" end point. Freud's formulation that the end point of libidinal development comes down to the "subordination" (sic.) of all sexual partial drives to genital primacy and thus to the "subjection" (sic.) of sexuality to reproduction, leaves little doubt about the fact that he considers genital sexuality to be the optimal and final point. (S. Freud, *SE XVI*, p. 328.) In his *Three Essays on the Theory of Sexuality*, "Character and Anal Eroticism," "The Disposition to Obsessional Neurosis," and "On the Transformation of Instinct as Exemplified in Anal Eroticism," the same message can be found: once one has passed through the genital stage, pregenital drives are outdated. All libidinal investments of the anal and oral zone, of looking and hearing, have to serve the function of genital sexuality.

26. "Freud never succeeded in conceiving the said sexuality otherwise than as perverse. . . . perversion is the essence of man" ("Freud n'a jamais réussi à concevoir ladite sexualité autrement que perverse. . . . la perversion est l'essence de l'homme." J. Lacan, *Le Séminaire XXIII, Le sinthome, Ornicar?*, 11, 1977, p. 8.

27. J. Lacan, 1998, *Seminar XX, Encore: On Feminine Sexuality. The Limits of Love and Knowledge*, 1972–73, translated with notes by B. Fink, New York and London: Norton, p. 80.

28. J. Lacan, 1966–67, 1/17/67: ". . . pulsion génitale que quiconque serait bien incapable de définir comme telle."

29. This idea of the Real as an internal exteriority, a central lack, was elaborated by Lacan in Seminar VII with his topology of *Das Ding*. The Real is "at the centre only in the sense that it is excluded" (Lacan, 1992, p. 71).

30. This is already clear with Freud, especially in the paper that Lacan considers as Freud's legacy: *Analysis Terminable and Interminable*.

31. J. Lacan, 1974–75, *R.S.I.*, in *Ornicar?*, 3, 1975, pp. 106–107.

32. *Ibid.*, lesson of 2/18/75: "Je définis le symptôme par la façon dont

chacun jouit de l'inconscient en tant que l'inconscient le détermine" (our translation).

33. *Ibid.*, lesson of 1/21/75.

34. There is a beautiful Freudian example of this process: the famous "Glanz auf der Nase" (shine on the nose) of the Wolf-man, where it is the translation that takes care of the transition from letter to signifier. In the original German version of the symptom, the kernel of the drive is central, while in the defensive translation, the process of "significantisation" takes place. Cf. S. Freud, *Fetishism* (1927), SE XXI, pp. 152–153.

35. See F. Deutsch, *op. cit.*

36. "Les points de suspension du symptome sont en fait des points, si je puis dire, *interrogatifs dans le non-rapport*. C'est ce qui justifie cette définition que je vous donne, que ce qui constitue le symptôme, ce quelque chose qui se bécotte avec l'inconscient, c'est qu'on y croit." (Lacan, *R.S.I.*, *Ornicar?*, 3, 1975, p. 109).

37. "Une préférence donnée en tout à l'inconscient," J. Lacan, *Ornicar?*, 12/13, 1977, p. 15.

38. "La réciprocité entre le sujet et l'objet a est totale," J. Lacan, 1998, *Seminar XX*, *op. cit.*, p. 127.

39. "La raison en est que ce que le discours analytique concerne, c'est le sujet, qui, comme effet de signification, est réponse du réel" ("The reason for this is that, concerning the analytic discourse, it is the subject that, as an effect of signification, is an answer of the Real," J. Lacan, *L'étourdit*, *Scilicet* 4, 1973, p. 15).

40. "Body" not in the sense of the Symbolic or Imaginary body, but the body as organism, as Real. See P. Verhaeghe, "The Subject of the Body," paper given at the UCLA conference, March 1999 (to be published).

41. "*Sinthome*" is an equivocal neologism, combining at least three different signifiers: *symptôme* (symptom), *saint homme* (holy man), *Saint Thomas* (the one who didn't believe the Other—Christ—but went for the Real Thing).

42. J. Lacan, *Seminar XI*, *op. cit.*, p. 250.

43. *Ibid.*

44. It is quite remarkable that not one of these three notions was fully elaborated by Lacan himself. The last one—"destitution subjective"— (J. Lacan, *Proposition d'Octobre*, *Scilicet*, 1, 1968, p. 23) is today the most well known, but this is mainly due to Slavoj Žižek's extensive commentaries on it.

45. J. Lacan, *Seminar XI*, *op. cit.*, p. 214.

46. "Well, the names of the father come down to this: the Symbolic, the Imaginary and the Real insofar as, to my sense—with all the weight I gave above to the word 'sense'—that's what they are, the names of the father, the first names to the extent that they name things" ("Eh bien, les noms du père

c'est ça: le symbolique, l'imaginaire et le réel en tant qu'à mon sens—avec le poids que j'ai donné tout à l'heure au mot 'sens,' c'est ça les noms du père, les noms premiers en tant qu'ils nomment quelque chose."), J. Lacan, R.S.I., 3/11/75, *Ornicar?*, *op. cit*. For an excellent overview of Lacan's development on this difficult topic, see E. Porge, *Les noms du père chez J. Lacan: Ponctuations et problématiques*, Paris: Editions Erès, 1997.

47. S. Freud, *Moses and Monotheism* (1939), SE XXIII, p. 118. In a fascinating essay, John Brenkman discusses the difficulties in education when one wants to raise his children without religion. The main difficulties do not reside in the dichotomy between reason and faith, but in the question of which narratives, symbols, and discourses to use if one does not believe (J. Brenkman, "The Labyrinth of Accusation," in *Venue*, 3, 1998, pp. 144–156).

48. See P. Verhaeghe, "Trauma and Hysteria in Freud and Lacan," in *The Letter: Lacanian Perspectives on Psychoanalysis*, Autumn 1998, no. 14, pp. 87–106.

49. J. Lacan, *Ornicar?*, 17/18, 1979, p. 7.

50. S. Freud, 1937, SE XXIII, p. 25; C. Soler, "Aimer son symptôme," *La Cause Freudienne, Revue de Psychanalyse, La passe: fait ou fiction?*, 1994, pp. 103–114.

51. "Nous savons bien que nous ne pouvons pas non plus opérer dans notre position d'analyste comme opérait Freud, qui prenait dans l'analyse la position du père. . . . Et c'est pour cela que nous ne savons plus où nous fourrer—parce que nous n'avons pas appris à réarticuler à partir de là quelle doit être notre position à nous." J. Lacan, *Le Séminaire, Livre VIII. Le Transfert*, Texte établi par J.-A. Miller, Paris: Seuil, 1991, p. 345.

52. See A. Kardiner, *Mon analyse avec Freud*, Paris: Belfond, 1978, p. 103.

53. J. Lacan, 1966, p. 818 (our italics); *Écrits: A Selection, op. cit.*, p. 316.

54. J. Lacan, *Écrits: A Selection, op. cit.*, p. 316.

55. J. Lacan, *Le Séminaire XXIII, Le sinthome, Ornicar?*, 8, 1976, p. 20. "Ce que pour la première fois j'ai défini comme un sinthome, est ce qui permet au symbolique, à l'imaginaire et au réel, de tenir ensemble. . . . Au niveau du sinthome, . . . il y a rapport. . . . Il n'y a rapport que là où il y a *sinthome*."

56. J. Lacan, *Le Séminaire XXIV, L'insu que sait de l'une bévue, s'aile a mourre, Ornicar?*, 17/18, 1979, p. 21. "Ce que j'énonce en tout cas, c'est que l'invention d'un signifiant est quelque chose de différent de la mémoire. *Ce n'est pas que l'enfant invente—ce signifiant, il le reçoit*, et c'est même ça qui vaudrait qu'on en fasse plus. *Nos signifiants sont toujours reçus*. Pourquoi est-ce qu'on n'inventerait pas un signifiant nouveau? Un signifiant par exemple qui n'aurait, comme le réel, aucune espèce de sens?" This quote sums up the first difficulty we discussed above: how to become independent from the (signifiers of the) Other (italics added).

57. It is no coincidence either that his removal from the IPA coincides with the seminar on the names of the father. Neither is it a coincidence that he gave only one lesson. The lack of this seminar provides us with a perfect mirror-image of the lack of the Other of the Other. In this context, the subsequent course of Lacan's institutional history is very revealing as well. In spite of his efforts to take up the position of the object *a*, both in his School and during his analytic practice, Lacan underwent the same fate as Freud. His concepts did not provide the impetus for a new knowledge, but became embalmed as well. Finally, to escape from the position of founding father, and to open the possibility for inventing a new knowledge, Lacan dissolved his School and took up the position of object *a*: he interrupts the seminar and stays at bay during the founding of the ECF in 1980; see also J. Lacan, *Lettre de Dissolution, Ornicar?*, 20/21: "This problem demonstrates that, in order to have a solution, one has the dis-solution. . . . It is enough that one goes in order to liberate all the others, and that goes for every one in my borromean knot; in my school, it has to be me." "Ce problème se démontre tel, d'avoir une solution: c'est la *dis*—la dissolution. . . . Qu'il suffise d'un qui s'en aille pour que tous soient libres, c'est, dans mon noeud borroméen, vrai de chacun, il faut que ce soit moi dans mon École" (Lacan, 1980, p. 9).

58. J. Lacan, *Le Séminaire XXIII, Le sinthome, Ornicar?*, 6, 1976, p. 18.

59. J. Lacan, *Le Séminaire XXIII, Le sinthome, Ornicar?*, 7, 1976, p. 15.

60. J. Lacan, *Le Séminaire XXIV, L'insu que sait de l'une bévue, s'aile a mourre, Ornicar?*, 12/13, 1977, pp. 6–7 (our italics).

61. *Ibid.*

REFERENCES

Freud, S. (1894). The neuro-psychoses of defence. *SE* III.

——— (1896). Further remarks on the neuro-psychoses of defence. *SE* III.

——— (1909a). Analysis of a phobia in a five-year-old boy. *SE* X.

——— (1909b). Notes upon a case of obsessional neurosis. *SE* X.

——— (1918). From the history of an infantile neurosis. *SE* XVII.

5

Weaving a Trans-subjective Tress or the Matrixial *sinthome*

Bracha Lichtenberg Ettinger

TRESS, *SINTHOME* AND THE "IMPOSSIBLE" FEMININE RELATION

Right up to the end of his teaching, Lacan claimed that "there is no sexual relation (*il n'y a pas de rapport sexuel*)." Psychoanalysis itself, in his view, was proof of this. The lack of such a *rapport* is the very basis of psychoanalytic discourse (but if such a relation had existed, he implies, it would have been feminine). In some of his very late seminars,[1] however, Lacan is led—by logical and topological considerations, and also by some aesthetic ones—to imply, enigmatically, the possibility of a psychical zone where the feminine sexual *rapport* has not been appropriated and "killed" by the signifier, or mastered by the phallic dimension, cut out and kicked away by castration. This "supplementary" feminine non-conscious zone is stretched out of, and retreats back into, art, and is separated from psychosis, occultism, initiation, telepathy and mysticism by less than a hair's breadth.

At this late stage in his teaching, Lacan describes the psychical registers RSI (Real, Symbolic, Imaginary) as rings linked together by a knot, a kind of triangular warp-and-woof weave, or a tress made up of three strings, where the string of the Real is—in principle, structurally and primarily—inseparable from the strings of the Imaginary and the Symbolic. In such a tress, with the Real conceived of not only as the third string but as the triple tress itself, some kind of knowledge is written "and should be read in deciphering it."[2] If bodily traces of jouissance and of trauma (in the Real), their representations (in the Imaginary), and their significance (in the Symbolic) are woven in a tress around and within each psychical event, their knowledge in/of a Real marks the Symbolic with its sense and its thinking, no less than the Symbolic gives meaning to the Real via signification and concepts. We may therefore suppose a resonating significance between no-meaning and sign, intermingled with the fourth term that knits the three registers together and corresponds to the tress as a unity: the *sinthome*. The *sinthome* and the tress refer to the feminine-other sex and its impossible *rapport*.

> It is in so far as there is *sinthome* that there is no sexual equivalence, which is to say there is a relation. . . . Where there is a relation, it is in so far as there is *sinthome*, which is to say . . . it is by *sinthome* that the other sex is sustained. . . . The *sinthome*'s direct link, it is this something which must be situated in its doings with the Real . . . It is the *sinthome* we must deal with in the very relation that Freud maintained was natural—which doesn't mean a thing: the sexual relation. . . . All that subsists of the sexual relation is that geometry which we alluded to in relation to the glove. That is all that remains for the human species as a basis for the relation.[3]

The three registers are knitted together in a tress that harbors the possibility of a feminine relation coming to be, emerging from its proper impossibility. "What is it, a tress?" asks Lacan in 1973.[4] Everyone weaves its knots, he says, or rather, each "woman" plaits her tress. Everyone is weaving, but when you are weaving and succeed something inside the failure of plaiting, you are a "woman." She is weaving together the Real, the Symbolic, and the Imaginary in order to give psychical events a sense from the side of the Real. The weaving of the knot in the phallic arena is necessarily faulty (failure, *ratage*) for both men and women. What fails is more then the knotting of *being* with *knowledge* by the Imaginary; what fails is the process of knotting itself, which would be love. What fails is love, insofar as love is the impossible relationship between the Real (with its phallic jouissance and its jouissance beyond-the-phallus) and knowledge as articulated in/by the Symbolic, as well as an impossible relation between two bodies because one's jouissance is unable to reach, to form a bridge across to the other.

This failure is necessary, because what fails is a link that would, if materialized, threaten to bind the death drive, concealed beyond the pleasure principle, to jouissance and therefore to put *being* in relation with *death*. What a woman sometimes succeeds in, despite this failure, is a sexual union where jouissance binds up the death drive in a primal scene. Indeed, a fabric of hidden connections between the death drive and the feminine underlies Freudian psychoanalysis in general and Lacanian theory in particular, allowing us to see that the foreclosure of the feminine-beyond-the-phallus is vital for the phallic subject: it stands for the split of what is living from the death drive. Sometimes, through a work of art, the failure fails and its meaning almost appears. Then the death drive borders upon jouissance and the borderline is called beauty. Beyond beauty lies fragmentation, tied up with regressive self-annihilation before any psychical order.

The tressage, its knotting and its holes offer us, states Lacan, "the Real that is before order . . . which makes three with the Imaginary and the Symbolic. Sexuality is linked to the death of the body, to reproduction . . . the body goes towards jouissance . . . death . . . is not in the scope of Truth . . . for having to do with death, it can only go together with the Beautiful; it is there that it touches . . . in so far as it glorifies the body."[5] "The real of the Borromean knot is not a *three* but a *tress*."[6] In the tress, three strings are united, like the triple rings bound in a Borromean knot, and such a triplicity is in itself a Real—the Real of the tress that treasures a special kind of knowledge revealed not by truth but by beauty, a knowledge working not through concepts but through affects, or through what Lacan calls the pathetic: "It's in the knot itself that resides all that is for us, finally, no more than pathetic."[7] Pathos as meaning is a knowledge in/of the Real "which functions without us knowing how its articulation happens in what we are used to seeing realised . . . This dimension of the Real touches the borders of the Real" and "bears witness to the Real."[8]

An unconscious knowledge that is "topological"—supported only by proximity in space, not by any order derived from a law—is what

Lacan means by the knowledge of a knot or tress: a knowledge of the Real that articulates itself affectively. This is quite different from the knowledge of an unconscious structured by language, but at the same time it is not an "instinctive" knowledge. This knowledge is simply produced or not, "inscribed or not inscribed."[9] The inscription of a tress, the writing of this knotty knowledge—each time newly invented out of and inside an unexpected relation that is otherwise impossible—can be revealed by artistic writing, by that which only later Lacan named *sinthome*. If and when we do succeed in tearing off a string from that Real in deciphering it, something written in it can surprisingly be read. But language itself is an obstacle to this knowledge of a tress-like Real, just as language is an obstacle to the sexual relation. It is an obstacle insofar as it is at the service of the phallus. But beyond the phallus, via the *sinthome*, however much of this knowledge can be translated by language or carried inside language would not necessarily become its want-to-be, but be rather sliding along the intercoiling of the tress.

Where the phallus returns and turns around itself, the relation that would be sexual and feminine must turn into a nonrelation, and the unthought-of sense of the tress into a nonsense:

> Masculine knowledge in the speaking being is irremediably a route of wandering; it is a cut, alluring a closure, precisely, that of a departure . . . this is the ring-shaped string. It turns around in a ring. In it there is the One at the departure, as a stroke that is repeated with no counting, and from turning around in rings it gets closed upon itself, without even knowing that from these rings, there are three. . . . Happily, for that, there is a woman. *The* woman—this doesn't exist . . . but a woman, this . . . this can be produced, when there is a knot, or rather a tress.[10]

The failure of knotting in the phallic arena is that "due to which the woman doesn't exist." But at the same time,

> this very thing is exactly that through which she manages to succeed at sexual union. Only this union is the union of one with two, or of each with each, of each of these three strings. The sexual union, if I may say so, is internal to its weave. And that is where she plays her part, in really showing us what a knot is, by which the man, for his part, succeeds to be three. That is, the Imaginary, the Symbolic and the Real are only *simply distinguished* by being three. . . . Without him finding itself in it, [the sub-

ject] starts from this triplicity, of which a woman, sometimes, makes her success in missing it, i.e., of which she is satisfied as realising *in herself* the sexual union; it is starting from this that the man begins to grasp slightly the idea that a knot can be useful. . . . She doesn't know that sexual union exists only in herself and incidentally. She knows nothing. . . .

She is ignorant of *the impossibility* of the relation, while "the man knows that there is the impossible." In him, the sexual relation "never writes itself except through the lack of his desire, which is nothing but his being locked-up and squeezed inside the Borromean knot."[11]

The nonrelation, then, is not a matter of contingency but of impossibility, of a certain function, and the feminine, neither a matter of function or of being, but of *linking*. She doesn't exist, she doesn't signify anything, but she sometimes realizes an impossible link. "The function of the woman in relation to a man and the function of the man in relation to a woman can't be inscribed—this is the sexual non-relation . . . there exists no function that links them."[12] So how can a woman give an-other sense to the otherwise non-relation and realize the impossible link between separate individuals? We are reminded here of an analogous question Lacan had expressed some ten years earlier, where an impossible intersubjectivity is connected to aesthetic experience, where the impossible is in fact the archaic union of which I am the result, the moment of the subject's birth that is forever absent for him; a birth that can't be inscribed in language and thus can only appear as lack, translated in language as a "want-to-be," allowing us to link the successful union of the primal scene to the unary stroke, in the background of any creation and emergence:

And also remember what I said the painting was: the *real painting*. It is gaze. That it is the painting that gazes at whosoever is caught in its field and brought into its snare, that, from the Other, the painter is the one who makes the gaze fall before the other. . . . [T]he projected figure before him, from the one who no longer knows from what position he sees himself, the point from which he sees himself, for the S of the schema which I have shown to be the constitutive site of primordial identification, identification of the *unary stroke*, identification of the I[Imaginary], and from which somewhere everything is positioned for the subject, this S of course, has no point, it is that in which that *outside* which is the *point of birth*—the *point of emergence of some creation* which can belong to the order of reflection, to the order of the secretly organised, to that which is positioned, to that which is instituted as *intersubjectivity*, that light—suddenly appeared on the image itself of s/he whose name is lost, of s/he who is presented here as the *lack*. It is really—and on this subject Freud leaves us with the thing in suspense, leaves us kind of tongue-tied as we say—it is the *apparition of the point of emergence into the world* from that point of insurgence which, in language, can only be translated as the *want-to-be*.[13]

Lacan leans on the topology of the Borromean knot and the tress in order to articulate and demonstrate something concerning this impossibility: the writing of the otherwise want-to-be, the articulation of this point of emergence in the world that masculine knowledge can't apprehend but around which the phallus turns and returns to establish this point as its blind emergence, an isolated unary stroke. This spot of archaic emergence, with its impossible relationship, converges with the impossible sexual relation, for we are in the dangerous domain of the parental primal scene, the origin of the prehistoric incestuous mother–child relationship, a scene that is necessary for giving life and entering life, essential for the emergence of subjectivity and yet necessarily foreclosed by the phallus and therefore divorced from culture, endlessly designified by the operation of castration.

In his seminar *R.S.I.*, Lacan finally states in so many words that the link of the incest taboo with castration is "what I call *my sexual rapport*."[14] Now "there is no sexual relation" means that symbolic castration creates the nonrelation to the archaic incestuous mother–infant bond that has of course occurred in experiential reality, but when such a reality exists, the condition of symbolic castration doesn't (yet) exist. This is immemorial for the subject. And for the already humanized subject, it is this experiential reality that doesn't exist (any more); unbreachable borders surround it.

So the theory goes; but isn't *that* human subject, for whom such an experiential reality no longer exists, clearly a *masculine* subject operating within an individual male body? The fatal condition of a male individual regarding the incestuous bond is that, after the Oedipus complex, he has no more *real* contact with it, except in hallucinations, dreams, or fantasy. Of course, as a baby, before the Oedipus complex, both the male and the female subject cross the borders of the infant–mother incest taboo. But of course at that point these borders don't yet exist, so the word "transgression" is unfit to describe such a crossing of borders, if the taboo is not yet in play. In infancy, before the Oedipus complex, the law of castration does not yet function, so there can be no transgression.

By contrast, although the female subject crosses the borders of this not-yet-existent taboo before the Oedipus complex in the same sense as the male subject—that is, without "transgression"—she later transgresses it, actually or potentially, when coming into motherhood. In any case, any female embodies a being that transgresses this taboo in a potentiality that becomes a real possibility after puberty. In this sense, in the sense of this *potential*, embodied transgression, *the body—female or male—makes a difference* and transgression itself becomes a meaning in or of the feminine. Regarding this kind of transgression, the body makes a difference *for* subjectivity. And so, as an adult, a male subject will have no direct corporeal contact with the infant–mother incest relation that borders on the primal scene, and he will only be able to transgress the taboo partially—to a certain extent and in imagination, by means of love or an aesthetic experience, as the shadow that accompanies love, as the shadow of beauty. But a female adult subject can in potentiality—and sometimes must in actual reality—transgress this taboo by coming into motherhood and through her relations with her potential preoedipal baby, who will have no knowledge of this taboo when crossing the borders within her.

Under these circumstances, for the adult female this taboo melts away, but to transgress it is not simply meaningless, because this subject, like the male subject, is now postoedipal. In other words, transgression and the opposing taboo paradoxically coexist in her unconscious. She at once respects the taboo and transgresses it, in different but simultaneous dimensions of her body-psyche time-and-space. Transgression for her is thus not only regressive, not only meaningless. Transgression is the meaning of what in the phallic dimension is meaninglessness itself, and of what for a male subject can only stand for regressive fragmentation into partial subjectivity in the Real, on the way to annihilation and psychosis, to a fatal encounter with the death drive. Crossing the borders is a kind of knowledge for both the oedipal and the preoedipal female subject (here we must cast doubt on Lacan's assertion that a "woman" knows nothing of this knowledge), and it is the meaning of social meaninglessness for this same subject operating on the phallic level simultaneously, because it is what in the phallus is the opposite of meaning carried by language. This same transgression is meaningless for the male preoedipal subject because it is not-yet forbidden, and it is crazy or mystical for the postoedipal masculine subject who is split off from it.

Can we treat this feminine transgression, where castration meets with incest, where the nonrelation stops not-being and not-being-written, as just as senseless for a woman as it is for a man and as the early, not-yet-transgressive ignorance of the infant–mother incest taboo experienced by an infant? If not, then she knows something, and some knowledge must pass from this Real to the Symbolic, from "nature" to "culture," and such a knowledge will necessarily be "an invention" each time it appears, in Lacan's terminology: something that appears in the Symbolic for the first time, because it appears in a conjunction that is unexpected and different each time. The knowledge is not restricted to the original past transgression, but to the re-emergence in present reality of transgressive links that trigger the unconscious pathways affectively opened by the original transgression and are inscribed (or not-inscribed) in these pathways.

Let's put the question again in a different way. If the sexual relation is defined in this way, as a relation partly linking the traces of the archaic coupling of the primal scene (a relation "before the subject's conception") to an archaic infant–mother non-prohibited-yet-incestuous relation, and if such a sexual relation might occur under certain circumstances in adult life in a feminine subjective dimension, the question arises: Can this feminine transgressive relation be sublimated, can it constitute a social link, can it be "elevated" to a level of ethical knowledge? Or does it only operate at the level of occultism and initiation, mysticism and psychosis, something that surges into the Symbolic as a rupture, unless its close links to the death drive bordering on jouissance allow it to emerge as beauty in a work of art?

Lacan's reply is clear: "the link of castration with the incest taboo . . . is what I call my sexual *rapport*. . . . The beginning of any social link is constituted from the sexual non-relation as a hole, not two, at least three. Even if you are only three, it makes four. The Plus-one is there."[15] In other words, the link between two individuals, according to the infant–mother prototype, without a third (the oedipal father), and the Name of the Father (Plus-one, the symbolic phallus), which guarantees the phallic law and introduces castration, has no social value, though it is the constitutive starting point of the social.

At this inception of the social, the Woman-archaic-m/Other-Thing, moistened by her archaic jouissance, saturated with pain or pleasure and in contact with the sexual *rapport* that engages the subject's own conception, is for Lacan forever situated behind originary repression; we can perceive nothing of it. This Woman-Other-Thing, between conception and the incestuous infant–mother relation, is the Impossible itself. This impossibility includes the time between conception and birth, a time beyond phallic-subjective time and equally a space beyond phallic-subjective space, which Lacan considers to be outside the limits of psychoanalysis. In the same way that he emphasizes the impossibility of the feminine relation, he also insists on the foreclosure of prenatal experience and of pregnancy. But still . . .

As Lacan himself claims in 1975–76, although it is outside the limits of psychoanalysis and even poses a threat to it, something of this impossible sexual relation can be accessed in or by the feminine and articulated through art as *sinthome*. Not through analysis, but through art—the art, in Joyce's case, of writing, but also perhaps through the visual arts, via the gaze as object *a*. The *sinthome* is therefore the other sex, it is what "woman" is to "man," and it is a product of art. And we would add that if art can in turn be symbologenic, if it can not only transform a non-relation into a relation but also allow the transfer of the effects of this transformation and the working through of this passage from affects to ideas, then it can put into operation not only the difference between "woman" and "man" but also the difference between "woman" and woman, that is, an originary feminine difference.

In this last difference, as we shall see, what we will term a matrixial *sinthome* can become a site where traumatic feminine jouissance can be partially shared, and where the transgressive feminine relation can be sublimated and "elevated," not only into aesthetic experience but also into the borders of ethical knowledge.[16] It can even indirectly inform a model of a social bond that cannot be regulated by the phallic law but can be nourished by an ethical inclination and must therefore be reinvented for each encounter, but which, however, is inseparable from such an ethical inclination, where ethics exceeds the social only to be its guiding light. Here, in each encounter, with its product as matrixial *sinthome* and knowledge, the borders between aesthetics and ethics need to be constantly renegotiated.

THE COMING TO RELATION OF
THE NON-RELATION IN A *SINTHOME*

Under certain circumstances, an "impossible" feminine sexual relation coexists with the usual nonrelation. This is what the *sinthome* conveys. What might be another mode of inscription and meaning-resonating that would correspond to the coming to relation of this nonrelation? What might be a mode that could allow the passage of the supplementary feminine jouissance and its sexual relation into culture following the dissimulated incarnation of these in a *sinthome*, so that they would not be solely experienced in the Real, enacted in mystical phenomena, or realized in psychosis? What could make us discover this passage as an-other knowledge, a knowledge that would not imply the foreclosing split of the feminine from the subject? What would evade even the constitution of the *sinthome* as a failure in knowledge? If the Real, and not only the Symbolic, already harbors some knowledge, a feminine difference based on bodily specificity and links not only simply occurs as always-too-early for knowledge and always-too-late for access, but can also make sense inside a *sinthomatic* weaving.

The archaic jouissance saturated with pain or pleasure, the traumatic wound beyond the border of an originary repression of the incestuous bond with the archaic m/Other, is certainly inaccessible to the subject in the dimension where each subject—male or female—is phallic. From the phallic point of view, the elimination of the archaic m/Other is the sacrifice necessary for masculinity to become productive and to sublimate, and thus occupy the place of subject, and for femininity to find its place as object. But the phallic structure of the subject (disguised as neutral) and with it sexual phallic difference (disguised as neutral), which becomes the measure of any sexual difference, refer both directly and indirectly to the male body, to its pleasures and pains and to the phantasms attached to it. Even Lacan, who endlessly sought to establish the neutrality of the phallus, admits in his late theory that the phallus is deeply rooted in the Real of the male body and notes the profound consequences of this enracination. The symbolic One, states Lacan, is what makes an obstacle to the sexual relation, that is phallic jouissance. It is in so far as phallic jouissance is there, let's say that I make it an organ, I make the supposition that it is incarnated by what, in man, corresponds to it as an organ—it's in so far as this jouissance takes up this privileged accent, privileged in the way it imposes itself in all that is our analytical experience; it is there around the individual in itself sexuated which supports it, it's in so far as this jouissance is privileged that the entire analytic experience gets set in order. [The signifier is] secretly stolen, subtracted, borrowed from phallic jouissance itself, and it is in so far as the signifier is its substitute that the signifier itself is found to cause an obstacle, so that what I call the sexual relation will never be written.[17]

The sexual relation is thus itself the negation of the phallic function, and as such it can't take place. Phallic jouissance and its signifier cause an obstacle to the sexual relation, but there is another jouissance, belonging to a different order: "The minimum we can say is that there are two. It's to the extent that in the level where this 'not-all' (*pas-toute*) is articulated, there is not only one jouissance." We need to distinguish between phallic jouissance, which has stolen "the whole function of signifying," and another jouissance, another way by which the body is affected, an-other jouissance. The latter concerns the "impossible *rapport*," the relation of two bodies—as in the primal scene or mother–infant incest—and refers enigmatically to the experience of love. It is a jouissance that reaches across to the other, and not only satisfies one's own organs.

In the feminine, *something in the body can give support to the reference to the other as such*. "It's as long as the Symbolic is secretly stolen from and subtracted from the order of One, of phallic jouissance, and as long as there is a relation of bodies as two, from this fact we must pass through a reference to, a reflection on, something which is other than the Symbolic, which is distinct from it, and it is what already, from before, as three, appears in any minimal writing." If something of this jouissance is shown forth in writing, the signifier not only signifies but also shows; it "shows that precipitation by which the speaking being can have access to the Real."[18] The entwining and coiling of the tress, away from the phallus, as a tutoring of/from a relation to the other enabled by the *rapport* of two bodies provided by a different, feminine jouissance, is an opening onto the Real. By way of the intercoiling and intertwining of the tress, an unconscious knowledge of the Real is found or invented.

When the Real, the Imaginary, and the Symbolic intertwine around a feminine encounter, according to the parameters of the Real revealed in/as a tress, the tracing of the knot somehow "goes wrong" and the knot appears to "slip," a lapsus of what is already not language, or not yet language. In the tress, the phallus fails, or this feminine-other-potential-knowledge fails the phallic unconscious order, and an-other sense, disordered, based on *originary* feminine difference, emerges. Is it not this failure of the phallus in/by the feminine—its failure to seize femininity itself—that Lacan calls "*sinthome*"? Only this failure, as he says, is the same for men and for women. It represents what is a "woman" to the subject as a "man"—it represents femininity for the phallus-structured subject. This "feminine" is not "nothing," it is quite "something" already, though disordered; it is already an "invention" where a sexual relation, usually foreclosed, suddenly lunges out and seizes you. "She" is therefore the unexpected event beyond the phallus, a surprise occurrence discovered via a writing that is a work of art, which reaches you from otherness and alters your knowledge in an affective collision.

> . . . the *sinthome* [is] something that allows the Symbolic, the Imaginary, and the Real to continue holding together . . . what I call, what I designate . . . the *sinthome*, which is marked here with a circle . . . of string, is meant to take place at the very spot where, say, the trace of the knot goes wrong. [It's a] 'slip of the knot.'
>
> I allowed myself to say that the *sinthome* is, precisely speaking, the sex I don't belong to, which is to say a woman. Because a woman is a *sinthome* for every man, it is perfectly clear that we need to find another name for what becomes of man for a woman, since for that very reason the *sinthome* is characterised by non-equivalence.
>
> There is no equivalence, that's the only thing, that's the only recess where what the speak/through-being[19] the human being, sexual relation is sustained . . . the *sinthome*'s direct link, it is this something that must be situated in its dealings with the Real, with the Real of the unconscious.[20]

For Lacan, "when there is equivalence, it is due to this very fact that there is no (sexual) relation. If for an instant we assume that from then on there is a failure of the triple knot, this failure is strictly equivalent—there's no need to say it—in both sexes."[21] Yet it is also clear that a "woman" can't only be defined by a failure in the phallic system. And so to this I add: if a woman is a *sinthome* for every man, it is perfectly clear that we need to find not only another name for what it is to become a "man" for a woman (masculine sexual difference from a feminine point of view), but also of what it is to become *a "woman" for a woman* (an originary feminine difference from a feminine point of view). A "woman" for a woman cannot remain radically Other, as she can for a man, or else all women would become psychotic when they come into contact with their "own" originary difference, or when the potential transgression is reembodied. For a woman, a "woman" must at certain moments be a border-Other, and transgression must be meaningful. "She" cannot be radically absent in the subject but *non-absent* or *ab-present*, and so her difference also locates a state of *pre-ab-sence* which transgresses both pure absence and pure presence, transgresses the conditions of both existence and non-existence.

If in the no-place of the Thing in art Lacan identifies via the *sinthome* something of the revelation of "absent" femininity and her "impossible" sexual relation, I see in the *sinthome* a possibility of the sublimation of transgressive *pre-ab-sence* in/from foreclosed aspects of the feminine, on condition that we give the notion of the *sinthome* a new twist in the light of matrixial difference,[22] in order to discover what a "woman" can become in-difference for a woman, and also for a man who would risk positioning himself in the unconscious matrixial borderspace.

SINTHOME AND SYMPTOM

When we reflect on the difference between a creative artifact produced as a symptom—be it a formal expression with the help of "artistic" tools, or in the language of writing, painting, or music—and a work of art that appears as what Lacan names a *sinthome*, marking a slight but definitive difference from the symptom, a seemingly paradoxical idea imposes itself: it is the symptom, and the creative artifact produced as symptom, that in fact makes sense in and through the Symbolic. And such a making-sense in the Symbolic, creative as it may be, cannot be a measure of art because it takes shape through a signifying process that is *already* culturally accepted. It is an articulation of suffering *already in the language of the Other*, an articulation made for the Other, a message aimed at a symbolic Other, and finally perhaps also apprehended by those who can analyze it and return its sense to the subject who created it. If the symbolic Other already contains all the clues required to decipher the message contained in the work-as-symptom, this work has no potential to *transform* this same Symbolic. The work-as-symptom stems from the unconscious and aims at an unconscious "structured as a language," at what is already there but dissimulated, or cut away, castrated, repressed, temporarily lacking.

A form comes to life and exercises its effects as work of art on a level which, at least to begin with, subverts this signification, a level equivalent to that of events erupting in the Real. And so we may say that the work of art, any work of art fabricated as *sinthome*, is in a way crazy; it is produced at the level of jouissance and it is meant to create jouissance and to make sense through what is left of it (an object *a*, a *plus-de-jouir*). The work of art as *sinthome* is a unique response that contains the enigma it corresponds to and that brings it about, an enigma that resonates with a lacuna of a quite different status than that of the Symbolic. It corresponds, not to a lack defined by the phallic mechanism of castration, but to what is not yet there, what is yet to come, what resists the Symbolic, to the mysterious and fascinating territory of that which is *not yet even unconscious* or which for cognition is impossible.

A symptom that corresponds to a lack in the Symbolic aims to defy castration and points to a lack or a failure *in* the phallic structure. A *sinthome* that points to the dark margins of the Unconscious, struggling to resonate with the traces of a Thing, lies *beyond* the effects of castration. It is indifferent to castration; it does not even defy it as the foreclosed. It indirectly hints at the failure *of* the phallic structure as such, or at some kind of psychical world where the phallic structure is simply irrelevant.[23] In this sense, and in others, it has to do with a dimension of the feminine *beyond* the Phallus. And it is precisely here—in the site of the relation to such a feminine, and in the non-place of such a feminine difference—that Lacan's very late idea of the *sinthome* steps forward to mark a deviation from both his early and his later notions of the symptom.

Lacan's symptom, following Freudian guidelines, has two facets. One is that of the articulated message at the service of the symbolic Other. This was emphasized by Lacan in his early theories. Here what comes to light is what the symptom "says" to the Other where the subject cannot speak for itself. Under this aspect, if the symptom participates in creation, it does so by way of metaphor, by a displacement of whatever is already a compensation for a lack, a subjective split, a separation from one's own partial corpo-reality and from one's own archaic m/Other. The second facet is that of jouissance, increasingly given emphasis by Lacan in his later theory. Here what comes to light is the ways drives are satisfied through the symptom and the pleasures derived from an Imaginary satisfaction of the desire of the Other. Under this aspect, the symptom participates in creation by metonymy, repudiating signification by rejecting any recognition of lack.

A symptom as such is not a work of art. However, as J.-A. Miller remarks, it does, according to Lacan, backtrack on itself in effects of creation. If in its facet of articulated message "the symptom harmonises with castration,"[24] it is perhaps more in its other facet that it backtracks on itself in effects of creation: through following the trails of *jouissance*. Here, something is satisfied by the symptom; something in the speak/through-being is gratified even if the subject is suffering. Something is delighted "beyond the pleasure principle," in what also causes suffering. But if we want to speak of art-object and art-working, even in terms of reading the symptom in its second facet, that of jouissance, which introduces the operation of the death drive in repetition, something is missing from the picture, something that concerns an artistic creativity that transgresses cultural sublimation: the intrinsic potentiality of a work of art to tear apart the world in order to embrace the new, to transform the world's current frontiers and open thresholds capable of receiving new meanings.

Where a message of suffering—a symptom—can be transformed into a work of art, another sense is created beyond its symbolic signification, and a supplementary jouissance not only penetrates the scene or the space of the work but is invented in/by it, a jouissance capable of reaching others. An unimagined trail of jouissance is then invested, but not simply followed by a working through. With the matrixial *sinthome*, something *more* is added to the domain of jouissance, something I think of as a diffracted trace-imprint of trauma-and-jouissance which, as in a reversed movement of time, turns the trace of an imprint that would usually be an effect into an imprint of a trace that presents

itself as a cause, a cause to which, as an effect now, it would also seem—
as trace-imprint—to be a response. This trace-imprint of trauma-and-
jouissance joins in the creation of a work of art because the latter is neither a codified message nor a pure jouissance. It is neither simply an
expression of trails of suffering or pleasure, nor is it a pure marking of their
traces. The work of art is an incarnation of the body-and-psyche in matter, with representation in the external world. It is the unfolding into time
and place of a psychical space-out-of-space at the borders of the Real, in
a visible form or an object which, though inanimate, does, like a subjective substance, *make* suffer/enjoy and *make* sense. It makes sense, it over-
whelms, it touches and fascinates—*it* and not the subject behind it.

A trace-imprint of trauma-and-jouissance makes suffer/enjoy, but
not only by metonymy, in terms of clinging onto an object and turning lack into being. And it makes sense, but not as a metaphor, not by
becoming want-to-be and by passing through the battery of existing
signifiers, and therefore not via the Symbolic or via public and social
recognition—not, at least, to begin with; not, at least, as its defining
criterion. The Symbolic is thereby initially dethroned, only to reappear
by the back door, but only on condition that it becomes a receptive
texture able to give access to and receive what I call the Event-Thing
and the Encounter-Thing of the body-psyche—that affective body-
psyche, denuded and lusting—open, open to oneself and to an-other.

Within the phallic framework, the Woman-Other-Thing screened
off by originary repression is to be understood as a psychical phenomenon that may, of course, enter intersubjective relationships, but as
something separate and distinct. The subject, forever split from the
Woman-m/Other-Thing and facing a woman/object, mourns its loss of
and separation from the former and celebrates its heroic inspiration in
the face of its subjugation by the only-One sexual difference, leaning
on the mechanism of castration anxiety, in order to gain creativity and
symbolic significance. For such a subject, the archaic m/Other is to be
symbolically eliminated or foreclosed, and any part-object, belonging
to the archaic constitutive but evaded dimension of subjectivity is
equally—to use Kristeva's term—an abject. With this originary feminine difference, we approach the Woman-Other-Thing in its insepa-
rability from subjectivity by way of a fundamental transsubjectivity
where what is impossible is not the relation, but the nonrelation.

WEAVING A MATRIXIAL *SINTHOME*

She is weaving. "She manages to succeed at sexual union. Only this union is the union of one with two, or of each with each, of each of these three strings. The sexual union, if I may say so, is internal to its weave. And that is where she plays her part, in really showing us what a knot is."[25] She is weaving. She is being woven. But weaving the Real, the Symbolic, and the Imaginary together and being woven by them in a *sinthome* is not enough to shift the phallic paradigm. Because the *sinthome* is still the phallic failure to tie them up, while "woman" is not just a failure of/in the phallus, not even if taken up by the poetics of the *sinthome*. In a matrixial *sinthome* she is weaving and being woven by strings that are not "hers." She is plaiting her *not-I*'s tresses together with her own, she trans-weaves a work of art.

For Lacan, the question of the aesthetic engages death in its conjunction with the outrageous and beauty. "Outrage" is transgression into the horrible, and the beautiful is the limit that keeps us distant from such a transgression in reality but also allows us to glimpse its unique value, and the "effect of beauty derives from the relationship of the hero to the limit"[26] and to the unique value that hides behind it. I argue, then, that not only death as the horrible conjoined with the "supplementary" jouissance of the Woman-Other-Thing as abducted and foreclosed, but also the subject's trauma and jouissance experienced beyond the Phallus, in *jointness* with the archaic m/Other-Thing-Event-and-Encounter are the values behind the limit.

Moreover, in the matrixial sphere it is the limit itself that is each time transformed by such a jointness and turned into a transgressive threshold. I also propose, in a matrixial perspective, to bring the idea of nonlife and not-yet-life alongside that of death, and of feminine borderswerving, borderlinking, and borderspacing alongside the feminine "impossible" sexual relation, in order to account for the beyond-the-phallus subjective domain that informs the aesthetic and the effect of beauty in a different way. In this perspective, Woman-m/Other should not be understood, as Lacan suggests we understand her, only "in the field of the Thing" and as the "other-Thing lying beyond"[27] but also *in the field of Event and Encounter* and as an *almost-other-Event-Encounter of a not-I that is borderlinked to the I.*

If, then, the question of the aesthetic engages with the question of the relation between jouissance, death, and foreclosed femininity, in the feminine-matrixial dimension it also arises from the problem of traumatizing co-emerging and co-fading within non-foreclosed feminine jouissance working through the passages in between life and non-life in the passage to the other. The artist desires to transform death, non-life, not-yet-life, and no-more-life, in co-emergence and co-fading, into art as the theater of the soul, with its jouissance and its trauma. Where the subject coemerges with an event-other and is constituted in relation not to an other-as-object but to the trembling experience of oscillation between *I* and *not-I* in their encounter, it cannot recognize its trans-subjective objects in any voyeuristic way. It joins the other-encounter and witnesses the other's event: it wit(h)nesses in weaving.

The matrixial borderspace is a sphere of jointness modeled upon an intimate feminine/prebirth sharing of jouissance, trauma, and phantasm beyond the limit of the not-yet-prohibited feminine relation. Here, pre-maternal begetting stands for a passage to the Other in jouissance and trauma, that is a psychical capacity for shareability created in the border-linking to a female body—a capacity for differentiation-in-coemergence that occurs in the course of separation-in-jointness, where distance-in-proximity is continuously reattuned. I(s) and not-I(s) interlace their borderlinks in a process that I have named *metramorphosis*, created by, and further creating—together with and by matrixial affects—relations-without-relating on the borders of presence and absence. A web of movements of borderlinking, between subject and object, among subjects and partial subjects, between me and the stranger, and between some partial subjects and partial objects, becomes a psychical space of trans-subjectivity relating to trans-subjective objects. Via metramorphosis, affects, events, materials, and modes of becoming and encounter infiltrate the non-conscious margins of the Subsymbolic. Metramorphosis is a process of inter-psychical communication and transformation that transgresses the borders of the individual subject. It is a joint awakening of unthinking knowledge on the borderline, and the inscription of the encounter in traces that open a space in and along the borderline itself. Metramorphosis is a *poiesis*, a process of affective-emotive, "pathetic" swerving. The swerve is a measure of difference in the field of affectivity that produces a "pathetic meaning."

Borderswerving, from the outset, is transgressive. It is a process of differentiating in borderspacing and borderlinking, a process of inscriptive exchange between and within several matrixial entities. It dissolves the individual borderlines so that they become transgressive and as thresholds allow a passage that for each participant, becoming a perceptible grain, captivates what I call a *surplus of fragility* in the passage to the other. The knowledge of the passage between at least two bodies-and-psyches is a crossed transcription of one body-and-psyche in another. It is a subknowledge of which we gain a sense in visual arts by inventing or joining a screen, a texture, or a textile where an originary matrixial repression—a fading-in-transformation—is partially lifted or bypassed to allow the originary matrixial transitive trauma (of myself or others) some veiled visibility by way of a touching gaze.

We have realized by now that female bodily sexual specificity allows for thinking primary co-affectivity, which supplies an apparatus of sense making. Sexual difference is in itself an apparatus of thinking and sensing and a level of subjectivation. Metramorphosis is both a coaffectivity and a coactivity at the level of a borderline, which opens up the borderline between subjects and between subject and object into a space that occasions a linking and does not enable the pretense of absolute separation between subjects upon the pattern of cut/split/castration from the Other-Thing, a separation that is in fact the pattern of elimination of the archaic m/Other-Event-Encounter.

It takes a special kind of weaving to create the feminine relation from/on the side of the woman. It takes swerving and borderlinking to create a matrixial *sinthome*. We then discover that a "woman" is not confined to the One-body with its inside and outside, but is always some-bodies tracing knowledge and weaving knots with one another's threads. A movement of borderlinking among several partial subjects, and an affective swerve germinate directly from/with-in and in contact with a Real "touched" by the feminine Thing-Encounter and Thing-Event. These swervings and borderlinkings comprise a matrixial sexual difference, for both men and women. This alignment of sexual difference is independent from the phallic organization of difference. It is created from the beginning as an originary dimension of potentiality in a weave of affects and information interwoven in a trans-psychical web. If both the knot and its slippage remain inside the boundaries of the individual, they link, or fail to link, its different psychical dimensions. A matrixial weaving of a tress, on the other hand, is a borderlinking between several individuals and therefore a borderlinking of the "impossible" relation between at least two body-psyche entities.

According to my interpretation of Freud's "The Uncanny," we may posit a differentiating potential on the level of affection, implied by Freud's analysis when he discusses the anxiety that may go along with our experience of art. The matrixial affect as a primary differentiation introduces a difference on the level of the Thing as it indicates that some-Thing happened, and that a transition from Thing to object is taking place *without a total separation from the Thing*. Matrixial affect indexes a transformation and an exchange, and a matrixial phenomenon testifies to the fact that such a passage has taken place and to the creation of a minimal meaning and its diffusion across the different partial subjects that share the experience. A tremulous meaning, a differentiation-in-togetherness, is tracing itself, and if so, partial and shared subjectivity are both already involved and in the process of being created. Some subjects are there to be affected, and these are not objects to one another, not abjects to be rejected. They are not fused either. The matrixial affect is the affect of the Thing as it inscribes traces in the I and the not-I. Differential affectivity at this level is inseparable from this passage from the Thing to a subjective or objective grain. This passage is a minimal sense, and it works for meaning through the work of art, where the pathetic makes sense together with other human "ruins" and traces.

"The Real itself is three, that is jouissance, body, death, as long as they are knotty, as they are of course knotty only by this unverified deadlock of sex."[28] The object *a* situated "on the border of the Real" is the "waste product," the "ruin" of the human being, it is a "pathetic witnessing,"[29] an affective knowledge of the Real. Is the passage from Thing to object-and-subject on the partial dimension accompanied by affect or created by it? To this we can have no answer, because differential affectivity at this level is inseparable from the passage itself. Their coincidence is fatal, it works for meaning through a work of art as a matrixial *sinthome* that is able to transmit its desire to be acknowledged. The matrixial *sinthome* is symbologenic in principle, but it waits for the artist to stage it for meaning in the externalized theater it produces for the internal and trans-subjective traces of the soul. Passions arising in direct connection to the Thing dwell in the aggregated, enlarged border-Other, in whose constitution they also take part. They act directly as unthought sub-knowledge in a sub-Symbolic connectionist web, and they open primary measures of difference between Thing and object, but also between Thing and subject. Because *some ones* are already there, attracted by the artwork, as silent witnesses.

In the matrixial stratum, a subject exhibits intersections of knots in a trans-psychical web, and therefore "woman" is not a radical Other but a border-Other that can be encountered if we follow upon her threads in the texture and the textile of the web. In other words, if the knot accounts enigmatically for the failure to inscribe feminine desire in Lacan's still (and until the very end) phallic paradigm, and if with the concept of the "knot" it becomes clear that for Lacan the possibility of describing the "supplementary" feminine within the phallic framework has reached its limits, in the passage to a matrixial apparatus, the metramorphosis remembers, inscribes, and transfers the feminine jouissance and swerve during its borderlinking with the other. Via art, this process spreads its specific mode of thinking, sensing, and understanding across the threshold into culture.

Metramorphic processes of webbing and wit(h)-nessing, of exchange of affect and phantasm based on conduction of/in trauma or jouissance in jointness, and of transmissions-in-transformation of phantasm release knowledge from blanks and holes in the shared Real plaited by few tresses. Swerving and contacting become themselves a kind of knowledge; they are, in a spiraling movement back and forward, the inscriptions of traces of borderlinking. We can consider them as manifestations of a matrixial *sinthome* that releases/creates/invents/reveals, in an encounter, some knowledge of the tress from a feminine side, as potential desires whose sense, which does not depend on the signifier, will be revealed in further encounters.

The feminine weaving tells us the story of decentered severality, of unpredictable occurrences, of asymmetrical reciprocity, if we can read between the threads. If the matrixial *sinthome* cannot yet describe what a "man" is to a woman, it can describe what a feminine difference is to a woman and to a man who renders himself fragile inside the Matrix, because the matrixial difference operates in/for men no less than for women, but not in the same way, in that the treatment of its constitutive elements is different for male and female subjects. For men, the maternal prenatal Thing can go through an originary repression and remain the absolute absence, inasmuch as it remains the forever before and outside. For women, inasmuch as their own bodily specificity vibrates and echoes the prenatal Thing as a potential present or future as well, and as both archaic outside and invisible inside, the archaic-m/Other-to-be as a partial subject is never severed like a total absence or like a radical Other, and the maternal prenatal Thing is non-consciously ab-present in-be-side its phallic foreclosure. The difference here is not a result of having/not having an organ, but of relating, as a subject-to-be, to a becoming-mother, perceived in bodily terms as different (and later not even "opposite") in the case of a male infant or as similar-yet-not-the-same in the case of a female infant, in the two-body "impossible" *rapport*.

The manifestation of this difference comes to *ab-pre-sence* in the potential return in the Real, of encounters that are similar—by their affect, by their phantasmatic quality, and by their events-marking—to the original encounter. Thus, depending on whether your sexual embodiment is the same as, or different from, that of the archaic-m/Other-to-be, the *same* events can take this or that route of unconscious tracing. An event that will correspond to weaning-and-separation for a male subject, for example, might correspond to separation-in-jointness for a female subject. The "same" event will then create different minimal sense and be mounted on different nonconscious tracks. Thus, not only does feminine sexual difference traverse every subject, but also transitivity itself in the human is a feminine sexual difference.

The matrixial *sinthome* plays differently for males and for females, because for a male-incarnated human being, difference has a corporal evidence of opposition, of having or not having, that is accessible for sense making. Separating from Her-Thing or clinging to Her-Thing is his painful "choice," but when you separate from Her-Thing you still have evidences of your own different liminal body-Thing. A female person must separate-in-re/in-fusing Her-Thing in the sense that accepting Her-body must still mean opening, otherwise the distance of the similar-but-not-same. Inasmuch as rejecting Her-body is rejecting my body, which can become a deadly blow, difference of the alike-but-not-same is not the difference of the opposite-that-can-be-rejected. Another difference becomes available for her and through her, which does not follow the path of either rejecting or fusing with the m/Other, and which does not question the having/not having opposition but is in-different to it. The matrixial difference is created by/for the alike, not for the same (which doesn't exist), not for the opposite. It indexes the differences in the linking in-between I and not-I, and not the difference (same or opposite) from the not-I. It can only occur in jointness. This nonoppositional difference that operates in borderlinking can be sublimated; it can make an artist, and this is what is revealed to us in the weaving of I and not-I in a transsubjective tress that precedes the distinct I *or* the distinct not-I and transgresses the inter-psychical R.S.I. individual weaving.

The trauma of the loss of archaic transsubjective events is immemorial for the male subject, it is its prehistory; but for a female subject, since it might take new *bodies* in the Real, even this immemorial par excellence is not totally immemorial, is not a total alterity to the subject. It makes sense in/by the Real of the tress. Through the encounter with-in the feminine, traces of this immemorial in men and in women, since they are already created in the encounter with a woman, can be seized in another encounter and be reinvested. Therefore, through the matrixial *rapport*, men have access to this immemorial too. If the linking between I and not-I opens a measure of differentiation in/of/from the feminine, then the initial occurrence confronts me not with how to meet you and share with you, but with the painful question of how to not-share with you, and how to give meaning to our difference-in-jointness that precedes and coincides with my being One-self.

The point of emergence is immemorial for men and for women, but a woman potentially or actually goes through this point again, positioned as its Other with another other, and therefore she is closer to the immemorial, to the hole in the Real. If the Real is "that which is marked out only by writing," the hole in the Real is "the impossibility of writing the sexual rapport." This hole is determined by the Real itself, and it "doesn't stop not-being-written," yet sometimes, it stops being not-written. Something "stops not-being written between two subjects" for "some rare and privileged cases."[30] In this writing, the unconscious invents itself. "There is nothing to be perceived, one needs to invent: to see where is the hole, one has to see the border of the Real."[31] Along the border of the Real that is the intercoiling of the tress, subjectivity is woven with the immemorial and becomes its witness and writer in a feminine "impossible" dimension.

Matrixial subjectivity refuses opposition or fusion because it is woven—a textile and a texture. Yet matrixial subjectivity does not

mean an endless multiplicity of singular individuals but a limited multiplicity—a severality—that traverses subjectivity. Severality is a necessary result of the affective shareability that underlies it. If sharing
knowledge via concepts is by definition limitless, opening a difference
via affects is by definition limited to few encounters at a time. Some
ones must pass through the event and work it through.

She weaves the Real, the Symbolic, and the Imaginary so that no
definitive separating frontiers between them can be established. To this
extent, the failure in/by the *sinthome* brings about the same "woman" for
women and men, on the phallic side. But there is something more. She
is also weaving partial objects and partial subjects in a trans-subjective
texture by/with her borderlinking antennae. Her non-gendered feminine
difference makes sense in the textile, where no identity can work through
its destiny *alone*. In the texture, the relation between at-least-two bodies-
and-psyches carries a difference that, although impossible, is yet possible,
because partial subjects do not accumulate into a subject; they remain
grains. The assemblage of partial subjects is at once less than a subject
and more than one. Partly a subject, partly a veil, the impossible relation turns into trans-textuality, half veiled, that carries knowledge that
can only, to use Lacan's expression, be half spoken (*mi-dit*).

She is weaving and being woven with an-other body-psyche. She
bears witness in the woven tress and texture. Wit(h)nessing makes another sense—the sense of the nameless Thing (Lacan), the immemorial
(Levinas), the originarily repressed (Freud), of the Thing-encounter-
event.

"The desire to know meets obstacles. In order to embody the obstacle I have invented the knot."[32] With the notions of *sinthome* and
knot, Lacan looks for ways of knowing "woman" beyond mere affirma-
tions of her existence. However, this "woman" beyond-the-phallus
exhibits the psychical knot while remaining, as we have shown, a radical
Other. In the Borromean knot, the unconscious is disharmonious; the
knot leads us to deal with knowledge in/of the Real. Surely, says Lacan,
women are less closely committed to "the unconscious as a disharmonious knowledge," they are somewhat more free in relation to it, they
are "more strangers" to it, because this kind of unconscious arrives to
them from the phallic side, or as Lacan says: "from the man."[33]

The knots account enigmatically for the failure to inscribe feminine desire in Lacan's persistent—and until the end—phallic paradigm.

However, with the concept of the knot it already becomes clear that for Lacan the possibility of describing the "supplementary" feminine within the phallic framework reaches its limits. In the passage to a matrixial apparatus, a "woman" exhibits intersections of knots in a trans-psychical web and therefore she is pres-ab-sent as a border-Other. If knowledge stored in the Real is not a host of data awaiting decoding by means of signification that will also constitute a cleft from it, but an "invention, that's what happens in every encounter, in any first encounter with sexual rapport";[34] then a swerving at the heart of a joint event opens a minimal distance between partial elements and links between them by affect, inscribing traces of the borderspacing and borderlinking. Such can be the work of a feminine *sinthome* emerging from a shared and partial, assembled and diffracted subjectivity. It inscribes traces in the psyche and transmits them to the world via artworking, enabling a *border shareability in trauma and phantasm* while it resonates meaning and creates feminine-Other-desire via metramorphosis, which also creates and contacts knots directly in a trans-subjective non-conscious web.

A work of art produces, to borrow a late Lacanian expression, a *jouis-sense*, a sense emerging from a unique jouissance but whose vestiges are treasured by its traces (*plus-de-jouir*). These traces can be transformed into a work that will make *its* sense for the first time and that, rather than being interpreted by the Symbolic, will *transform* the Symbolic by that which was never, up to that point, known by or in the Other or known by the I. The *jouis-sense* is not of the artist's experience but of the artwork itself in its process of transitive working through. Instances without the signifier make sense through the artwork. Some-Thing, some-Event, some-Encounter, are not just being expressed or "represented." They keep being made-present and keep resonating their designified meaning while attracting the viewer's gaze to join them and to join in with them. And this some-Thing, some-Event, or some-Encounter has to do with the becoming-sense of that which is for the phallic-Symbolic something impossible to signify. Thus artworking, articulated via the *sinthome* and twisted by a matrixial touch, has to do with the coming-into-sense of what for Lacan is the "impossible feminine *rapport*" and what is for me an originary matrixial difference that can't make sense without a trans-subjective transmission, and whose imprints-traces emerge in/by artworking.

NOTES

1. J. Lacan, *Les non-dupes errent* (SXXI, 1973–74), unpublished; *Le sinthome* (SXXIII, 1975–76), unpublished.

2. J. Lacan, *Les non-dupes errent*, February 12, 1974.

3. J. Lacan, *Le sinthome*, February 17, 1976.

4. J. Lacan, *Les non-dupes errent*, November 18, 1973.

5. *Ibid.*, March 12, 1974.

6. *Ibid.*, January 8, 1974.

7. *Ibid.*, March 19, 1974.

8. *Ibid.*, May 14, 1974.

9. *Ibid.*, January 15, 1974.

10. *Ibid.*

11. *Ibid.*

12. *Ibid.*

13. J. Lacan, *Les probems cruciaux de la psychanalyse* (SXII, 1964–65), January 6, 1965.

14. J. Lacan, *Les non-dupes errent*, April 15, 1974.

15. J. Lacan, *R.S.I.* (SXXII, 1974–75), April 15, 1974, unpublished.

16. In speaking of *a matrixial sinthome*, we are taking Lacan's notion beyond the work of Joyce to address a special kind of artworking, beyond the art of writing and the problematic of language to speak mainly of painting and the problematic of visual art.

17. J. Lacan, *Les non-dupes errent*, May 21, 1974.

18. *Ibid.*

19. [*parlêtre*, usually translated as "speaking being"].

20. J. Lacan, *Le sinthome*, February 10 and 17, 1976.

21. *Ibid.*

22. [Editor's note: For more on the concepts of "matrix" and "metramorphosis," see B. Lichtenberg Ettinger, *The Matrixial Gaze* (Leeds: Leeds University, Dept. of Fine Art, 1995); "Metramorphic Borderlinks and Matrixial Borderspace," in *Rethinking Borders*, ed. J. Welchman (London: Macmillan, and Minneapolis: University of Minnesota Press, 1996), pp. 125–159, and "The With-In-Visible Screen," in *Inside the Visible*, ed. C. de Zegher (Cambridge, MA: M.I.T. Press, 1996)].

23. See J.-A. Miller (1985), "Reflections on the Formal Envelope of the Symptom," *Lacanian Ink* 4 (1991), 13–21.

24. *Ibid.*, p. 14.

25. J. Lacan, *Les non-dupes errent*, January 15, 1974.

26. J. Lacan (1959–60), *Le Séminaire de Jacques Lacan, Livre VII. L'éthique*

de la psychanalyse, ed. J.-A. Miller. Paris: Seuil, 1986. *The Ethics of Psycho-Analysis*, trans. D. Porter, London: Routledge, 1992, pp. 260, 286.

27. *Ibid.*, pp. 214, 298.
28. J. Lacan, *Les non-dupes errent*, March 19, 1974.
29. *Ibid.*, April 9, 1974.
30. *Ibid.*, February 12, 1974.
31. *Ibid.*, February 19, 1974.
32. J. Lacan, *Le sinthome*, February 10 and 17, 1976.
33. J. Lacan, *Les non-dupes errent*, June 11, 1974.
34. *Ibid.*, February 19, 1974.

6

Acephalic Litter as a Phallic Letter

Véronique Voruz*

The Truth about Sancho Panza

Without making any boast of it Sancho Panza succeeded in the course of years, by feeding him a great number of romances of chivalry and adventure in the evening and night hours, in so diverting from himself his demon, whom he later called Don Quixote, that this demon thereupon set out, uninhibited, on the maddest exploits, which, however, for the lack of a preordained object, which should have been Sancho Panza himself, harmed nobody. A free man, Sancho Panza philosophically followed Don Quixote on his crusades, perhaps out of a sense of responsibility, and had of them a great and edifying entertainment to the end of his days.

—Franz Kafka

Happiness, in the reduced sense in which we recognise it as possible, is a problem of the economics of the individual's libido. There is no golden rule which applies to everyone: every man must find out for himself in what particular fashion he can be saved.

—Sigmund Freud

*I would like to thank Philip Dravers for his insightful suggestions as well as for many a stimulating discussion, Heather Menzies and Barry Collins for comments on early drafts, and Luke Thurston for his patient editorial work.

INTRODUCTION

The three moments of my paper will reverberate in the resonances of its title. As such, it anticipates what I will elaborate of the Joycean fragmentation of the apparent unity of the signifier via homophony, while also retracing the itinerary of Lacan's travels through Joyce's letters in a journey that will map the logical moments of the constitution of the symptom, of any symptom, as knotting. Indeed, the few years Lacan dedicated to the study of Joyce can be divided into three phases, each leading to a number of crucial advances for psychoanalytic theory in general, and the notion of the symptom in particular.

The first phase is marked by Lacan's interest in Joyce's wordplay: "The letter! The litter," in which a letter ruptures a *semblant*[1] with the consequent revelation that the signifier is a means of jouissance over and beyond that traditionally associated with the signified. In a second moment, this rupturing brings to light the duplicity of symbol and symptom, elucidating the twin aspects of the Symbolic order: meaning and jouissance. In passing, this duplicity of the Symbolic will show how the phallus[2] is articulated to the letter. Last, Lacan's near fascination with the writer comes to an end when he realizes that the Joycean solution leads its author to the same impasse as the rest of us: that of the sexual relation, although in Joyce it can be seen to emerge in the particularity of his *sinthomatic* relation to language. This last moment of the symptom is the point at which it can no longer be reduced to meaning: the moment of the letter as it returns on itself, and simultaneously that of the alterity of the Other sex.[3] It is through such an encounter with otherness that the limitations of the symptom emerge, the noninscription of the sexual relation echoing with the irremediable alterity of the letter, *a* being the letter par excellence: (*a*)*utre*.

Before I begin to tell of Joyce's littering of his letters—or of the Lacanian lettering of Joyce's litter—let me indicate from the outset the purpose of my article. I am not claiming to explain away Joyce's life through a psychobiographical analysis of his writings, for my interest lies in Lacan's work on Joyce: to be precise, his elaboration of how the speaking being[4] is interwoven in language, of how the symptom knots the Real to the body by means of the unconscious. The work of Joyce, because of its very specific use of language, comes to be the vehicle Lacan borrows for his exploration of a new way of articulating RSI, which comes to supersede his previous concern with the structure of discourse. This conceptual shift, which takes the emphasis away from the *signifier* and places it on the *letter*, is concurrent with a definite modification in Lacan's ethical position, for from then on, he no longer strives to define a *transcendental* aim for psychoanalysis but rather leans on the side of *pragmatism*.

This is why the topology of knots now comes onto the scene of Lacan's teaching. Knots indeed are *not* of the order of the signifier, quite the contrary;[5] they are the logical consequence of Lacan's acknowledgment of the impossibility of *representing* the subject's *particularity* by means of the signifier. This major theoretical step is accompanied by a progressive rehabilitation of the Imaginary: the body. If the Symbolic is outside the body (*hors-corps*), what now interests Lacan is the body itself: *en-corps*, one of the resonances of the title of his Seminar *Encore* (1972-73); and Lacan's last definition of the end of analysis underlines the necessary conjunction of knowledge (*savoir*) and action (*faire*): "To know how to make do (*savoir y faire*) with one's symptom: such is the end of analysis."[6]

From the Signifier to the Letter

Lacan's absorption in Joyce provides the timely support necessary for this radical transformation, which he initiates in his *Seminar XX, Encore*, a seminar which, in more ways than one, echoes *The Ethics of Psychoanalysis* (Seminar VII, 1959–60), and which is no less of a turning point in his teaching. Arguably, indeed, until then Lacan had been pursuing the possibility of a complete treatment of the Real by means of the Symbolic, one that would culminate in a true awakening of the subject. In *Seminar XX*, however, Lacan's own elaborations leave him little choice but to accept that the analytic discourse,[7] despite its ciphering of the Real in the position of agent, is itself contaminated by the irremediable duplicity between symbol and symptom. The inclusion of object *a* in the 1969 formulae of the discourses, Lacan's attempt to integrate the Real within discursive structures,[8] proves insufficient, for the Real remains glued to the heel of discourse. This leaves Lacan no other alternative than to accept that language itself is in the service of jouissance, while the unconscious is cast as its "accomplice." Lacan's new definition of the unconscious; "the unconscious is the fact that being, by speaking, enjoys" (SXX 95, 118–119[9]), testifies to a crucial differentiation of his approach.

Once the impossibility of calculating the effect of one's action on the symptom is recognized, by the same token Lacan's project of speaking from a given position of enunciation in order to have a determined effect on the Real is undermined. Seminar XX then hosts the partial failure of this ambitious enterprise,[10] for the duality of the signifier and jouissance, which cohabit the same body, the body of the symptom, implies that the only Real attainable by means of discourse is a Real tainted by the Symbolic. And, since the signifier is an elaboration of the letter, the Symbolic must be understood as itself tainted by the Real.

Confronted with the incapacity of the Symbolic to treat the obstinate density of the Real, Lacan finds himself faced with the following conundrum: the only way of treating the Real is through language; yet language itself is in the service of jouissance. How, then, can we hope to break the vicious circle of the symptom's hold on the subject? It is at this point that Lacan begins to look to the *letter* as the only logical anchoring point for his thought, the letter being that which in language is closest to the Real. Lacan now re-elaborates the letter as the vehicle of object *a*, however understood as pure drive-object: hence the *intransitive* jouissance inscribed by the letter, which insists beyond any *conjugation* of the subject with the drive that the fantasy implies. For the fantasy is a signifying elaboration of the drive, the classical example of which is "a child is being beaten."[11] Having thus reduced object *a* to intransitivity, Lacan logicizes its function by presenting it as the material element in language that supports thought—he even coins the term *l'appensée* to indicate that thought (*pensée*) has to lean on (*appui*) object *a*.[12] From this point on, Lacan's work is an attempt to use what in language is material, noncalculable, in order to learn how to *make do* with the Real of the symptom, while the topology of knots strives to elaborate a mode of representation that does not make use of the signifier, "accomplice of jouissance."[13]

The stake in studying Joyce's writings therefore lies in the possibility of grasping the skeletal structure[14] of the symptom[15] (cf. *Joyce le symptôme I*, 25), for *this is what knots RSI*, not the Name-of-the-Father as Lacan first believed. Progressively, this bare structure reveals itself to be the coupling of two elements of a different order: a letter and a signifier.[16] Such is the status of the symptom now reduced to its logical core by

Lacan: the coalescence of jouissance and meaning, *arising from a letter, leaning on a signifier*. Hence the solution proposed in *Le sinthome*: to make do with the symptom one has *to use a signifier, leaning on a letter*. This neat reciprocity is, however, fragmented from within by the different implications of the letter in its three moments—moments that echo those of the symptom: *inscription, articulation, and impasse*.

ACEPHALIC LITTER

THE LETTER! THE LITTER! AND
THE SOOTHER THE BITTHER!

In my introduction, I argued that the third decade of Lacan's teaching was centered on a concern with knowing how to use the Real in language, a Real to be used to quell the delirious productions of language in its signifying aspect. The function of the letter is thus to bring an end to the endless motions of ciphering and deciphering that flow from the dual effect of the discourse of the Master. Indeed, the effect of such a discourse is to lull us endlessly on the seesaw of the jouissance of the *semblant*, which takes us from phallic jouissance to *joui-sens* and back again; from a deciphering of the unconscious, which obeys the command of the signifier "to be," to an enjoyment in the signifying equivocations that allow one to escape from petrifaction beneath a signifier through the emergence of *a* in the space between signifiers.

But why would one want to move away from the soothing rounds of semblance and its circuit? Because this endlessly revolving circle is animated by the fact that in it the subject is nothing but the *dupe of his symptom as signified of the Other*.[17] To live in semblance, although it is not without enjoyment, does not free us from the fiction of the Other's existence and the corresponding subjection to fantasy, *a phrase that enjoys itself*[18] *at the expense of the subject*.

Joyce's writings, therefore, harbor the opportune prospect of a way out of the self-serving enjoyment of the symptom, insofar as it is Other to the subject. Here is a writer who seems to enjoy without the Other, without being subjected to the discourse of the Master, to fantasy (SXXIII, November 18, 1975). Could we possibly learn from him? Four years before *Le sinthome*, Lacan's hope is clear from his conviction that

Joyce reached the equivalent of the end of an analysis through his writing: "Had he taken part in our game, [Joyce] would not have gained anything from it since, with his *a letter, a litter*, he went straight to the best of what one can expect of an analysis at its end."[19]

From 1971 on, then, Lacan takes on the study of this alluring symptomatic form, one that is to teach him many things. Indeed, it may be in the work of Joyce that Lacan first discovers the possibility of a symptom functioning independently of the Other, a possibility that is, however, coupled with the realization that the symptom endures even after the subject is freed from his oppressive belief in the Other. For, although Lacan's teaching may be marked by a number of failed attempts to treat the symptom completely, it is only with Joyce that Lacan comes to accept its irreducibility as *structural* and to envisage the symptom as a necessary residue of the very fact that we speak. Thus, logically, this new direction in Lacan's elaboration leads him to explore the potential for deployment of this symptomatic residue.

To rephrase our advance so far, let me say the following: *the first moment of the symptom, its irreducible core, is a soldering of jouissance to meaning in language.*[20] At this stage, there is no play between its two constituting elements, a letter and a signifier. The symptom, after this moment of *inscription*, must then come to be elaborated in its moment of *articulation*. The still predominant oedipal structure is the neurotic way of treating this fixation. It does so through the introjection of the phallus, namely the signifier that symbolizes lack for the subject and, consequently, introduces the possibility of play. The result is an articulation of this moment of fixation in the signifying chain, itself progressively unraveled according to the subject's interpretation of the desire of the Other. The flip side of the neurotic's solution is his subsequent alienation in this chain of signifiers. Gradually, Lacan develops the idea that one must use the *letter* in order to break loose from this entrapment in one's incessant reconstruction of this primordial Other. This would explain his interest in the Joycean treatment of the Real of the symptom by means of the letter, a solution that manages, concurrently, to produce movement and to de-suppose the Other, exposing it as fiction.

We will return to the question of how Joyce reaches such an enviable position—namely, the ability to enjoy his symptom beyond the Other and the fantasy—after a brief exploration of what is entailed by the traditional oedipal subjection to the signifier. The signifying operations of *alienation* and *separation*,[21] which Lacan elaborates in Seminar XI (1964), will support my account.

Alienation and Separation

First of all, then, alienation. The subject, once marked by language—the letter—is void (*évidé*), and as such characterized by lack-of-being. He finds a way out in an identification with a nonsensical signifier, S_1, which subsequently represents him. But this identification has the lethal effect of petrifying the subject beneath a signifier, this petrifaction being coupled with lack-of-enjoyment. To make up for this new ailment, the subject calls to the Other, the "treasury of signifiers," namely, the locus of meaning: S_2. This linking with the binary signifier completes the operation of alienation insofar as the meaning returned to the subject is infused with the desire of the Other. "What the subject has to free himself from is the aphanisic effect of the binary signifier [the S_2] and, if we look at it more closely, we shall see that in fact it is a question of nothing else in the function of freedom" (SXI: 219). One of the aims of analysis is thus to separate S_2—knowledge—from the desire of the Other, which in the meantime has been transformed into a *demand* by the subject. Indeed, in order to dam up the anxiety flowing from the enigma of the desire of the Other, the subject transforms it into a constellation of signifiers, and from then on dedicates a respectable share of his energies to the elaboration of subtle strategies that will defeat it.

The second insidious consequence of the operation of alienation, lack-of-enjoyment, is remedied in the operation of *separation*. The subject will identify with an object *a*, constructing a fantasy that will allow him to make up for the *mythically* lost jouissance. This enables him to achieve a degree of separation from the desire of the Other by devising an imaginary scenario in order to recuperate some enjoyment. The dual goal of analysis is to free the subject from his subjection to both the binary signifier and the fantasy: from the binary signifier, for its originating in the Other nails the subject to his status as signified of the Other, and from the fantasy, insofar as it implicates the subject in a repetitive staging of his enjoyment that requires the support of the existence of the Other, the indispensable partner of his symptom. To bring about this liberation of the subject implies that the Other be revealed as nonexistent, or, more precisely, as a *fabrication* of the subject.

How can analysis guide the subject on the pathways leading to the destitution of the Other? To address this question, we need to look at the various modes of interpretation,[22] bearing in mind that the theory of interpretation retraces the circuit of the logical operations of alienation and separation.

Different Modes of Interpretation

The classical mode of analytic interpretation is situated on the axis of metaphor, in a deciphering of the discourse of the subject that culminates in a *You are this*. Such a mode of interpretation reinforces castration, as it makes the subject fade beneath a signifier that represents him for all other signifiers. It consolidates the alienation of the subject in the semblance of being, itself the product of the metaphoric effects of the master signifiers that govern his life.

The mode of interpretation favored by Lacan, on the other hand, aims at producing object a through the use of the cut in the analytic session. It implies that the analyst make use of the metonymical axis in the unconscious, the axis of separation and desire. Such a mode of interpretation allows the subject to ex-sist *qua* enjoyment rather than exist in meaning: a is the letter that ruptures a *semblant* inasmuch as the subject is no longer the mere signified of a binary signifier. At this point, and as a partial answer to the question of what analysis can do to alleviate the weight of the symptom, we can think of Lacan's phrase: "For, after all, our only weapon against the symptom is equivocation" (SXXIII, November 18, 1975).

An elucidation of this Lacanian assertion could take the following route: the symptom, in its bare structure ($S_1 + a$), is a moment of fixation. This moment of fixation is buried at the heart of the signifying chain (S_2), which is so constructed that it tirelessly produces serialized significations of the Other's desire. We then understand why equivocation is the only weapon against the symptom—understood as repetition of its moment of fixation in a signifying elaboration—as it is that which allows for the resurfacing of the drive-object as pure enjoyment, unmediated by the phantasmatic staging of the Other. At this stage, *equivocation* is thus the only moment where the subject's enjoyment is not dependent upon the existence of the Other.

The necessity of doing away with the Other is, without a doubt, present in Lacan's work from early on, but I would argue that it is Joyce's writing that offers Lacan his first insight into the possibility of transforming the symptom into something *positive*, a possibility that throws some light on his enigmatic phrase of 1976 to the effect that the concluding moment of an analysis may be an identification with one's symptom.[23] Such a transformation—from symptom as cause of suffering to symptom as knotting of identity and enjoyment—is nowhere better illustrated than in artistic creation, which produces effects going well beyond the fleeting escape from the symptomatic grip produced by mere equivocation.

A Literary Traversal of the Fantasy

The Joycean solution seems to echo with Lacan's devising of a different mode of separation, this time from the fantasy: *construction*. Equivocation is to be taken up in the process of construction as its impetus. In this sense, construction refers to the construction of a way of relating to object *a* as drive-object, divested of the burden of the fantasy. How does one construct object *a* as distinct from the fantasy? It is a question of analytical technique, but it seems to require a shedding of identifications, which brings about a progressive effacement of the Other and culminates in an act of self-nomination.[24]

Bearing these three moments of interpretation in mind—*alienation, separation, construction*—let us take up our question again: How is it that Joyce reaches the equivalent of the end of analysis? Such are the elements of the equation so far: for Lacan, Joyce does *not* have a neurotic structure, and yet, he has a symptom that functions *like* that of a neurotic, and even like that of a neurotic at the *end* of an analysis. This implies not only that Joyce has successfully knotted a letter with a signifier and that he is able to articulate this otherwise repetitive linking through a mode of equivocation of his own invention, but also that he is able to detach himself from the fiction of the existence of the Other (and thus to go beyond the need for equivocation). Indeed, the Other does not appear to exist for him, either as locus of truth or as phantasmatic Other.

The Joycean equivalent to more traditional equivocation is produced in an incessant interweaving of sounds and letters. Joyce uses sonorities to produce equivocal sense, and equivocal sense, no doubt, is a necessary treatment of fixation. Yet he leaves this way of handling the symptom behind once his invention of a new way of writing is completed. If the first form of equivocation is a defense against jouissance, then Joyce's later writing testifies to the possibility of a form of equivocation that no longer functions as a mechanism for the deferral of a certainty in relation to jouissance, but as a mode of enjoyment. According to Lacan, such writing demonstrates a way of relating to the drive-object that is no longer indexed on the necessity of meaning and amounts to a "traversal" of the fantasy. Such a *désabonnement* (disinvestment) comes about after an exhaustive exposure of the fictitious nature of the Other of meaning through the use of the letter.

Indeed, in his final work, *Finnegans Wake*, Joyce bypasses the Other and its corollary, the fantasy. His writing no longer produces equivocal sense, but rather seems to be concerned with canceling the possibility of making sense in its willful multiplication of resonances. The product of this intentionally meaningless[25] interweaving of phonemes and letters is what I call acephalic litter—Joyce's writing insofar as it is pure drive-enjoyment, a writing that does not condescend to signification, short-circuiting the dimension of the symptom *qua* signified of the Other. This is how Joyce "makes do" with language: he creates a cipher that cannot be broken and thereby acquires a *savoir-faire* with *lalangue* that is not indexed on the One of the logic of exception (that of the neurotic), but on the infinite and multiple unicity[26] of the letter.

These letters are then littered (*poubliées*).[27] This littering of his letters, his art, allows Joyce to mobilize his jouissance beyond the horizon of equivocation. The letters as *encaisse-jouissance* receive it and circulate it in the flow of his writing. And, like every drive-jouissance, this is an acephalic—headless—jouissance, it turns back on itself.[28]

Our next question concerns this mysterious duplicity of the Symbolic that Lacan introduces in his Seminar XXIII: that of symbol and symptom.[29] This duplicity will illustrate how the Joycean knotting remains different from a traditional neurotic knotting, for the latter is supported by the phallus as *agent équivocateur*, coupled with the function of the oedipal father as agent of universalization, while the former is an extension of the structure of the symptom to the whole of language.[30] In effect, each letter has to be knotted to a signifier (here, understood as a phoneme), *for there is no possible factorization of a pre-inscribed phrase in psychosis.*

AS A PHALLIC LETTER

THE DUPLICITY OF SYMBOL AND SYMPTOM:
JOYCE LE SYMPTOME AND JACQUES LE SYMBOLE

In Seminar XXIII, *Le Sinthome* (1975–76), the symptom is defined as that which knots RSI for each subject. Lacan, who calls Joyce *Joyce-le-sinthome*, argues that the writer reveals the "essence of the symptom"[31] and proceeds to study his writing in order to observe how a symptom is constructed.

Epiphanies and Quilting Points

In the previous section, I put forward the hypothesis that one could identify two stages in Joyce's writing: one stage where there is sense, albeit equivocal sense, and another where there is no longer any need for sense. The first period of his work, that of *knotting*, is punctuated by little tales that Joyce calls *epiphanies*, while the second, to indulge in an easy wordplay, is more of a seamless *knitting*.

The Joycean "epiphanies" are presented by Jacques Aubert, a distinguished Joycean scholar who was Lacan's "other" in this matter, as a "kind of splitting in two of experience."[32] Aubert takes the definition of the epiphany from *Stephen Hero*, noting that Joyce transforms a "sudden spiritual manifestation" into a writing experience, and thereby provides a puzzling moment with a kind of resolution. In the scholar's terms, a "realist" experience, likely to be disturbing—Aubert indicates the frequent connection with religion, indirectly touching upon questions of parenthood and sexuality—is coupled with a "poetic" experience, the result being the "elision" of something and its replacement with something else. In the example Aubert gives, a poem is written following a conversation with the mother on the topic of religion and is elided, being replaced with a dialogue between a young man and a young woman.

Lacan reads these epiphanies as moments at which "the unconscious is knotted to the Real."[33] Arguably, they fulfill a similar function to quilting points (points de capiton),[34] and have a comparable mechanism, in that an elision and a substitution are involved in both. There is, however, one crucial feature that differentiates the neurotic quilting point: unlike the Joycean epiphany, it is an effect of the extimate agency of the Name-of-the-Father, an overarching metaphor that names the subject, producing a certain number of anchoring points within language. The function of these is double: to distribute jouissance and to produce a number of fixed significations that allow the subject to find his way in language. Quilting points prevent the endless slipping of the signifying chain, providing moments of arrest where a signification is produced. The fact that there are several such points gives the subject a place within a constellation of significations, while he himself remains without a signification. This is the drama of the neurotic: he is given a name by the Other, but does not know what this name means. Classically, his haunting question, *Who am I?*, takes the form of a quest: *Who am I for the Other?*, and can sometimes be resolved in an act of self-nomination through which the neurotic gives up the fiction of the Name-of-the-Father and becomes *father to his name*.

If, following Lacan, the Name-of-the-Father is not operative in a psychotic structure, a replacement mechanism has to operate at both the level of jouissance and that of sense. Joyce's particularity is that, unlike most psychotics, he is not constructing a delusional metaphor—that is, his own overarching naming device—bypassing the need for an extimate agent. However, before he is able to simply interweave—knitting—the two constituents of language, namely matter (inscription) and air (phonation),[35] the epiphanies—knotting—had to have a "quilting" function, insofar as a number of definite resolutions seem to emerge for Joyce. Arguably, it is thanks to these that Joyce can avoid being pinned down to the signification that would materialize the certainty of jouissance. Indeed, for the psychotic there is only one signification, and it is that of jouissance; for the Name-of-the-Father, that which articulates the letter as *mark of language* to the signifier by means of the *lack* that it instates, is rejected.

Literature, the *act* of writing, is a most efficient means of the treatment of jouissance for both psychotics and neurotics, but it will operate in reverse. Writing,[36] for the neurotic, seems to function as a deferral of jouissance—a stalling strategy—that provides substitutive satisfactions. For the psychotic subject, on the contrary, writing itself circulates jouissance, alleviating its unquilted concentration in the one place, and may even lead to a resolution.[37] Joyce, taken as a Lacanian paradigm of psychosis, offers us an example of how the treatment of the Real occurs in writing. He uses the letter in its *multiplicity* in order to treat a *singular, isolated* S_1—the mortifying mark of language on the body, the "imposition of language," the "parasite of speech" (SXXIII, February 17, 1976)—and to escape from the identity it imposes on him; whereas the neurotic may use the letter in its *unicity* to rupture his alienation to the *multiplicity* of signifiers, the Other, in order to obtain a sense of identity. This may be what Lacan implies when he opposes *Jacques le symbole* to *Joyce le symptôme* (*Joyce le symptôme* I, 21). We can even imagine that the term Lacan coins to refer to his *Écrits: poubellication*— a condensation of the terms *publication* and *poubelle* (rubbish bin)— could be a Lacanian equivalent of Joycean littering.[38]

If Joyce's writing as acephalic litter—that is, as drive-enjoyment detached from the Other—functions as a phallic letter, logically my next questions will concern the nature of the *letter*, the relation between the letter and the signifier, and the function of the *phallus*.

The Letter: Scription, Inscription, Writing

The Lacanian exploration of Joyce's world begins with A *letter!* A *litter!* the famous wordplay from the volume orchestrated by Joyce as a preface to *Finnegans Wake*.[39] Lacan leans on it—*l'appensée*—in order to elaborate his theory of the letter. In his article "Lituraterre" (1971a), Lacan posits the incommensurability of the signifier and the Real, and indicates that the signifier is on the side of the *semblant*, while the letter is on the side of the Real. The letter is that which partakes—takes a/part[40]—in both orders.

"Lituraterre" opens with some cryptic comments on the letter in literature. We then encounter this mystifying formulation: one has to use a letter to rupture a *semblant* (Lacan, 1971a, 7). One of the many ways to read this pithy statement is to take it *literally* (*à la lettre*): *by replacing the letter* e *with the letter* i, Joyce ruptures the *semblant* of the signifier "letter" and exposes its jouissance-value: namely, that it is a container of enjoyment, an *encaisse-jouissance*,[41] both that which hollows out the Real, and the waste object that comes to fill it: "litter." In other words, the rupturing of the signifier—that which in language is universal—reveals the particularity of each subject's investment of it.

To recast this unexpected tale of the letter in a more familiar Lacanian idiom, we could state that the letter fulfills a dual function: first, it pierces the Real, it is the unary trait that cuts out a hole for the Symbolic in the Real, thus barring the subject ($\$$)—this notation indexes an *évidement*, an emptying-out. In a second moment, this hole in the Real, this *manque-à-jouir* (lack-of-enjoyment) comes to be filled by object *a*, the *plus-de-jouir* (surplus-enjoyment). It subsequently becomes the "blind angle" of knowledge (the "border of the hole within knowledge," Lacan, 1971a, 5); the missing signifier—that of jouissance— comes to be replaced by surplus-enjoyment.

The letter is the Real of language, then. And yet, "the letter is, radically speaking, an effect of discourse" (SXX, 36), for it comes from the Other. It is the inscription of the mark of language on the body, core of the symptom in its Real *demansion*, as Lacan writes it in "Lituraterre"—no doubt to remind us that this inscription is later used to channel the jouissance ascribed to the Other by transforming it into a *demand*—this is why the symptom is the signified of the Other. Then, of course, at a third level, the letter is the material support of language, one that also ruptures the auditory unity of a signifier by inscribing it, by damming up the flow of *lalangue*.

To summarize: the three moments of the letter are *scription, inscription*, and *writing*. *Scription* is a term sometimes used by Lacan to refer to a sign, a gesture that marks the "living." This "blotting"[42] does not cover anything and is the trace of the first encounter with the Other; yet Lacan calls it a blotting because it becomes retroactively invested with the phantasmatic reconstitution of the primal trauma. *Inscription* is the coalescence of this mark with sexual reality,[43] which also provides the matrix of the symptom as meaning. As for *writing*, it is the alphabet, both recipient and support of the drive-object.

This is the letter, then: *a coalescence of three different moments.*

My next question is the following: How does Joyce's art function as a phallic letter, namely that which enables the neurotic subject not to be fixated to the One of jouissance: the phallus operating as *agent équivocateur?* This wordplay on *agent provocateur* indicates that the phallus is the possibility of alternation between lack-of-being and *plus-de-jouir*, ($) and (*a*) respectively: the phallus allows for movement between being as signified and being as enjoyment and is thus the possibility of equivocation. Again, if our only weapon against the symptom is equivocation, without this *agent équivocateur* the psychotic is without equivocation: he *is* the signified of the signifier that represents him. Joyce, however, through his use of phonation and the letter, manages to achieve a similar effect of equivocation, though not between senses but *within the word itself*: homophony mobilizes the letter as mark of jouissance while *letters* rupture the unity of the signifier.

The Phallus

Let us attempt to circumscribe the concept of the phallus, cutting through its many fortunes and the countless number of functions it has been assigned in a single century of psychoanalysis. In the session of June 9, 1971, Seminar XVIII, *D'un discours qui ne serait pas du semblant*, Lacan returns to one of his *Écrits: Die Bedeutung des Phallus*, "The Meaning of the Phallus" (Lacan, 1966, Sheridan, 1977). He says the following:

> Language derives its structure from the fact that it is constituted of a single *Bedeutung*, and this structure results in the fact that, because one lives within it, it can only be used for metaphor, from which all the mystical inanities on which its inhabitants feed result, and for metonymy, from which they derive whatever little reality they have left under the guise of the *plus-de-jouir*.

The term *Bedeutung* is a reference to Frege's binary *Sinn/Bedeutung* (sense/referent) and implies the ex-sistence of a referent organizing the existence of interconnected representations. For Lacan, not all is textuality, and the differential order of meaning is sustained through a logically anterior moment of attachment that will sustain the order of language. This moment is the nonsensical mark of the letter, and the phallus as lack comes in its place.

In the first instance, then, the function of the phallus redoubles that of the letter by symbolizing the *mark* of the former on the body of the subject as *lack*; this redoubling of the letter transforms the body into a drive-body (*corps pulsionnel*), that is, a body-in-language. In a second moment, the phallus becomes the signifier of difference, the bar that separates signifier from signified. In its third moment, it may come to be articulated with the paternal insignia, resulting in a classical oedipal structure indexed on the paternal ideal, but this does not concern us here.

This reading of the phallus also provides us with a way of reading the "Seminar on *The Purloined Letter*" (Lacan, 1966). A phallic letter alone is a letter that merely symbolizes a lack in the Real, and it only acquires a meaning when coupled with a signifier that represents the subject for other signifiers. The letter in Poe's tale is itself mute and can mean anything. Indeed it is never read; its mysterious content is never elucidated. All we know is that it harbors some forbidden jouissance, but it modifies the position of whoever holds it: the Queen, the King, the Minister, Dupin. All are defined in relation to the letter, yet this letter itself only takes on meaning when it is coupled with a signifying position. This is why whoever holds the letter is feminized, defined in relation to a nonsensical alterity that is not *one-ified*, not subjected to the logic of exception[44] that would turn the letter into a *semblant*, thereby universalizing it. When this operation does not occur, we remain at the level of the *not-all*.

Arguably, in a psychotic structure, the mark of the letter is not *symbolized by lack*, the phallus as *signifier of difference* is not instituted, and the possibility of equivocation is consequently missing. For the psychotic, the letter pierces the Real, tainting it with something of language, of the Symbolic, but it remains at the level of a mere inscription of alterity in the subject—imposition but no position—never given a "substitutable" signification.

Lacan seems to intimate that, for Joyce, the letter remained at the level of this mere inscription. He jokes that [Joyce] "*avait la queue un peu lâche*" (SXXIII, November 18, 1975) or "had a little bit of a loose prick." Yet, Joyce's psychosis remains latent and is successfully defused through his construction of a symptom and his subsequent use of the letter. For such is the duplicity of symptom and symbol, knotting the subject in language: a letter, mark of the Real in language, coupled with the signifier that represents the subject, articulated by lack. For Joyce, although there may be no lack symbolized by the phallus, *phonation* serves a similar function, for it is by means of *homophony* that Joyce defuses the certainty of sense.

The Phallus Is a Name for All

A phrase of Lacan's—"it is phonation which transmits this specific function of the name"[45]—indicates that the phallus is also important with regard to the act of naming. If the phallus is that which introduces a distance between the signifier that represents the subject and the signified that the subject is for the Other, then the phallus prevents the subject from being the signified of the Other, and thus the object of his jouissance. The phallus, associated with phonation (for it is a *signifier*), must therefore have a substitute in psychosis.

How does Joyce replace the phallus? In his work, particularly in *Finnegans Wake*, the letter is used to dismantle the signifier from within through a mechanism involving the sonority of the words used. The signifier is shorn of its identification-producing effects of meaning and returned to its pure sound-value through the fragmenting of the letter. This operation takes place in order to eliminate the certainty of signification, which could bring about the looming identification with it that would glue the subject to his position as signified of the Other, turning him into an object. The phallus separates signifier and signified, and the subject ex-sists in the interval. Similarly, Joyce's writing, by "stuffing[46] the signified" with the signifier,[47] defeats any potential identification with it. His art thus functions like the phallus in a certain sense, although a phallus not coupled with the Name-of-the-Father.

As a final point on the function of the phallus with regard to the name, let us note that the phallus, although it is a concept that indexes a structural necessity, does not entail any invariable signification. However, it nevertheless institutes the immutable basis for the subject's identity, and in this sense, the phallus is a *name for all*. By extension, we see that in neurosis the phallus functions as the *universal* signifier of *particularity*; this seeming paradox implies that it is thanks to the phallus that the subject will always be able to locate his *particularity* in the *universal* order of the world. In psychosis, this is not the case: we note that psychotic delusions need to account progressively for *every single event in the world*, to rearticulate *all* the knowledge available in the universe around their own being; in paranoia, megalomania, or persecution, any one event concerns the subject and him only. Similarly, in Joyce's *Finnegans Wake*, Tim Finnegan's song encompasses the whole of world history, and we can interpret this as another mode of remedying the absence of the phallus, *universal* marker of the subject's *particular* position in language. Joyce thus also needs to use his letters to make a name for himself, a name that does not come from the Other. And if one of the functions of the phallus is to unify the subject under a *semblant*, then Joyce equally succeeds in creating a name as-one for himself: he turns his proper name into a common name or noun: *un nom commun, un nom comme-un.*

ASSEZ-PHALLE JOUISSANCE

CANCELLING ONE'S SUBSCRIPTION TO THE UNCONSCIOUS IS NOT A SIGN OF LOVE

Le semblant dénoncé par la vérité est, il faut le reconnaître, *"assez-phalle."*
Jacques Lacan[48]

The pun in my title, acephalic/as a phallic, can be supplemented by yet another: *assez-phallique*. Lacan puns on *assez-phalle* jouissance in Seminar XVIII, *D'un discours qui ne serait pas du semblant* (1970–71). The French phrase means "quite phallic," or "phallic enough," punning *acéphale*, "headless." In the quotation used as epigraph above, Lacan seems to be referring to the hysteric's discourse, for she famously wields truth in order to expose the Master as impotent (see SXVII, chap. VI). In other words, the hysteric's discourse aims to reveal the status of semblance of the jouissance we all derive from the discourse of the Master, which is that of the unconscious: phallic jouissance or the jouissance of castration.

Three Forms of Jouissance

In Seminar XXIII, *Le Sinthome*, Lacan identifies three forms of jouissance: phallic jouissance ($J\Phi$), *joui-sens* and the Other jouissance ($J\cancel{A}$). Phallic jouissance is the jouissance that one derives from alienation, from one's fixation under the S_1. *Joui-sense* is the jouissance of equivocation, linked to the operation of separation, and feeding into the illusion that one is escaping from the *manque-à-jouir* of castra-

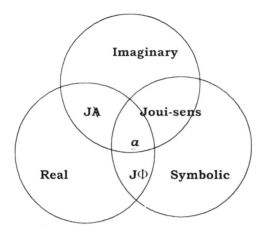

Figure 6–1. Three forms of jouissance

tion. Both are "idiotic" forms of jouissance in the sense that they are solipsistic—hence the *acéphale/assez-phalle* homophony. As for the jouissance of the Other, it does not exist because the Other does not exist, the Other jouissance being, by definition, beyond language: it may only ex-sist.

Joyce's writing is *assez-phalle* in this sense. In other words, it is akin to the jouissance of the idiot, the enjoyment that bars the Other—understood as the Other sex, since the Other of meaning does not exist—from its field, the only other that is tolerated being the mirror image, the guarantor of Joyce's eternal self-identity: the university, which will cite him universally: *l'univers-cité, cité-universellement*. Joyce creates a name for himself by transforming his proper name into a common noun—Joycean—or again, *un nom comme-un*: a name or noun *as-one*, and he uses the university as the guarantor of his unity: University, *a turning towards the One, which takes the place of the neurotic's père-version*.[49] By making a name for himself, Joyce also abolishes the possibility of being attributed a fixed signification by the Other. The result is the identity Joyce = Joyce, in *a single trait*; but this name nevertheless retains the mobility necessary—as common noun, Joycean, for example—to avoid the identification with the object, the psychotic's sword of Damocles, through his use of writing.

Canceling One's Subscription to the Unconscious

What characterizes Joyce's writings is that we see him use S_2 in order to cancel his subscription to the unconscious, understood as lucubration[50] (*élucubration*) on the desire of the Other, his *Che vuoi?* This is why Lacan claims that Joyce is a *saint homme* (a holy man), even a *sinthome-madaquin*.[51] For indeed, Thomas Aquinas's device, *Velle bonum alicui*, is interpreted by Lacan as follows: it indicates that one wants the good of the other insofar as the other is necessary for one's own good, rather than wanting it to further the sovereign Good (SXI, chap. XV). A *saint homme* is thus someone who does not give up on his desire, that which defines him intimately, and holds on to it, as opposed to being subservient to the Other's desire and its corresponding fiction of an Other of the Other, locus of universal truth.

By writing his name in a *single* trait, *Joyce-le-sinthome*, Lacan indicates how Joyce makes himself one without being alienated to the desire of the Other (*saint homme*), for he turns himself into what makes the Other desire, instead of trying to guess what the Other wants. This is why Lacan can say that Joyce "cancelled his subscription" to the unconscious, that he was *désabonné à l'inconscient*. Joyce is not interested in the knowledge that the Other could have about him. He is identified with his *sinthome*: he *is* this *sinthome*. "[Joyce] is he who occupies the privileged position of having pushed to the extreme the attempt to incarnate the symptom, thanks to which he escapes from all possible death, for he has reduced himself to a structure which is that of man (*lom*)"[52] (Lacan, 1975a, 28).

In this sense, Joyce's symptom functions like a neurotic's, except in reverse: he creates a name for himself, an S_1 that is *désabonné* from the S_2, although he uses S_2 in two successive ways. First, he uses it to defuse the danger of an identification with S_1, to silence the echoes of the Voice in his body, and second to enjoy language. To an extent, this is what a neurotic may hope to reach at the end of analysis: to construct his identity on the basis of an S_1 that does not sustain itself through the S_2 of the Other. In order to free himself from the Other, the neurotic needs to create his own signification [*significantiser*] for his S_1. Such a trajectory echoes with the reduction of the symptom to its structure: if Lacan could say that there is no other father than the symptom, arguably, once the symptom is freed from the fiction of Other, then the subject must become father to his name, following in Joyce's footsteps.

This, then, is what the Joycean symptom can tell us about a possible end of analysis. Truth is to be half-spoken, *mi-dite*, a combination of being *qua* jouissance—a letter—and being *qua* meaning—a signifier: the symptom as semantic part of the Real, or as real part of the Symbolic, freed from fantasy and the signifying efflorescence that goes with it. And "the true is a saying in conformity with reality, reality being, here, what functions truly" (SXXIII, April 13, 1976): this designates a *savoir-faire*—knowing how to deal with one's jouissance—coupled with a *mi-dire*—knowing how to name oneself independently from the Other's desire, the Other being revealed as nonexistent. In other words, the desirable end of analysis is the coupling of a real truth and a true Real (SXXIII, April 13, 1976), a symptomatic knotting evacuated of its excessive jouissance, whether it be joui-sense or phallic jouissance. But is such an identification with one's symptom all that can be hoped for in analysis?

An Impasse for the Symptom

One question indeed remains open: Is this knowing how to make do with one's symptom sufficient to enable the subject to face up to the impossibility of the sexual relation?

Indeed, Joyce's writing goes full circle. It is not *assez-phalle* in order to allow him to go beyond this inscription of identity; the letter has to work constantly to contain his jouissance. No liberating effect is produced that would allow him to recognize the particularity of the Other sex. He becomes the scribe through which the letters flow, like water flowing through the wheel of a mill: *riverrun, the river runs....*

> But still, *Finnegans*, this dream, how can one say that it is finished, since already its last word can but attach itself to the first, the *the* on which it terminates, by agglutinating itself to the *riverrun* on which it starts, which indicates the circularity? To say it bluntly, how could Joyce miss out, to that extent, on what I am introducing of the knot at the moment?[53]

Here, Lacan indicates that although the symptom functions, it has its limitations: one thus has to try to go beyond the necessity of structure—that which does not cease writing itself, as indeed we can see with *Finnegans Wake*, which did not cease being written for seventeen years—toward the impossibility of the sexual relation, the contingency of love.[54] There must be another form of creation then, one that goes beyond a *savoir-faire* with *lalangue*, and this must involve the other.

If, following the example of Joyce, to reduce the symptom to its core articulation is the way to learn how to live without the Other, it is nonetheless only the starting point of knowing how to live with the other.

CONCLUSION

FROM THE IMPASSE OF THE SYMPTOM TO LOVE

Despite extensive reading, I was not able to confirm this hypothesis. There is no doubt, however, that Lacan, in the last period of his teaching, picks up on the impasse of the symptom and explores ways of articulating it that would carry the subject beyond the confines of repetitive jouissance. One of the numerous possible significations of the title of Seminar XXIV (1976–77), *L'Insu-que-sait de l'Une-bévue s'aile à mourre*, supports my hypothesis. This Seminar, which directly follows *Le Sinthome*, could be another reference to the Irish writer, as *l'Une-bévue* [the one-slip] arguably refers to Joyce. Indeed, not only does his writing have the same effect as a neurotic slip[55]—namely, to allow the subject to ex-sist, to escape his being as signified—but it also operates similarly (although in reverse). It is by using the auditory resonance of the signifier that Joyce treats the letter, while in a neurotic slip it is the letter that returns to release the jouissance incarcerated in the signifier.[56]

Let us take the title of the seminar step by step. *L'Insu* I take to refer to the letter: the unknown in the unconscious, itself the cause of the unconscious, the fundamental inscription of the xenopathy of language. Thus we have *l'Insu*: the unknown; *que sait*: that knows; *de l'Une-bévue*: of the unconscious—or of Joyce, who *is* his unconscious.[57] In other words: the unconscious knows the unknown of its inscription, or the unconscious is a *lucubration* of knowledge[58] on an inscription that does not belong to the order of the knowable. The unconscious is now revealed as the conjunction of knowledge and the mark of jouissance, and Joyce has reduced himself to this articulation by identifying with the structure of language. There is a subsequent *ossification* of his symptom, as the foreclosure of the Other prevents the recognition of any alterity other than that of the letter, an alterity that the writer successfully domesticated and diverted so that it would bring water to the wheel of his jouissance. The possibility of any other movement is eradicated, and Joyce can only circulate within his revolving circuit of letters, caught up in the exigency of drive satisfaction that always demands more writing.

Thus, the failure of Joyce—*L'Insu-que-sait* is homophonic with *l'insuccès* (failure)—despite his one slip, the *organized and exhaustive substitutability in language of all its components*, is a failure to love: *c'est l'amour* being homophonic with *s'aile à mourre*. How does Joyce fail? He is frozen in his *art-gueil* ("art-pride," *Joyce le symptôme II*, 33), his artificial narcissism[59] has alienated him to his reflection in the shimmering Other, and he is condemned to eternal self-identity. And, in effect, Lacan contends that Joyce did not allow for the alterity of the Other sex.[60]

> [Joyce] knew very well that his relations with women were merely his own song. He tried to situate the human being in a way that has the sole merit of differing from what has been asserted about it previously. But in the end, all that, it's the same old story, it's the symptom. What I'm the most inclined to say, is that this is the human dimension proper. That's why I spoke of holy Joyce-the-symptom [*Joyce-le-sinthôme*], like that, in a single trait. [Lacan, 1975b, pp. 23, 26, English translation modified]

This would thus be the impasse of the symptom, neurotic and Joycean alike: that it leaves no room for a certain form of love.

Love in psychoanalytical theory has three dimensions: Imaginary—love invested in the reversible movement of ego-libido (the classical Freudian interplay between identification and object-choice); Symbolic—love as supposition of knowledge (at the heart of transference and thus of the possibility of analysis, although it supports the fiction of the existence of the Other); and finally, *of the Real*—love of absolute difference, the one that makes "jouissance condescend to desire." The "failure to love" ascribed to Joyce would refer to this third kind of love which, Lacan tells us, sometimes comes about at the end of analysis: "love beyond the law," embodied in the desire of the analyst.[61]

If we are to believe in this third kind of love, a love no longer addressed to either the imaginary other or the symbolic Other, a more forward-looking reading of *L'insuccès de l'Unbewußt*[62] *c'est l'amour*—a strictly phonetic one—is: the failure of the unconscious is love. The most evident understanding of this reading is that it is a statement to the effect that the unconscious, although it provides the subject with a means of being-in-language, also locks him up in solitary jouissance and obliterates the possibility of love. Secondly, to pick up on this reading on a more positive level, it is an implication that love can defeat the unconscious.

This second resonance can be deployed in two directions: first, if equivocation is the only weapon against the symptom, then love is the only weapon against the unconscious, and the analytic process must therefore make use of it. Lacan tells us that "love, in the service of psychoanalysis, is the Imaginary taken as a means for the relation of the Real to knowledge to be written." (SXXI, December 18, 1973). In other words, the three forms of love—all partaking in the Imaginary as they involve the other as *support*—must be incarnated in turn by the analyst in a handling of transference aimed at loosening the hold of the symptom.

Second, *L'insuccès de l'Unbewußt c'est l'amour* could also be read as follows: love may challenge the insistence of the jouissance of the One, byproduct of the subjection to the *Un-conscient* (the One-conscious: a lucubration on the master-signifier, the one signifier). To believe in one's unconscious, to be fascinated by it, excludes the possibility of recognizing the other as other. Did Freud not clearly indicate, in his *Civilization and its Discontents* (1930, SE XXI, chap. II), that man organizes his psyche so that it provides him with substitutive satisfactions, built-in compromise formations that bypass the dependency on external reality? Such substitutive or hallucinatory satisfactions protect man against potential suffering coming from external reality, loss of the love object being singled out by Freud as the main cause of pain.[63] The danger is that one may find so much satisfaction in the process that one's only partner ends up being one's symptom. At this point, we need to remember that satisfaction is far from being antinomial to suffering and leaves the subject defenseless in the face of the death drive.

Love, on the contrary, is that which ceases not to write itself, an inscription of contingency that comes to replace castration[64] as what is necessary in order to make do with the impossibility of the sexual relation. This form of love, arising from an acceptance of the sexual nonrelation, is of the order of invention, of a *savoir-faire* that enables one to make do with the impossibility of the Real without being the slave of the unconscious.[65]

NOTES

1. The concept of *semblant* has been introduced by Lacan to designate an imaginarized semantic element, the function of which is to make up for the fact that there is something that cannot be symbolized by the subject: castration in the real. Although Lacan tells us that the signifier itself is of the order of the *semblant* (Lacan 1971a), *semblants par excellence* are the phallus, the Name-of-the-Father and object *a* insofar as these three concepts name the three complementary aspects of the function of exception, a function that organizes the structure of language for the subject by decompleting the Other, the set of signifiers.

2. The phallus is not to be confused with anything anatomic; it is the signifier of the absence of sexual relation, namely of the fact of sexual difference, to be understood as *incommensurability*. By extension, it is the signifier of difference, which introduces the disjunction necessary for there to be *desire*, that between subject and language.

3. Throughout Seminar XX, Lacan elaborates the argument that since the Other of meaning, as place of truth, the Other of the Other, does not exist, the only Other (understood as distinct from the Other of the signifier) is the Other sex. For example: "The Other, in my terminology, can thus only be the Other sex" (p. 40; 39); "There is no Other of the Other" (p. 76; 81); "the partner of the opposite sex remains the Other" (p. 109; 121).

4. The French term is *parlêtre*, a condensation of speaking (*parler*) and being (*être*), and is sometimes used by Lacan in his later teaching; it is broader than the term "subject," which implies subjection to the signifier. *Parlêtre*, on the other hand, in its homophony with *par lettre* (through the letter), designates the human being as branded by language in its materiality rather than in its signifying dimension, that is, *lalangue* as opposed to language.

5. Cf. Lacan 1971a, p. 7 for an explicit linking of the signifier to the universal. Knots, on the other hand, are particular to each subject.

6. *Le* sinthome, SXXIV, November 16, 1976. Most of Lacan's works referenced in this chapter are not available in English and the translations are my own.

7. "'Discourse" is to be understood as a mode of subjective articulation in the social bond and not merely as a linguistic construction. Generally, on the discourses, see Seminar XVII.

8. Cf. Lacan SXX, 1972–73, pp. 79–95.

9. When both are available, the French page number will come first, followed by the English one.

10. As argued by J.-A. Miller in his 1998–1999 course, unpublished.

11. S. Freud, "A Child is Being Beaten" (1919), *SE* XVII.

12. *Le sinthome*, SXXIII, May 11, 1976.

13. After J.-A. Miller (1995).

14. I refer to the hidden structure of the symptom. This bare articulation is usually fleshed out by family romance and other explanatory narratives pervaded with fantasmatic imaginings.

15. Joyce's *sinthome* functions like a neurotic symptom. In the seminar of December 16, 1975, Lacan makes clear that the "*sinthome* is neurotic," and he uses the words *sinthome* and symptom indifferently. Thus the work of Joyce can show us, paradoxically, how a *neurotic* symptom functions.

16. In Lacanian algebra, a and S_1, bearing in mind that they are liable to take on diverse significations, depending on which logical moment of the symptom is considered.

17. Inscribed as s(A) on the graph of desire, in "Subversion of the Subject and the Dialectic of Desire" (*Écrits* 1966, 1977).

18. This is a possible translation for Miller's expression, *une phrase qui se jouit* (Miller 1996), one that brings to light the fact that enjoyment derived from the fantasy is self-serving drive-circulation, albeit clothed, through the very fact of fantasy, in the semblance of love.

19. J. Lacan, SXVIII, May 12, 1971.

20. Generally on the symptom, cf. *Geneva Conference on the Symptom* (Lacan 1975b).

21. My understanding of these operations owes a lot to P.-G. Guéguen's commentary on Lacan's *Position of the Unconscious* (Freudian Field Seminar, London, May 8, 1999).

22. On these different modes of interpretation, see J.-A. Miller's seminal text "Interpretation in Reverse" (1996).

23. J. Lacan, SXXIV, November 16, 1976.

24. Cf. J.-A. Miller, "Le sinthome, un mixte de symptôme et de fantasme" (1987).

25. No doubt, the text harbors countless possibilities of interpretation, but it defeats the imposition of a *narrative* unity. Joyce's writing refuses to be reduced to the signification of the reader, to truth as symptomatic production.

The only "truth" that offers itself is not to be read *between the lines* but *in the lines* of his writing; it is that of his enjoyment of *lalangue*.

26. This seemingly opaque phrase refers to the fact that, while the signifier is imposing the *semblant* of oneness onto the subject through its universalizing function, the letter, that which cannot be ruptured in its unicity, is an infinite collection of irreducible particulars, tireless containers of jouissance (*encaisse-jouissance*) which, unlike signifiers, are disconnected from the ideal of Eros, of unification.

27. The Lacanian condensation of *oublier* (forget) and *publier* (publish) indicates that there must be an evacuation of jouissance for it to circulate, a separation from one's enjoyment then.

28. Cf. J. Lacan, Seminar XI, *op. cit.*, chaps. XIII and XIV.

29. J. Lacan, SXXIII, November 18, 1975.

30. Cf. *Joyce le symptôme* I, p. 27.

31. *Ibid.*, p. 25.

32. January 20, 1976, in Aubert 1987, pp. 58–59.

33. J. Lacan, SXXIII, May 11, 1976.

34. Generally, see J. Lacan, "The Agency of the Letter in the Unconscious" and "On a question preliminary to any possible treatment of psychosis" (*Écrits* 1966, 1977).

35. J. Lacan, *Joyce le symptôme* I, p. 27.

36. Or not writing, as Lacan indicates à propos of the writer's block in "The Subversion of the Subject and the Dialectic of Desire" (*Écrits* 1966, 1977).

37. See the notorious case of President Schreber, Freud's paradigmatic study of paranoid psychosis (*SE* XII), elaborated on the basis of Schreber's memoirs; or of Aimée, one of Lacan's hospital patients, on whom he wrote his doctoral thesis (1975). Some of her writings were published in the surrealist journal *Minotaure*.

38. J. Lacan, Seminar XX (29, 26).

39. Cf. Samuel Beckett et al., *Our Exagmination Round His Factification for Incamination of Work in Progress*, Paris: Shakespeare & Company, 1929.

40. To clarify my use of this trope: the letter is not real, it is *of* the Real. The Real itself is that which is incommensurable with the order of the signifier, while the letter is that which separates while uniting both orders, thus takes a/part: the letter takes the Symbolic and the Real apart—as it is the introduction of language in the Real—while being part of both. Further, one can read it as a/part as well, as the first moment of the letter is also that which inscribes the rim of the drive—object *a* is cut out as such. There is thus a distinction to be drawn between the Real in language and the Real "outside" of it (SXXIII, April 13, 1976).

41. *Encaisse-jouissance*: an expression used by Lacan to describe object *a*. It evokes a till: that which absorbs jouissance through the "holes" of the body, the rims of the drive inscribed by the encounter with the jouissance of the Other. The phrase he uses in "Lituraterre" is *"le godet de la jouissance"*: the recipient of jouissance (1971a, 7).

42. *Rature d'aucune trace qui soit d'avant* (1971a, 7): "a blotting of no trace that would be prior to it."

43. J. Lacan, 1975b, p. 14; 16.

44. On the logic of exception, see J. Lacan, Seminar XX, *op. cit.*, chap. VII.

45. J. Lacan, SXXIII, January 20, 1976.

46. The French here is *truffer*, which refers to the intrusion in a body of a foreign element, for example a body can be *truffé* with bullets, a text can be *truffé* with errors, and so on. Thus something material, real, intrudes in a body—an entity—and ruptures its unity.

47. J. Lacan, SXX, p. 37, 37.

48. "It must be said that the *semblant* denounced by truth is 'quite phallic.'" Seminar XVIII, June 9, 1971.

49. Or turning toward the father, a concept introduced in Seminar XXII, 1974–75 (*RSI*), to replace that of the Name-of-the-Father after Lacan theorizes the pluralization of the names-of-the-father in his Seminar XXI, 1973–74, *Les non-dupes errent*.

50. A word used by Lacan in Seminar XX (p. 127, 139) to refer to language—namely, the Freudian unconscious—as an elaboration of knowledge on *lalangue*.

51. Echoing *St. Thomas d'Aquin*, the French for St. Thomas Aquinas.

52. Here Lacan spells "man" (*l'homme*) *lom*, which echoes his tale of the lamella in *Position of the Unconscious* (Lacan 1966; *Reading Seminar XI*, 1995): namely, man at the stage of his most basic articulation between jouissance and signifier.

53. J. Lacan, *Joyce le symptôme I*, in Aubert (Ed.), 1987, p. 29.

54. On these various logical propositions, used by Lacan in order to approach the Real, see Seminar XX (mainly chap. XI).

55. In Seminar XX (p. 37, 37), Lacan indicates that the writing in *Finnegans Wake* is very close to neurotic slips insofar as they are to be *read*, not for what they *signify* but for the indications as to jouissance that they contain.

56. See the famous Freudian parapraxes: *Signorelli, famillionnaire*. They are taken up by Lacan in the first chapters of his Seminar V. It is the fragmenting of the signifier by means of the letter that allows us to release the truth of the repressed in the neurotic, while in the work of Joyce it is the return of the

phonetic equivocation that prevents the stagnation of the letter in the place of its fixation of jouissance.

57. Joyce does not have an unconscious in the classical sense, as there is no slipping of the signifying chain that would produce equivocation at the level of sense, pointing at the "truth" of a secret jouissance. His unconscious is an unconscious that does not have to do with the repressed; there is no hidden meaning to be deciphered. In that sense, his unconscious is reduced to a means of enjoying *lalangue*.

58. J. Lacan, Seminar XX, *op. cit.*, p. 127, 139.

59. Cf. *Joyce le symptôme II*, 34, where Lacan plays on the resonance between two words: *Escabeau* (stepladder), a word used by Lacan to refer to Joyce's prosthetic narcissism, in which he gets stuck: *hissecroibeau* thus (homophonically resonating with *y's'croit beau*: he thinks he is beautiful).

60. In the Seminar of February 10, 1976, for example.

61. Cf. the closing lines of Seminar XI.

62. *Unbewußt* being the German term for the unconscious.

63. "Against the suffering which may come upon one from human relationships the readiest safeguard is voluntary isolation, keeping oneself aloof from other people." (*Civilization and its Discontents*, SE XXI, p. 265).

64. *Ce qui cesse, de s'écrire*: that which ceases because it writes itself. (SXXIII, November 18, 1975).

65. The other equivocations (*s'aile à mourre*) of Seminar XXIV's title certainly support this new idea of love, no doubt linked to Lacan's rethinking of the Imaginary, but this lies beyond the scope of this article. See also his *Télévision* (1974).

BIBILOGRAPHY

Aubert, J., ed. (1987). *Joyce avec Lacan*. Paris: Navarin.

Feldstein, R., Fink, B., and Jaanus, M. (1995). *Reading Seminar XI*. New York: SUNY Press.

Freud, S. (1911). *Psychoanalytical Notes on an Autobiographical Account of a Case of Paranoia*. SE XII.

——— (1919). *A Child Is Being Beaten*. SE XVII.

——— (1930). *Civilization and Its Discontents*. SE XXI.

Kafka, F. (1988). *The Collected Short Stories*. London: Penguin.

Lacan, J. (1932). *De la psychose paranoïaque dans ses rapports avec la personnalité*. Paris: Editions du Seuil, 1975.

——— (1953–54). *Le Séminaire, Livre I. Les écrits techniques de Freud*. Paris: Editions du Seuil, 1975.

—— (1957–58). *Le Séminaire, Livre V. Les formations de l'inconscient*. Paris: Editions du Seuil, 1998.

—— (1959–60). *Le Séminaire, Livre VII. L'éthique de la psychanalyse*. Paris: Editions du Seuil, 1986.

—— (1966). *Ecrits*. Paris: Editions du Seuil.

—— (1971a). "Lituraterre." In *Littérature* vol. 3.

—— (1971b). *Le Séminaire, Livre XVIII. D'un discours qui ne serait pas du semblant*, unpublished.

—— (1972–73). *Le Séminaire, Livre XVII: L'envers de la psychanalyse*. Paris: Editions du Seuil, 1991.

—— (1972–73). *Le Séminaire, Livre XX. Encore*, trans. Bruce Fink. Paris: Editions du Seuil, 1975; London: Norton, 1998.

—— (1973–74). *Le Séminaire, Livre XXI. Les non-dupes errent*, unpublished.

—— (1974). *Télévision*. Paris: Editions du Seuil.

—— (1974–75). *Le Séminaire, Livre XXII. RSI*, unpublished.

—— (1975a). *Joyce-le-symptôme I & II*. In Aubert, 1987.

—— (1975b). "Conférence à Genève sur le symptôme." In *Le Bloc-Notes de la psychanalyse*, no. 5, 1985, or "Geneva Lecture on the Symptom," trans. Russell Grigg. In *Analysis*, vol. 1, 1989.

—— (1975–76). *Le Séminaire, Livre XXIII. Le sinthome*, unpublished.

—— (1976–77). *Le Séminaire, Livre XXIV. L'Insu-que-sait de l'Une-bévue s'aile à mourre*, unpublished.

—— (1977). *Seminar XI: The Four Fundamental Concepts of Psychoanalysis*, trans. Alan Sheridan. London: Penguin.

Miller, J.-A. (1987). "Le sinthome, un mixte de symptôme et fantasme." In *La Cause Freudienne*, No. 39.

—— (1995). "La disparate." In *Quarto* No. 57, June 1995.

—— (1996). "L'interprétation à l'envers." In *La Cause Freudienne* No. 32, or "Interpretation in Reverse," trans. Véronique Voruz and Bogdan Wolf. In *Psychoanalytical Notebooks*, vol. 2, 1999.

—— (1997–98). *Le Partenaire-Symptôme*, unpublished.

—— (1998–99). *L'expérience du réel dans la cure analytique*, unpublished.

Sheridan, A. (1977). *Ecrits: A Selection*. London: Routledge.

7

In the Wake of Interpretation: "The Letter! The Litter!" or "Where in the Waste is the Wisdom"

Philip Dravers*

> The Other is the refuse dump of the representatives of the representation of this supposition of knowledge, and this is what we call the unconscious in so far as the subject has lost himself in this supposition of knowledge.
> —Jacques Lacan, Seminar IX, Identification

> The letter! The litter! And the soother the bitther.
> —James Joyce, Finnegans Wake

In chapter five of *Finnegans Wake*, the hen Biddie Doran scratches up a letter from where it lies buried in a midden-heap. The letter subsequently becomes an object of mock scholarship, providing the mate-

*I would like to thank Luke Thurston for the opportunity to write this paper and for providing a provisional translaton of *Le sinthome*, from which all quotations derive except where a slightly different inflection seemed appropriate for the use I was making of it. I would also like to thank Véronique Voruz for her invaluable comments and for opening a space for me beyond the encapsulated equivocations of my own enjoyed sense.

rial for countless elaborations as it is drawn up into the hare-brained lucubrations of knowledge. In order not to be drawn up into the flails of this interpretative mill, let us pose the following question: What do such lyrical elaborations have in common with the lucubrations of the unconscious, and thus with what might be referred to as the "dreaming up" of the unconscious itself?[1]

Such a question encourages us to consider the function of interpretation, not merely as a secondary elaboration of a primary text, but as the very process through which the formations of the unconscious proceed. We might refer ourselves here to the way Freud conceives of transference in *The Interpretation of Dreams* as the mechanism that allows the formation of the dream to occur as a push-to-meaning or wanting-to-say in an interpretation that itself wants to be interpreted. Here both the dream and the symptom share the same structure in relation to the signification they suppose, namely the substitution at work in their formation. Indeed, both dream and symptom proceed through an interpretation that elaborates a path passing through the fantasy, which links it, through the opacifications of the sexual, to sense. From this, it might appear that the formations of the unconscious open the way to the pleasures of an endless hermeneutic inquiry. However, if we begin to formulate our question in the light of the later Lacan, where the signifier is both cause and elaboration of jouissance, then such formations must also appear, in a reformulation of what is at stake in transference, as a ciphering in the service of jouissance.

In this way, the "dreaming up" of the unconscious can be considered as an interpretative elaboration that proceeds along its dual axes of meaning and jouissance, and these two dimensions of interpretation, as both signification and ciphering, will be the two axes orienting my article. They will lead us to account for Lacan's distinction between language and *lalangue*, in which the unconscious, though remaining "structured like a language," now appears as a knowledge formed through the delirious elaboration of the signifier, or as Lacan says in *Encore*: "knowledge's hare-brained lucubration about *lalangue*."[2]

But, here a second question poses itself to redouble the first: What if interpretation, based as it is on just such an elaboration of the signifier, itself implies the very structure of delusion? What if all interpretation, that said to be analytic included, proves to be nothing but a delirium, the only effect of which would be the progressive entanglement of the subject in the defiles of the signifier, ineluctably drawn by the lure of truth?

After all, such an equation is drawn by Freud in his paper *Constructions in Analysis*, where he finds himself "unable to resist the seduction of an analogy," namely that between the "delusions of patients" and the "constructions which we build up in the course of analytic treatment."[3] In this paper I will draw out some of the consequences of this remark and ask: In view of the equivalence between interpretation and delusion, how can we free the subject from his delirium, cancel our subscription to the Freudian unconscious, and proceed into the wake of interpretation?

To indicate my direction from the outset, I will say that it is here in a dimension both anterior to elaboration and beyond it that a new form of interpretation emerges to separate the subject from the phantasmagoria of which he has become so fond. This form of interpretation, an "interpretation in reverse," is one that aims to return the subject to the elementary signifiers upon which, in the trauma of his encounter with language, he has had a delirium.[4] Such a definition of interpretation will imply a reappraisal of the value we assign to knowledge in our well-turned phrase, for if it is not identical to the "hare-brained lucubrations" that proliferate from it in the name of a symptomatic truth, then knowledge, far from being based upon the order of the signifier and the signification it supposes, would find itself inscribed in a different register as knowledge in the Real. It is in this way that one can be freed from a raison-d'être resonating with the pathos of the inexistence of being, and that the *sinthome* can emerge as an art of savoir-faire about the knowledge inscribed in *lalangue*.

Lalangue will thus be an indispensable term in accounting for the relation between language and jouissance in the late Lacan. How can we begin to approach it?

THE UNCONSCIOUS, LANGUAGE AND *LALANGUE*

The concept of *lalangue* emerges in Lacan's seminars with a shift in the orientation to the Real, no longer departing from the Other, but from the One with its problematic of jouissance. In this way the structuralist emphasis on language as differential structure in which meaning effects are supported by syntax and grammar, gives way to the concept of *lalangue*, disjunct from the Other and indexed on the One. *Lalangue* answers to the necessity of rethinking language as an "apparatus of jouissance."[5] It thus becomes the precondition for the relation to the Other and the elaboration of language as structure. *Lalangue* subtends the dimension of differential structure—as sound beyond sense and ciphering without signification, for "the signifying inventory of *lalangue* supplies only the cipher of meaning."[6]

Lalangue is where jouissance is deposited and where it is held in reserve;[7] it is the place where the residues of signification accumulate as a kind of alluvium produced in the flow of speech, a *saidimentation* of the dimension of speech in which the signifier reveals itself as "enjoying substance"[8] beyond any meaning its signification may support. With this in mind, and in order to grasp something of the spirit of Lacan's neologism with its willful inmixing of the infantile babbling of *lallation* with the French word for language (*la langue*),[9] we might refer to it, in a modified Joyceanism, as the *ulalluvial* dimension of speech.

One can easily see the importance for the clinic of this concept, especially, for example, in relation to what Lacan calls "*lalangue de famille*," which refers to the way in which jouissance is suspended in the language circulating in the family, an enjoyment located in a particular pattern or practice of speech that conditions the body of the child and inscribes the jouissance that he will later be heir to. *Lalangue* thus emerges as a kind of non-sense language in which the most elementary and enigmatic sense effects can be heard babbling beneath the meaning produced in signification. In this way one could even define *lalangue de famille* as the jabbering in which the "slithy toves" of a free-form familiarity gyre and gimble in the cross currents of the family's most secret enjoyment.[10]

Just how a letter comes to be precipitated from *lalangue* is crucial for the advent of the subject. *Lalangue* is the fluidity of the mother tongue as it flows over the subject, the ululation that through some chance encounter leaves a contingent mark or trace on the body. Or, to be more precise, *this mark leaves a body in its wake*, for the body is produced in this primordial encounter with language. This mark is the trace upon which the letter will form, while its elementary articulation with sound and sense allows for the elaborations of the signifier, upon which will be built the lucubrations of the unconscious linked to sexual reality. It is here that the symptom forms in a pure relation to *lalangue*, and emerges from the debris of a contingent encounter to be caught in the defiles of signification.

It is in this separation of ciphering and signification that the distinction emerges that ruptures the unity of the signifier: that between the signifier and the letter. To parallel this distinction, two versions of the unconscious appear: one that remains indexed on the signifier, the other on the letter. I will provisionally say that if the letter is what of writing has to do with the Real, then the signifier remains bound to the signification that it supposes—a signification which, from a certain perspective that I would like to explore, is nothing but the Freudian unconscious itself!

But this is not the only definition of the unconscious, for as Lacan states in 1975, "the unconscious . . . is Real."[11] This definition of the unconscious is contemporaneous with his seminar on Joyce, but the formulation only comes as part of a dual affirmation, for where "the unconscious is real," the *psyche* appears as "a fiction of." Indeed, while, without the letter to structure its domain, the *psyche* would be nothing but the hot air its etymology implies, there would equally be no subject without the function of phonation to support the dimension of the speaking being and give air to its aspirations of a body. Fiction and the Real and the letter that knots them—what will we make of this? What indeed, in a detour through Joyce, if not an art of savoir-faire, a singular solution and a song.

However, before we can set out on such a journey, we need to take account of a major shift in Lacan's theory, one which will foreground the irreducible character of the symptom as the subject's response to the Real and the impossibility of the sexual relation. Here Lacan's path parallels Freud's, for both began by believing the symptom to be entirely soluble to interpretation while later testifying to its ultimate indissolubility to analysis. Thus, both Lacan and Freud indicate that at its most radical point the symptom is articulated with the Real.

PATHS TO SYMPTOM FORMATION: A POETICS OF THE FREUDIAN CORPUS

This is exactly what Freud indicates as he retraces the logical pathways to symptom formation back from the signification that opens it to analysis to the points of fixation in the unconscious where it begins.

Such points of fixation derive from "purely chance experiences in child-hood . . . [which] leave fixations of the libido behind them,"[12] and these are invariably traumatic encounters retroactively linked to the Real of sexual reality. Indeed, according to Freud, it is only by index-ing itself to these points of fixation that the "libido is lured into the path of regression" and "finally succeeds in forcing its way through to a real satisfaction."[13]

In this way both the symptom and its interpretation emerge in what we could call, following Lacan, "a poetics of the Freudian corpus"[14] linked to the practice of the signifier. Such a poetics, or practice, de-rives its efficiency from the fact that there is something in the body that resonates with the effects of speech, allowing the equivocations sounded out in analysis to strike a chord in the body by passing through points of fixation in the *psyche*. This something is, of course, the drive.

However, these pathways to symptom formation do not simply pass by means of the drive from source to symptom, for Freud finds it nec-essary "to insert a connecting link" between the points of fixation and the formation of the symptom, insisting that fixation can only be lo-cated through the intermediary of fantasy. And since the pathways of interpretation are identical to the formation of a symptom, we can de-duce that the fantasy is also where the drive acquires a semantic form. The symptom thus emerges as the product of a semantic circuit ulti-mately linked to a real point of fixation through fantasy:

> How does this libido find its way to these points of fixation? . . . the li-bido need only withdraw on to the phantasies in order to find the path open to every repressed fixation. . . . The libido's retreat to fantasy is an intermediate stage on the path of the formation of symptoms.[15]

Moreover, as Freud indicates here, the "repressed" points of fixa-tion are ultimately not given to interpretation but can be reached only by *construction*. In this way we can understand why Lacan insists that the fantasy is not to be interpreted but constructed, for while interpre-tation is always based upon a signifying substitution, and thus the struc-ture of repression correlative to the formation of a symptom, construc-tion aims at a logical consistency in the form of object *a*—which is to say nothing less than that "in construction there is a relation to the original repressed."[16] Indeed, it is this emphasis on logical consistency rather than truth that makes construction less delirious than interpretation, for while "truth has the structure of fiction" and is the dimension proper to interpretation, construction aims at a knowledge in the Real. Thus, the symptom, elaborated in the dimension of truth, is linked through fantasy to a knowledge unknown to the subject, a point of nonknowledge upon which all knowledge bears. In this way we can define the symptom, based as it is on the structure of repression, as "a truth . . . which is resisting a knowledge, that is to say a deciphering on the side of jouissance."[17]

FROM SYMPTOM TO *SINTHOME*

For Freud, who chose the path of a recuperative elaboration, this knowledge remained on the side of signification. Thus, while for Freud this residual real of the symptom merely attests to the impossibility of psychoanalysis as it runs aground on the rock of castration and negative therapeutic reaction, for Lacan it takes on a major role in a root and branch revision of his theoretical elaboration.

Indeed, in the later Lacan, when the Name-of-the-Father no longer appears as a necessary and sufficient mechanism for the inclusion of the subject within the social bond, and RSI appear as entirely discrete orders that require a supplementary knotting to secure their relation, it is the symptom that emerges to take on these roles. In this way, through a retroactive revision that accounts for this innovation, the Oedipus itself appears as just such a symptom, providing a supplementary knotting for RSI, with the caveat that "the Oedipus complex is like an Imaginary envelope of the castration complex,"[18] for it is at root this latter that designates the mark of language on the body and installs the drive.

It is thus only through the duplicity of symbol and symptom that the subject finds a place in the link that constitutes the social bond and thus the structure of discourse. How can we figure this forth?

The quotation that annotates the figure of the four discourses (see Figure 7–1) is drawn from "the finding of the letter" and the reception anticipated for it in the opening chapter of *Finnegans Wake*, while the two tetrads are as they appear in the opening session of *Le sinthome*. Thus they both concern the reception of the letter, for the four terms

Figure 7–1. *So This Is Dyoublong!*[19]

of discourse concern nothing but this, and so provide the subject with his most elementary structure of belonging in the social bond, while also demonstrating the use of the symptom in this process. Here, the subject (S/), with its essential link to S_1, is effaced in a movement of articulation as S_1 becomes the signifier that represents him for the Other, that is for all other signifiers (S_2). The duplicity of symbol and symptom appears as that between (S_2) and (a), the irreducible Real of surplus enjoyment produced by, but also intruding into, the realm of symbolization. In an extremely rudimentary but no less valuable reading, these four terms could be seen to figure the relation among the three registers and the fourth term that knots them. Here S_1 would be the unary trait as the essential mark of the Symbolic, the S_2 would be the imaginarization of this trait in a movement of articulation that has been resolved into a meaning, a would be the Real mark of excess produced in this coupling, while the subject would emerge as the place in which the three registers are tied in symptomatic form.[20] It is ultimately the symptom that installs the subject in the social bond, while linking him, through the structure of *père-version*,[21] to what is most particular to him at the level of his enjoyment.

Thus, by passing through the theory of discourse, we are left with the paradox that although the subject's inclusion within the social bond is indexed upon what is most particular to him, he cannot find his place without passing through the Other. Indeed, what is immediately apparent here in the structure of discourse is that the relation between the S_1, the unary trait or elementary signifier(s), and the S_2 or S *d'eux* (the signifiers imposed by the Other) obscures and interrupts the fundamental link between S_1 and a, submitting it to the wild imaginings of interpretative elaboration.[22] In other words, the symptom is produced by an equivocation that passes through the defiles of signification and the "entanglements of the true."[23] This signifying elaboration of S_2 implies, at least here in the discourse of the master (the discourse most frequently associated with the unconscious), an alienating identification of the subject in the order of representation, complete with the supposition of a knowledge in the Other—the source of his subjection. As Jacques-Alain Miller suggests, the construction of the *sinthome* implies that a relation be established between S_1 and *a*, which does not pass via signification, the Other, and fantasy. Such a relation is effected through the construction of the fantasy and a traversal coextensive with its reduction to drive. There is thus a "de-imaginarization of the fantasy" in this process. As Miller explains, the construction of the fantasy occurs "according to the rhythm at which the symptom interprets itself," in an elaboration that enumerates its elementary signifiers and thus opens a space for a radical separation to be performed as a *cut* realized in the analytic act.[24]

Such is "Interpretation in Reverse" as it is realized in an analysis in order to reach its final term, where, as we might say with reference to a comment by Lacan: "fidelity to the formal envelope of the symptom . . . has led us to this limit where it reverses itself in effects of creation."[25] This shift can be summed up quite simply as a shift from signifying alienation in the Other to the ciphering of the One of the symptom reduced to *sinthome*, or more elliptically as that from "Function and Field" to "Fiction and Song."[26] Although this latter implies a theoretical shift, in a certain sense it is also the movement of the analytical experience itself, a movement in a manner of speaking as the subject passes from its subjection in the field of the Other, through an enjoyment sounded in the equivocations of speech, to a writing that ruptures and that once written never stops writing itself. It is this movement that allows the subject's own unique song to emerge as an answer to that which can never be written: the sexual relation.

This shift takes us from Lacan's work on *Hamlet*, in his early seminar on "Desire and its interpretation" where he declares "desire is interpretation itself," to Jacques-Alain Miller's formulation in "Interpretation in Reverse," a paper that explicitly draws its inspiration from Lacan's Seminar on Joyce, that "interpretation is nothing but the unconscious, that interpretation is the unconscious itself."[27]

What is the difference between these two statements: "desire is interpretation itself" and "interpretation is the unconscious itself"? It is that while the former is grounded in the field of representation and fantasy, upon the *want-to-be* of the subject and the concatenation that answers to this lack, the latter concerns the ciphering of the symptom as the mode of enjoyment of the unconscious.[28] Broadly speaking, while the former concerns desire, the latter concerns jouissance.

However, these should not be conceived of as simple alternatives. For although different modes of interpretation are available to the analyst, no mode can disregard the inevitable duplicity of symbol and symptom or ignore that the unconscious is at root the "accomplice of jouissance":[29] thus, "the unconscious interprets, interweaving jouissance and sense in its formations."[30] Indeed, the interpretation of the analyst will always be secondary to that of the unconscious, and if the unconscious "wants to be interpreted" it is not because it is hoping for a change of scenery but because interpretation only further elaborates its mode of jouissance. In fact, interpretation belongs to the same order as what produces a symptom in the first place, for "[t]he deciphering of the symptom is correlative to a jouissance linked to [its] appearance, to the emergence of the signification of this symptom."[31] Thus to interpret at the level of desire, though it may be useful in mobilizing the signifying chain and evoking the subject's lack of being, ultimately runs the risk of returning the subject to "the jouissance incarcerated in *lalangue*."[32]

The reduction of this jouissance and that portion of it that is fixated in signification is, as Lacan declares in his lectures on Joyce, the only means possible for the subject to awaken from its dream;[33] and the impromptu reduction of a dream's *wanting-to-say* is precisely what is at stake in *Finnegans Wake*.

In this way, as our interpretative itinerary unfolds before us, we find ourselves on a trajectory that leads from Lacan's early work on *Hamlet* to his later work on Joyce: Joyce who sought, through a specific mobilization of the letter, to protect himself from the echoes of speech, in an art that forges a new relation to his body by airing the symptom and knotting it with a letter. We thus find ourselves on the verge of a traversal of sorts, and it is one that we will have recourse to call "literary," and even *litter aire*. Indeed, this traversal will bring us to such a pass that we will only be able to proceed by calling into question the very function of representation itself.

FROM THE OTHER TO THE ONE:
HAMLET AND JOYCE

"from tham Let Rise till Hum Lit. Sleep"[34]—Wake!

A long elaboration separates Lacan's work on *Hamlet* from his later work on Joyce. He refers to *Hamlet* in his seminar "Desire and its Inter-pretation" in the context of the development of one of the more com-plex of his early topologies, the graph of desire.[35] It must be stressed that Lacan's use of literature here is merely illustrative, insofar as "the story of *Hamlet* . . . presents a most vivid sense of this topology" in a portrayal that is, however, not taken to be equivalent to clinical structure.[36]

What Lacan emphasizes in his elaboration is that throughout the play Hamlet's desire is sustained at the level of the Other; indeed, ac-cording to Lacan it is this that constitutes "the permanent dimension of Hamlet's drama."[37] Hamlet is "in a certain position of dependence upon the signifier," and it governs his fate.[38] Whether in indecision or in action, indeed, from his earliest inky black musings to the conclud-ing Act, in which he is ready to find in the fall of a sparrow the cipher of his destiny, Hamlet remains constantly suspended on the Other. In this way his drama unfolds "at the hour of the Other . . . the hour of his destruction." Indeed, according to Lacan, "The entire tragedy of Hamlet is constituted in the way it shows us the unrelenting movement of the subject to that hour."[39] This fatal destiny, indexed on the Other, is of the order of repetition compulsion in which we discover a poetics of identification indexed on a truth of desire whose final term is death.

Thus, we can clearly see how the dramatic dimension of *Hamlet* is generated by the fact that its hero is caught up in the itinerary of the signifier and throughout the play remains riveted to the truth that it supposes. As such, Hamlet is "the reverse side of a message that is not his own."[40] He is thus in the position of a signified in relation to a sig-nifier that represents him for the Other. In this way Hamlet, like the neurotic, is alienated in the field of the Other, indexed to a truth trapped in the defiles of signification, and in this way we find uncon-scious knowledge elaborated and sustained in the dimension of an oedipal truth: the truth of Hamlet's desire.

Where can we find the reference for this truth? It is in fantasy, and fantasy is a way of maintaining a relation to the Real through an imaginarization of the object that protects the subject from the drive. Fantasy occupies center stage in the essay on Hamlet. Indeed, desire and interpretation are conceived entirely at the level of the fantasy in Lacan's early seminar, and what is stressed is the phallic signification that is given to the object of fantasy and desire. It is this phallic signification that conceals the subject's fundamental relation to the drive. It thus concerns the alienation of the subject in the very field of desire, and as Lacan declares, "the phallus is our term for the signifier of his alienation in signification."[41]

With this emphasis on the subject of desire in relation to the phallicization of the object in the fantasy, we arrive at what will retrospectively appear as an impasse: at the end of analysis the subject "remains suspended on the Other," for "it is in so far as the measure of the unconscious desire at the end of analysis still remains implicated in this locus of the Other . . . that Freud at the end of his work can mark the castration complex as irreducible, as non-assumable by the subject."[42] These remarks anticipate a reformulation of psychoanalytic theory that opens the way to a traversal of the fantasy, and what Lacan discovers in Joyce is a literary crossing of the fantasy, the littering of identifications that support the fantasy at the level of alienation.

Thus, if one can say, following Freud, that the difference between Hamlet and Oedipus is that Hamlet knows, then the difference between Hamlet and Finnegans Wake is that in the latter there has been a modification in relation to this knowledge. While in Hamlet, our young pretender and uncrowned king always remains heir to the known with "words, words, words," in Joyce, the letters that support its supposition have been littered on the flow of the signifier. Thus, the space for fantasy that sustains literature in its dream is no longer there in Finnegans Wake, for Joyce gives it a blow in the bread-basket, filling in its hollow with huge fistfuls of material.

Indeed, if Hamlet bears out the definition of the symptom as that which "represents the return of truth as such in the failure of a knowledge"[43]—a knowledge unknown to the subject, no longer "complex" as in Freud but indexed on a signifier that represents him for the Other and inscribes the cipher of his destiny—then how can we be sure that the action that brings the denouement of the play is not in fact an acting-out that falls under the aegis of the unconscious? Is it not just the gruesome end to a particularly lurid family romance: "too much in the sun," as Hamlet says? For if we can describe *Hamlet* as a play about a father who "did not know that he was dead,"[44] it is only because his son is a dreamer. It is thus Hamlet who can be caught cooking up leftovers, for, caught up in the imaginary of an all too familiar story, he remains forever in thrall to fixations that he will only ever be air to. He thus never moves beyond the dimension of fantasy and so keeps dreaming a dream that, like all dreams, ciphers in the service of jouissance.

"To die, to sleep;/ To sleep, perchance to dream," ah yes, there's the rub: "Good night sweet prince!" indeed, for Hamlet dies so that his audience can keep on dreaming. Joyce, on the contrary, wanted to wake literature from its dream, "he wanted an end to it," and thus both to put in place—and to be—the very final term of literature:[45]

> But by writing thithaways end to end and turning, turning and end to end hithaways writing and with lines of litters slittering up and louds of latters slettering down, the old semetomyplace and jupetbackagain from tham Let Rise till Hum Lit. Sleep, where in the waste is the wisdom?[46]
> *Wake!*

A LITERARY CROSSING OF THE FANTASY: FROM "A POOR TRAIT OF THE ARTLESS" TO JOYCE-LE-SYMPTÔME

With this littering of the letters that support the lucubrations of the unconscious and its supposition of knowledge, we can discern what we can describe as a *literary* crossing of the fantasy in Joyce's writing. This is not to say that what Joyce performs in his writing is identical to the crossing of the fantasy and the construction of the *sinthome* in analysis, but it will help us to locate its crucial terms, while also allowing us to situate what is particular to Joyce and his writing.

As is well known, and often notoriously so, in his seminar on the *sinthome*, Lacan indicates that Joyce had a psychotic structure. More specifically, Lacan states that because of a failure in the knotting of RSI, in which the imaginary slips away from the other two registers, Joyce's art became for him a way of constructing a supplementary knotting to secure their relation. Only at the end of his Seminar does Lacan isolate what he takes to be evidence of the crucial point at which Joyce's body slips away, namely the episode in *A Portrait of the Artist as a Young*

Man where Stephen is tied up and beaten by his classmates in an argument over poets. Here Joyce seems to describe a sudden libidinal disinvestment of the specular identifications that support the ego. According to Lacan, in this passage Joyce "metaphorizes nothing less than his relation to his body,"[47] which, along with his anger, is divested from him "as easily as a fruit is divested of its soft ripe peel."[48] In this way the imaginary slips its knot, and the body falls away as image.

This clearly preempts a kind of progressive de-imaginarization that occurs in Joyce's writing, one that, in a certain way, parallels what is involved in the crossing of the fantasy. What Lacan is exploring here is that for Joyce the relationship between the body as image and its being as significance—the ego—gives way to something that radically corresponds to the function of writing. Joyce's ego thus becomes his writing. Indeed, if one could say that the limit of the imagination is the body, insofar as the body is staged within fantasy, then Joyce oversteps this limit in the course of his writing, discovering a more fundamental relationship to the body in *lalangue*. In this way one moves from *A Portrait of the Artist*, where Joyce attempts to capture an image of himself in meaning and frame himself in a work of art, through the technical innovations of *Ulysses*, to the radical "unreadability" of *Finnegans Wake*, in which his former work strikes up an echo as just "a poor trait of the artless."[49]

As a landmark along the way, Lacan chooses a single example, the riddle that Stephen Dedalus poses to his class in the second chapter of *Ulysses*. The riddle is a poem:

> *The cock crew*
> *The sky was blue*
> *The bells in heaven*
> *Were striking eleven*
> *'Tis time for this poor soul*
> *To go to heaven.*[50]

It is clear that the very structure of this enunciation derives from the enigma that it poses. It is thus based upon the supposition of a knowledge and the possibility of a deciphering. We could take this enigma to be equivalent to that of the subject as it is supposed in the place of a concealed signification or "latent nomination." Here the subject of this supposition lies within what is elaborated of it in poetic form: the encapsulated equivocations of a sense enjoyed by its allusive subject. In this way the subject appears as a poem, inflated by poetic truth, resisting a deciphering on the side of jouissance. This is precisely what Lacan notes of the riddle, namely the poetic mode of its enunciation that renders it as a "consistent artifact," a kind of portrait in verbal form besides which the answer is "a truly wretched thing": "—The fox burying his grandmother under a hollybush."

As Lacan stresses immediately, "Analysis is just that—the answer to a riddle; an answer which is quite exceptionally stupid": the reduction of the fantasy's most poetic elaborations to its essential term, meaning reduced to the non-sense that supports it, a non-sense in which there is no room to equivocate before one's essential relation to the drive. Of course Lacan's example is merely illustrative, but it does demonstrate something of what he is aiming at when he says that in the course of his writing "Joyce deciphers his own enigma."[51] In the process, Joyce develops a mode of writing that has less to do with "interpretation" than "construction," for it no longer proceeds as an interpretation elaborated in the dimension of a poetic truth, but rather "draws scattered and heterogeneous elements together," if not in a linear causality, then in a practice of sense that, unconstrained by signification,[52] describes the arc of an infinite straight line—a writing returning to itself in the Real.

In this way, Joyce moves from the retrospective meaning-making of A Portrait, to the artistry of Finnegans Wake, which lies precisely in its reduction to the ciphering of unique trait or letter that supports Joyce's relation to language as such. This is the trait that names him and ciphers his identity throughout his work, for the letter, unlike the signifier, can be defined as that which remains identical to itself even in repetition, since it does not represent a subject for, or in the place of, anything else. Indeed, it is precisely because of this that one could argue that Joyce's writing does not belong to the field of representation at all. It is also why Lacan writes Joyce's name "at one stretch," or rather "with a single trait": Joyce-le-symptôme. Lacan's elaboration may seem rather cryptic, but Joyce spells it out in his work: "So why, pray, sign any-thing as long as every word, letter, penstroke, paperspace is a perfect signature of its own?"[53]

We are thus back once again to the relation between the signifier and the letter.

THE LETTER! THE LITTER!

If we define the letter as the material support of the signifier that allows the latter to perform a kind of "quilting" or *capitonage* that secures the subject's relation to language and modifies his relation to jouissance, we can begin to see what is particular to Joyce and his writing. "Quilting" is a metaphor used by Lacan to describe how language is secured by creating anchoring points that stop the subject drifting in the flow of the signifier, and it is through networking these points that language is elaborated as a structure that organizes the distribution of jouissance. At a more elementary level, it refers to the way language secures the relation between what Saussure described as the two fields of sound and ideation, visualized in its unstructured state as two amorphous masses sliding over each other in the following way (Figure 7–2).

From this diagram, we can see how such "quilting points" or *points de capiton* recall the way that horsehair mattresses used to be quilted in France.[54] Quilting is the mechanism that ensures that the material of the mattress, or "stuffing," remains evenly distributed or aired, thus providing the basis for a comfortable sleep. We can locate this quilting point by referring to the most elementary articulation of the graph of desire, which illustrates the flow of signification, and the operation that quilts it in a retroactive movement of articulation.[55]

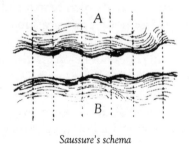

Saussure's schema

Figure 7–2. Diagram from Saussure's *Course in General Linguistics*

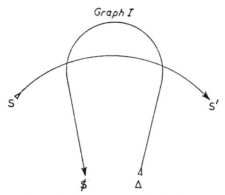

Figure 7–3. The graph of desire

It is just such an operation that organizes the structure of language, and since such effects of quilting are effected by the Name-of-the-Father, it is not surprising that the mechanism tends toward the fabrication of the oedipal bed and the dreaming that it supports.

For Joyce, however, there are no such quilting points effected by the Name-of-the-Father. There is rather a dereliction of the name, which commits him to wander amid the litter of his letters. In this way, Joyce *se fait litière de la lettre*; he makes a litter of the letter, constructing through his art a mechanism that makes up for the lack of a quilting point. He thus "makes a home for himself" in this litter by "making a makeshift bed" out of scraps and out of language.[56]

One could say that the frame improvised for this bed, that which gives it its form, is homophony, something that is revealed in Joyce's writing once what Lacan describes as Joyce's earlier belief in his symptom has been reduced to a pure apparatus. It is this that allows him to move from "bad poet" to supreme artificer. Indeed, in Joyce we find a whole structure of belief reduced to a relation of homophony with that which frames. Lacan refers to a privileged example of this in his seminar: a man goes to see Joyce and finds something perplexing about a particular painting on the wall. "Yes, I know, it's obviously the main square in Cork, I recognise it—but what is that around it?" To which Joyce replied "cork."[57] Thus in *Finnegans Wake*, not only does *Portrait* become *poor trait*, but, in a way that could not be more illustrative of this process, each of the *Apostles* becomes *a post* on a four-poster bed.

THE EPIPHANIES

In this way Joyce constitutes what Lacan refers to as a *suppléance*: "in his art Joyce, in a privileged manner, aimed at the fourth term of the knot."[58] A *suppléance* can be identified by three terms: a limitation of jouissance, something invented by the subject, and an indication or mark of the fault that it remedies. In Joyce's writing, this latter is fulfilled by the epiphanies. The epiphanies are moments of revelation of being, "sudden spiritual manifestation[s]" that, far from demonstrating any proleptic vision, elucidate no meaning and have the value of enigma. Here is one as it is recorded in *Stephen Hero*:

> A young lady was standing on the steps of one of those brown brick houses which seem the very incarnation of Irish paralysis. A young gentleman was leaning on the rusty railings of the area. . . .
> THE YOUNG LADY—(drawling discreetly) . . . Oh, yes . . . I was . . . at the . . . cha . . . pel . . .
> THE YOUNG GENTLEMAN—(inaudibly) . . . I . . . (again inaudibly) . . . I . . .
> THE YOUNG LADY—(softly) . . . Oh . . . but you're . . . ve . . . ry . . . wick . . . ed . . .[59]

If the Imaginary supports the meaningful dimension of communication, it is clear that here something very different is happening. For although this moment lays itself open to a delirium of interpretative elaboration, the crucial point is that the perplexing effect of making-present encapsulated in this encounter has little to do with any meaning one might suppose of it. Indeed, there is a pronounced element of decomposition here, in which the syntax and grammar that modulate the scansion of a phrase become distorted as the words break up into their constituting elements. This distortion gives a hint of what occurs in Joyce's later writing, where words break up only to be reconstituted in startling new forms. Indeed, as Lacan states in his seminar: ". . . in the continuing progress of his art . . . it is hard not to see that a certain relation to language is increasingly imposed on him, to the point where he ends up breaking or dissolving language itself, by decomposing it, going beyond phonetic identity . . ."[60] And he continues, "It is through the intermediary of writing that speech breaks up at the moment of imposing itself as such, in a deformation that is always ambiguous." But how can we begin to understand what it is that functions so specifically in Joyce's writing, and in particular in relation to his final work, *Finnegans Wake?*

HUSH! CAUTION! ECHOLAND!

As the "Outline" of Joyce's work suggests, the ineluctable lure of lucubration looms large in what might be described as the third time of the letter. First there is "*the finding of the letter*," where the letter is introduced; then, in the second time "*the letter is called for*" as it is summoned before a court in its dual aspects of *letter* and *litter*, the evidence of a sexual impropriety. Finally, in the third time, we find "*the interpretation of the letter*," where the first time is returned to in the context of a learned examination that cannot conceal its delusional nature.

As I will demonstrate, *the interweaving of these three times has the function of a certain knotting in Joyce's writing.* For the moment, suffice it to say that if Joyce had been any other writer, these three times might have resolved themselves in the normal run of the mill neurotic way. In other words it would have been possible to reduce them and scan them simply as: *finding, a vocation, in interpretation.* However, things turn out differently for Joyce. Indeed, an analysis of these three times and what Joyce does with them will not only help us to understand what is involved in canceling a subscription to the unconscious, but will also reveal what is at stake in the wake of interpretation, and the elaborations of the final Lacan.

To break our path toward this end, let us lean upon an artful use of analogy. For I wish to suggest that the three times of the letter in Joyce's writing, which can be captured and condensed in the three exclamations "Hush! Caution! Echoland!" sounded in the opening chapter, parallel the three times that for Lacan preside over the constitution of the signifier and the subject it hails in its three moments of inscription, vocalization, and an erasure performed in the service of a supposed sense.[61] These are the three times of the encounter with language.

In the *Hush!* of the first time, a time before speech, a unary trait strikes the body and is inscribed as a mark of jouissance. This trait is then vocalized in a call to a second signifier that holds out not only the lure of semblance, but also the possibility of discharge. This is a moment of "hesitancy" in which *Caution!* oversteps itself in anticipation and a reserve is constituted in the minimal creation of sense via homophony.[62] This minimal elaboration of the initial mark of jouissance is then resolved, or rather fixed in the third time, where a signifier appears fully constituted and what was absolutely identical to itself in the first time is effaced in a movement of difference and articulation. In this way, the neurotic subject is created as a lack, subordinated and alienated in an identification with the signifier it calls to, the master signifier that subsequently represents him in the Other.

Thus, these three times comprise the inscription of a mark that is covered over in a movement of phonation in which the phallus emerges as that which supports desire as a defense against jouissance. Indeed, at a push, we might even, with reference to Lacan's seminar on *Identification*,[63] define the phallus as the column of air formed in the guttural occlusive as the first signifier calls to a second signifier that it in part induces. It is this movement that allows the subject to escape petrifaction beneath a signifier, but at the same time commits him to the field of representation, precipitating him, under the sign of his erasure, into the delirium of interpretation.[64]

In this way, we see that writing functions as the support of speech in a movement that fixes the signifier in its signifying function. However, the letter is not only that which fixes; it is also what irrupts within speech to rupture the semblance of the signifier and the reserve constituted there. In this way the rupturing of a signifier in a modulation and rearticulation of these three times produces a stream of little letters, and in so doing opens the pathways to invention.

Lacan uses a beautiful metaphor to account for the modulation of these three times, one that indicates a capacity for fixation and a potential for change:

> One has a succession of alternations where the signifier comes back to strike, as I might say, the flowing stream with the flails of its mill, its wheel raising up each time something streaming, in order to fall back again, to enrich itself, to complicate itself, without us ever being able at any moment to grasp what dominates in terms of the concrete starting point or of equivocation.[65]

In order to see how Joyce builds this mechanism into every syllable of his writing, let us return to the three times of the letter in Joyce and take up the equivocation sounded in the second time between *letter* and *litter*, where the text offers a handy illustration of something that must ultimately be examined at the level of structure.

A TIME BEYOND POETICS

It is in the "hesitancy" of this second time that a letter quite literally erupts in Joyce's writing. For here, in the fourth chapter of *Finnegans Wake*, where the letter is called before the court, the text famously recalls the orthographic error committed in one of a series of letters forged to entrap Parnell. The author of the orthographic anomaly alluded to, the Irish journalist Piggot, in fact misspelled the very word "hesitancy" as "hesitency" (one letter slipping in in the place of another), in a slanderous attempt to further implicate Parnell in his extramarital affair with Kitty O'Shea.[66] It was thus the residual mark of *a letter* transformed into *a litter* that exposed the deception and, in fact, caused its perpetrator to break down in the witness box when it slipped in again under oath while he was testifying before the Parnell Commission. Here, in a historical precedent for the littering of the letter that Joyce takes up at the level of technique, we see the letter emerging as litter within the "hesitancy" of the second time—something that is echoed throughout *Finnegans Wake* in the stuttering that exposes the sexual misadventure of its hero HCE.

Moreover, that the historical precedent for such a littering of the letter concerns the most important figure in the history of the campaign for home rule in Ireland adds more than a touch of local color to Lacan's witty remark about "Sint'home rule." Indeed, this error seems to prescribe the very mechanism and logic of the *sinthome* constructed by Joyce in his later writing, where a letter slips in, not just as a signifier in the place of another signifier (the mechanism of substitution and displacement elaborated by Lacan in his commentary on *The Purloined Letter*), but within the signifier itself.

Thus, we can see that in Joyce there is a disturbance at the level of language that indicates an absence of a quilting point. Indeed, as Jacques-Alain Miller explains in "Lacan avec Joyce," the whole of Joyce's writing, as symptom, can be considered as a way of compensating for the lack of a quilting point.[67] We can see this in a reformulation of the graph of desire to account for the absence of a resolved

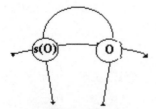 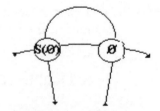

standard lower level
signification

Joyce: inconsistency
and the irruption of a signifier

signification at s(O).[68] Instead of the conventional first layer of the graph, in which a signification is produced through a retroactive movement, something quite different occurs. The Other that Joyce's writing addresses and articulates is not an Other completed by any supposed signification supported by a Real.[69] On the contrary, in Joyce's writing the inconsistency of the Other is laid bare, for the unconscious circuit, without the supposition that usually supports it, has collapsed onto the lower-level circuit that constitutes the message, and thus there is no room for any unconscious desire to equivocate between the two. The Other as not-all thus insists at the primary level, and the signifier, instead of answering for an effect of signification, attests only to the incompleteness of the Other. It is only because his writing has the value of a symptom that Joyce is able to establish a consistency through a knotting involving jouissance and *lalangue*. Indeed, as Jacques-Alain Miller declares: "It is its production which permitted him to re-situate the signification which he was lacking. It is his quilting point. He had to pass through this procedure which allowed him to liberate himself from the menacing echoes of signification, to put them on paper."[70]

As Miller states, although it is not easy to recompose the *Symptombildung* for Joyce, in other words its initial components, a "second time" appears in which it becomes possible to comment upon the mechanisms of his style. In this second time, the echoes produced by a particular word do not simply resonate in a poetic space evoked by the signifier, but rather return within the initial sound of the word itself.[71] Joyce thus writes in retroaction, in a time of *après coup*, for while the resonances produced in the first time could be described as poetic, Joyce con-

tinues "one step beyond" where the whole swarm of potential significations engendered by the S_1 return to be swallowed by it.

> In the moment where the reader must install himself within the text, be
> tranquil and able to dream a little, Joyce enters into the most intimate of
> cogitations, and kills all the literary effects. It is a "*coup du souffle*" of the
> dream, and it sends the reader off again on a different reading, almost
> the opposite of what one calls reading.[72]

In this way, we can say that Joyce writes in a time beyond poetics. How
can we understand what is at stake here?

In Joyce, there is a very particular mode of retroaction in which
the signifier, instead of "exploding with supreme alacrity—towards the
locus of the Other,"[73] returns upon itself, "producing a new symptomatic signifier instead of developing between signifier and signified"; it
is this that constitutes the artifice that makes up for the absence of a
quilting point.[74] Moreover, this fundamental reduction of the dimension of meaning fundamentally alters the relation with the subject-
supposed-to-know. "Joyce mobilises the supposed knowledge of the signifier . . . in an associative way and makes it pass to a level of exposé,
as if he could make all the echoes of the signifier explicit. . . . It is in
this way that he destroys the subject supposed to know and the very
space of interpretation."[75]

In this way, Joyce takes us back "to what there is of the real in the
relation to language, to what is the purest . . . the most elementary articulation of sense and sound"; but if Joyce returns us to the purest relation to language, he also returns us to the most impure, for he "calls
forth the hullabaloo, the jumble of culture, from all languages, from all
knowledges."[76] This occurs in a return to what I have located here as
the second time, for in Joyce there is a *convocation of cultures* that takes
place at a level both anterior to and beyond the delirium of interpretation. Joyce's art suspends the knowledge left over from diverse languages by stirring up the residues of its cultural activity.

Here we can make a connection between the psyche as "fiction of"
and literature as dream, for both concern fantasmatic residues recast in
the equivocations of speech. For the *saidimentation* of the dimension of
speech is also what makes of literature a collection of scraps, a calculated
accumulation or re-hashing of leftovers, or, as Lacan describes it in

"Lituraterre," an "*accomodation des restes*."[77] In this way literature appears as the art of suspending such *saidimentation*, as both the accumulation and recasting of the encapsulated equivocations of enjoyed sense that a culture keeps in reserve. It is only in Joyce's writing that these *saidimentations* appear for what they are, while at the same time having their "false seeming semblance" ruptured by a letter. In this way Joyce deflates the symptom by knocking the air out of its elaboration.

Indeed, if it is possible for Joyce to forge a new relationship to his body in writing it is because for him *lalangue de famille* appears to have been replaced by what we could call *lalangue litteraire*. In other words the *ulalluvial* dimension of Joyce's fundamental relation to language appears to be given in the *saidimentations* of literature; indeed it is with these that he aims at the *"allalluvial*."[78] Moreover, if we impose a rather arbitrary spacing we arrive at another dimension of Joyce's relation to language as *lalangue litter aire*, for in Joyce, the phallic function is supported only by the relic of an ob-literation.

Here I am referring to the phallus as a semblance linked to an effect of phonation. In the absence of a phallic signification resolved in a paternal metaphor by the Name-of-the-Father, the function of the phallus is secured for Joyce only in a constant littering of the letter, as it comes to support multiple effects of phonation.[79] My orthography for this ob-literation derives from Joyce's own in a passage where he refers to the letter as a "relic of pleasant Irish pottery."[80] This equivocation between pottery and poetry is well suited to illustrate how the relic of what we could also refer to as an *ob-litteration* comes to support the function of the phallus and phonation, since it is widely accepted that the letters of both ancient and modern alphabets derive from the markings on the base of pre-dynastic pottery. In this way we see that language comes to be supported by the broken fragments of a radical alterity, the relics of an other's relation to jouissance. Art and language thus always begin with ready-made "Phoenican wakes"[81] as Joyce puts it, but what is at stake in a *savoir-faire* is that it allows the subject to *faire-semblant*, beginning with his symptom—at root the mark of language on the body. *Savoir-faire* is thus an art in which the letter emerges as a receptacle for jouissance once the symptom has been reduced to its formal envelope.

However, as Lacan asks in his seminar, "Is [Joyce's art] a matter of breaking free from the verbal parasite, or rather, of being invaded by its phonemic qualities, by the polyphony of speech?"[82]

WHO AILS? A SINGULAR SOLUTION AND A SONG

Following Lacan, we might suggest that Joyce sought to install the paternal function, a mechanism with which to effectively organize his relation to jouissance by seeking a Name-of-the-Father in his relation to literature. Although such a function is never realized in Joyce, traces of the attempt are legible throughout his work, not least, for example, in the relation between Stephen and Bloom in *Ulysses*, or even in Stephen's extended discourse on *Hamlet*, Ann Hathaway, and William Shakespeare in chapter ten of the same work. Instead, in Joyce, an effective functioning of the Name-of-the-Father is replaced by a *dereliction of the name* that becomes the very principle of his writing, demonstrating that "one can do without the Name-of-the-Father as long as one makes use of it."[83] Indeed, this might be one definition of the *sinthome*. Thus, Joyce makes himself at home in the letter in a constant littering of the Name-of-the-Father, sounding out the diverse knowledges of the signifier while writing in a time beyond poetics, littering the letter in the very space of interpretation. In so doing, Joyce reveals the symptom as a pure relation to *lalangue* in a dimension both anterior to and beyond the fixations of language. Now that we have the definition of the way Joyce's writing functions, let us test it out in a reading.

In *Joyce-le-symptôme*, Lacan selects a single example of Joyce's writing: "Who ails tongue coddeau aspace of dumbillsilly."[84] As Lacan points out, this writing, supported by the rhythm and sonorities of *lalanglaise*, offers itself to the scansion of another tongue thus: "*ou est ton cadeau espèce d'imbécile?*" (where is your gift, you idiot?).[85] It is Lacan's example of how Joyce uses the letter to support a number of different phonetic effects. Also implicit here is the fact that one ails from the gift of language, for it is the initial encounter with language that constitutes the essential trauma for the speaking being and renders the human animal sick.[86] However, Lacan does not mention any other phonetic effects supported by this sentence.

"Who ails tongue coddeau" gathers its morphology from the encapsulated equivocations of *lalanglaise*, from Macbeth's encounter with the Weird Sisters who hail him three times in the prophecy that emerges from the babble of their speech: "*All hail, hail Macbeth, Thane of Cawdor!*" (I. iii. 49).[87] More precisely, it relates to how this event and its consequences are recorded in Macbeth's letter to his wife, as he recounts his reception of "missives" from the King, *"who all-hail'd me 'Thane of Cawdor'"* (I.v.7). The line thus concerns a letter between lovers in *lalangue litteraire*, a letter that, coupled with the "more than mortal knowledge" supposed of the sisters, inscribes a fatal destiny. By the end of the scene Macbeth's partner and accomplice of jouissance has clearly been taken up in the delirium of interpretation, provoked by a letter whose blemish she later finds she cannot remove:

> by the all-hail hereafter!
> Thy letters have transported me beyond
> This ignorant present, and I feel now
> The future in the instant.
> (I. v. 56–59)

But before we succumb to the wild imaginings of this ill-starred elaboration, let us backtrack a little and ask: What are the witches doing in the scenes in which they appear? They are making a body out of scraps and out of language.[88]

Returning to the context from which the sentence is drawn we discover more resonances still, for example, those that follow from the bawdy pun on *coddeau* (scrotum-water). If we look at the context from which this phrase is drawn, we discover that "Who ails tongue coddeau" is a response of the women, "the duncledames," to the men who ask "Elsekiss thou may, mean Kerry Piggy," which can be scanned variously in French as *Est-ce que tu m'aime* (do you love me), *Est-ce-que tu me manquerais* (would I miss you) and also *Et ce qui s'omet* (and that which is forgotten, or missing).

Moreover, the paragraph is an echo of the finding of the letter by the hen Biddy Doran, while an echo babbling at the back of the words tells the story of William Shakespeare *"dumbill"* and Ann Hathaway's courting, betrothal, and marriage, complete with the rapaciousness of Ann (hen) in relation to Bill's sexual substance (a crucial component of Stephen Dedalus's interpretation of *Hamlet* in *Ulysses*):

Menn have thawed, clerks have surssurhummed, the blond has sought of the brune: Elsekiss thou may, mean Kerry piggy?: and the duncledames have countered with the hellish fellows: Who ails tongue coddeau, aspace of dumbillsilly?[89]

Here the name of William Shakespeare, broken up and littered in the writing, is supported in *lalangue* by various phonetic effects playing rhythmically behind the words, some of which intertwine with his wife's name:

> Well may they wilt, marry, and profusedly blush, betroth . . . Lave a whale a while in a whillbarrow . . . to have fins and flippers that shimmy and shake.

The marriage is finally consummated on a makeshift bed, in a littering supported by *lalangue*:

> . . . Tim Timmycan timped hir, tampting Tam. Fleppety! Flippety! Fleapow! Hop![90]

No doubt it is difficult here not to fall into the delirium of interpretation; however, it is important to register the peculiarities of Joyce's style, and to demonstrate the artistry at work in his use of *lalangue*. It is above all the sonorities and the ciphering of *lalangue* that must be emphasized over and above any meaning effects that the text may—one might say to infinity—support:

> If reading [Joyce] is fascinating [it is because] this jouissance is the only thing that we can grasp in the text. This is the symptom, the symptom in so far as nothing ties it to what makes up *lalangue* itself, to that with which he supports this warp and woof, this interweaving of earth and air. . . . The symptom is purely what is conditioned by *lalangue*, but in a certain way, Joyce brings it to the power of language, without, for all that, anything of it being analysable.[91]

Indeed, it is in drawing the Real of the letter and the knowledge it inscribes up into the phonetic power of language that allows Joyce to treat the Real of jouissance, without any effective quilting to tie language to *lalangue* in symptomatic points of fixation. He thus gives *air to his symptom*, to that which constitutes his way of making up for the lack of the sexual relation as his own unique song.[92] For if the symptom is an event of the body, then Joyce certainly makes it sing. In his own words, it is a *songtom*,[93] the body's song, a body resonating with the effects of speech. He thus illustrates Lacan's untranslatable definition of the symptom as "un événement de corps, lié à ce que: 'l'on l'a, *l'on l'a de l'air, l'on l'aire, de l'on l'a'.*"[94] Here, Lacan is playing upon a having that is only the semblance of having (the phallus), while sounding out a score that supports the being of the body and the symptom whose notation knots it, and it is precisely here that the function of Joyce's art as *lalangue litter aire* takes on its value as a support for the phallic function.

How is this *songtom* to be sung? Perhaps the delirium of reading Joyce has truly set in, though to make sense of Joyce one often has to hear a coherent set of vocables and then sweep up from the phonemes that follow the litter of letters that have fallen from the missing morphemes,[95] but is it not also possible to read the following piece of advice murmuring within the lover's question—*Elsekiss thou may mean Kerry Piggy*: "Ask St. Tommy Aquinas!" As might be expected here, as in countless other occasions through *Finnegans Wake*, it is the paternal name itself that has been obliterated and littered upon the flood that formed it, indicating a dereliction of the name in Joyce in which autograph becomes a pure orthography, legible throughout, from *aperlogue* to *epellogue*, as "otherwise spelled, changeably meaning vocable scriptsigns."[96] It is this that demonstrates the *intransjouissance* of Joyce in relation to the enjoyment inscribed in the ciphering of his symptom: hence *Joyce-le-symptôme*, Joyce who made a litter out of the letter and who, by courting the University as partner of his jouissance, sought in his own unique way to become the "all-hail hereafter."

TO CONCLUDE: WITH LACK AND JOY

"The letter! The litter! and the soother the bitther."

Such is the mechanism of Joyce's writing, as it is constructed in the course of his work. For it is in the littering of the letter that Joyce supports the function of the name. Moreover, it is in the complex interweaving of what I have called, following Joyce, "the three times of the letter" that a supplementary knotting of RSI is secured through a *savoir-faire* concerning *lalangue*. Indeed, in Joyce there is what might be called a *transubstangeability* of the word, in which symbol and symptom are knotted around the floculations of the signifying material. Here it is the voice that gives consistency to the chord and the letter that knots it. Thus Joyce crosses the literary fantasy and secures a relation to his body out of scraps and out of language—out of the litter of knowledges inscribed in *lalangue litteraire*. In this way, a path opens to a new conception of the clinic that allows us to conceive of the possibility of canceling our subscription to the Freudian unconscious by littering the identifications that support it as an elaboration of knowledge.

How can we understand this sub-scription? We can understand it, through an effect of the signifier, as a signification produced as a supposed knowledge. This can be seen in the formula for transference inscribed in Lacan's *Proposition*:[97]

$$\frac{S \longrightarrow Sq}{s(S_1, S_2 \ldots Sn)}$$

From this we can deduce that to cancel one's subscription to the unconscious, one has to produce the signifiers below the bar above it, in a process of construction that operates according to the rhythm at which the symptom interprets itself.[98] As we have seen with reference to Joyce, this is tantamount to the deciphering of an enigma in which a poetics is reduced to the apparatus that supports it. For Joyce, who writes in a time beyond poetics, this occurs through a specific mode of retroaction in which the letter is littered in the very space of interpretation, interrupting and ob-literating what Lacan, in relation to the above formula, describes as "the supposing span of the . . . Signifier."[99] In analysis what is crucial is that the object *a* comes to replace the signification of the subject-supposed-to-know. This returns the idealizing dimension of transference, which proceeds at the level of identification and demand, to that of the drive. It is the latter that constitutes the properly analytic dimension of transference and it is this that Joyce's art forestalls by anticipating its final term. Thus, at the end of a long elaboration, we find ourselves returning to the distinction from which we began: between ciphering and signification. For it is only through this dimension of transference that one can claim that it is not to a signification but to the cipher that one returns at the end of an analysis.

The mechanism that Lacan invented to account for this end, the moment to conclude with lack and joy, is the *pass*. What it concerns is a canceling of one's subscription to the unconscious in the precipitation of little letters from *lalangue* and the inscription of a knowledge in the Real. Thus, the identifications that have hitherto supported the transference as a *want-to-be* supported by a lack, are littered on the flow of the signifying chain, and the analyst, as nothing more than the place in which this littering accumulates in the guise of a supposed knowledge, becomes a piece of waste and is dropped. It is this move from transference to *translitteration* that allows a new modality of libidinal satisfaction to appear in a modification of the subject's relation to *lalangue* and a Real deposited in the exclusion of sense. Such is the *sinthome*, constructed in the course of an analysis as an *art of savoir-faire*: "a knowledge of the knot and a tying it up with artifice." Thus, in the wake of interpretation we are led beyond the fantasy to an art of *savoir-faire* concerning a knowledge inscribed in *lalangue*, an art that is also a praxis supported by the inscription of the Real.

NOTES

1. I have borrowed this phrase from a translation proposed by Luke Thurston for "élucubration de l'inconscient," of *Le sinthome* (April 13, 1976). This dreaming up seems to illustrate perfectly the relationship between the unconscious and its formations, and that the unconscious proceeds only by interpretation.

2. J. Lacan, Seminar XX: *Encore*, trans. B. Fink, London: Norton, 1998, p. 139 (translation modified).

3. S. Freud, "Constructions in Analysis" (1937) SE XXIII, p. 226.

4. I take my lead here from Jacques-Alain Miller, "Interpretation in Reverse," *Psychoanalytical Notebooks of the London Circle*, 2 (1999), pp. 9–16.

5. J. Lacan, *Encore*, *op. cit.*, p. 55.

6. J. Lacan, *Television*, trans. Hollier, Krauss & Michelson, London: Norton, 1990, p. 9; glossed by Jacques-Alain Miller in the margin as, "*Lalangue* is the precondition of meaning."

7. "*Lalangue où la jouissance fait dépôt*," J. Lacan, *La Troisième* (internet text), p. 9.

8. J. Lacan, *Encore*, *op. cit.*, p. 23.

9. J. Lacan, "Geneva lecture on the symptom," *Analysis*, 1 (1989), p. 14.

10. My allusion here is, of course, to the privileged example of the so-called non-sense poetry of Lewis Carroll, *Jabberwocky*. Lacan refers to Lewis Carroll as an important precursor to Joyce for his use of puns and *portmanteau* words: "Joyce le symptôme I," *Joyce avec Lacan*, p. 25.

11. From the Preface to the English language edition of *The Four Fundamental Concepts of Psychoanalysis*, trans. A. Sheridan, London: Penguin, 1977.

12. S. Freud, *Introductory Lectures* (1917), SE XVI, p. 361.

13. *Ibid.*, pp. 359–361.

14. J. Lacan, "The Function and the Field of Speech and Language" (1953), *Écrits: A Selection*, trans. A. Sheridan, London: Routledge, 1977, p. 102.

15. S. Freud, *Introductory Lectures on Psycho-analysis*, *op. cit.*, pp. 373–374.

16. J.-A. Miller, "E=UKW: Towards the 9th International Encounter of the Freudian Field," *Analysis*, 6 (1995), p. 20.

17. J.-A. Miller, "Le sinthome, un mixte de symptôme et fantasme," *La Cause Freudienne*, No. 39 (1998), p. 16.

18. J.-A. Miller, "The Seminar of Barcelona," *Psychoanalytical Notebooks of the London Circle* 1 (1998), pp. 59–60.

19. J. Joyce, *Finnegans Wake* (London: Penguin, 1992, p. 13); J. Lacan, *Le sinthome* (SXXIII, November 18, 1975).

20. However, it is clear that this is only a very rough guide, as the three registers are implicated in each of the four terms, the recognition of which heralds the emergence of the more complex topology of knots.

21. Lacan's pun (on *perversion*) could be translated as "a turning toward the father," where the father as agent of the inclusion of the subject in the social bond no longer conceals the duplicity of symbol and symptom with an ideal.

22. J.-A. Miller, "Le sinthome: un mixte de symptôme et fantasme," *op. cit.*, pp. 7–17.

23. J. Lacan, *Le sinthome*, which also has a fractious quality to it brought in by the imaginary dimensions of S_2, indicated by the connotations of "tangle" in Luke Thurston's translation of *embrouille*.

24. J.-A. Miller, "Le sinthome: un mixte de symptôme et fantasme," *op. cit.*, p. 15. This cut that separates S_1 from S_2 could be figured with reference to the bottom line of the discourse of the analyst as $S_2 \mathbin{/\!/} S_1$, which in *Television* Miller glosses as "knowledge . . . without a master." Cf. J. Lacan, *Television*, *op. cit.*, p. 14.

25. J. Lacan, *Écrits* (Paris: Seuil, 1966, p. 66) (my translation).

26. Here the English cannot quite capture the resonance sounded in the French, where the theoretical movement is from Lacan's first Rome Report, "*Fonction et Champ*" to "*L'Etourdit*" where the phrase is reformulated as "*fiction et chant*," *Scilicet* 4 (1973), p. 18.

27. J.-A. Miller, "Interpretation in Reverse," *Psychoanalytical Notebooks of the London Circle*, 2 (1999), p. 9.

28. The allusion here is to Lacan's definition of the symptom in *R.S.I.* as "The way in which everyone enjoys their unconscious in so far as it is the unconscious which determines it." However, my own reference is Jacques-Alain Miller, "Le sinthome, un mixte de symptôme et fantasme," *op. cit.*, p. 17. Miller specifies that if the symptom is a mode of jouissance of the unconscious, it is precisely as a mode of jouissance of S_1.

29. J.-A. Miller, "La disparate," *Quarto* No. 57, June 1995.

30. P.-G. Guéguen, "Discretion of the Analyst in the Post-interpretative Era," *Psychoanalytical Notebooks of the London Circle*, 2 (1999), p. 22.

31. M.-H. Brousse, "Hysteria and Sinthome," *Psychoanalytical Notebooks of the London Circle*, 1 (1998), p. 68.

32. P.-G. Guéguen, *op. cit.*, p. 24.

33. J. Lacan, "Joyce-le-symptôme II," *Joyce avec Lacan*, ed. J. Aubert, Paris: Navarin, 1987, p. 36.

34. James Joyce, *Finnegans Wake*, op. cit., p. 114. That this phrase ciphers the name "Hamlet," only occurred to me after hearing a reading of the *Wake* by my friend Barry Collins.

35. The discussion of Hamlet in this Seminar is published as "Desire and the Interpretation of Desire in Hamlet," *Literature and Psychoanalysis*, ed. S. Felman, London: John Hopkins University Press, 1982, pp. 11–52.

36. *Ibid.*, p. 11.

37. *Ibid.*, p. 13.

38. *Ibid.*, p. 11.

39. *Ibid.*, pp. 17, 25. In French *l'heure* (the hour) is homophonic with *leur* (their)—thus Hamlet's attempt to find his own sense of time; to *"lire l'heure"* only precipitates him in a field of identification along the signifiers of the Other's demand.

40. J. Lacan, "Desire and the Interpretation of Desire in Hamlet," *op. cit.*, p. 12.

41. *Ibid.*, p. 28.

42. J. Lacan, Seminar IX, *Identification*, session of March 21, 1962, unpublished.

43. J. Lacan, *Écrits*, *op. cit.*, p. 234 (my translation).

44. The allusion here is to the "Dream of the Dead Father" in *The Interpretation of Dreams*.

45. J. Lacan, "Joyce-le-symptôme II," *Joyce avec Lacan*, *op. cit.*, p. 36.

46. J. Joyce, *Finnegans Wake*, op. cit., p. 114.

47. J. Lacan, *Le sinthome* (SXXIII), May 11, 1976.

48. J. Joyce, *A Portrait of the Artist as a Young Man*, London: Paladin, 1988, p. 84.

49. J. Joyce, *Finnegans Wake, op. cit.*, p. 114.

50. J. Joyce, *Ulysses*, London: Penguin, 1986, p. 22.

51. J. Lacan, *Le sinthome* (SXXIII), January 13, 1976.

52. An allusion to the definition Pierres-Gilles Guéguen gives to "construction" in "The Discretion of the Analyst in the Post-Interpretative Era": "Construction, unlike interpretation, draws scattered and heterogeneous elements together in a linear causality . . . [in] a discretionary practice of sense (but not of signification)." *Op. cit.*, p. 26.

53. J. Joyce, *Finnegans Wake, op. cit.*, p. 115.

54. I thank Professor Malcolm Bowie for this choice fragment retained after a flow of speech.

55. J. Lacan, *Écrits: A Selection, op. cit.*, p. 303.

56. These three significations are available in the French expression *se fait litière de la lettre*, which to my ear resonate in Lacan's text: to litter the letter, to make a home in the letter, and to make a makeshift bed in the letter.

57. J. Lacan, *Le sinthome* (SXXIII), May 11, 1976. This also demonstrates the reduction of a proper name to a common noun; however I will not draw this out further here.

58. J. Lacan, *Le sinthome* (SXXIII), December 9, 1975.

59. J. Joyce, *Stephen Hero*, London: Cape, 1969, p. 188.

60. J. Lacan, *Le sinthome* (SXXIII), February 17, 1976.

61. J. Lacan, *Identification* (SIX), unpublished.

62. This is illustrated in the French through an equivocation between *son* (sound) and *sens* (meaning). The word "hesitancy" has been placed in quotation marks for reasons that will soon become apparent, but it is also a reference to Lacan's description of logical time in *Écrits*.

63. See the session of January 24, 1962.

64. J. Lacan, *Le sinthome* (SXXIII), November 11, 1975.

65. *L'Identification* (SIX), January 24, 1962 (my translation). It is not surprising that, when there is too much jouissance *saidimented* in the flow of the signifier, this wheel gets stuck in one way or another. Perhaps the best literary example of the tragic effects that ensue when this wheel gets caught up in a compulsion to repeat is Ibsen's play *Rosmersholm*, and in the analysis Freud gives it in a discussion of "Some Character Types met with in Psychoanalytic Work" (1916), SE XIV, pp. 326–332. For in this play two lives are claimed by just such a wheel and its repetition of an oedipal trauma.

66. I have drawn this anecdote from Anthony Burgess's excellent introduction to the Faber edition of *A Shorter Finnegans Wake*, p. 12.

67. J.-A. Miller, "Lacan avec Joyce," *La Cause Freudienne*, No. 38 (1998), p. 13.

68. *Ibid.*, p. 17.

69. Such is the normal "symptomatic" dimension of the quilting that we would arrive at if we were to follow both the lower circuit and the second level of unconscious elaboration that the graph provides in its completed form (*Écrits: A Selection*, p. 315). For the logic that supports this elaboration see J.-A. Miller, "The Seminar of Barcelona," *The Notebooks of the London Circle* 1 (1998), p. 21.

70. *Ibid.*, p. 18.

71. *Ibid.*, p. 14.

72. *Ibid.*

73. J. Lacan, "The Function and the Field of Speech and Language," *op. cit.*, p. 61.

74. J.-A. Miller, "Lacan avec Joyce," *op. cit.*, p. 15.

75. *Ibid.*

76. *Ibid.*, p. 9.

77. J. Lacan, "Lituraterre," *Litterature* 3 (1971), p. 3.

78. J. Joyce, *Finnegans Wake*, *op. cit.*, p. 213.

79. "Tip": for a further elaboration of this point, see V. Voruz, this volume, "Acephalic Litter as a Phallic Letter," pp. 125–127.

80. J. Joyce, *Finnegans Wake*, *op. cit.*, p. 111.

81. *Ibid.*, p. 608.

82. J. Lacan, *Le sinthome* (SXXIII), February 17, 1976.

83. *Ibid.*, April 13, 1976.

84. J. Joyce, *Finnegans Wake*, *op. cit.*, p. 15.

85. J. Lacan, "Joyce-le-symptôme," *op. cit.*, p. 26.

86. This is emphasized by Jacques-Alain Miller in "Lacan avec Joyce," *op. cit.*, p. 11.

87. W. Shakespeare, *Macbeth*, ed. K. Muir, London: Routledge, 1964.

88. This represents the ghoulish counterpoint to the impotence of Macbeth and the "unsex me here" speech of Lady Macbeth. It is also interesting that Harry Blamires in *The Bloomsday Book* refers to the role of the Weird Sisters in Macbeth to account for the peculiarities of the "Circe" episode in *Ulysses* because they prefigure the question of how "disorder and disintegration in the system of Nature may be *concretised and bodied in dramatic form*" (my emphasis). Cf. H. Blamires, *The Bloomsday Book*, London: Routledge, 1966, p. 152.

89. J. Joyce, *Finnegans Wake*, *op. cit.*, p. 15.

90. *Ibid.*; it does not take too much imagination to hear in this line the tip-tapping of a typewriter, or to speculate that the Tim in question is the eponymous hero of the original American Irish ballad from which Joyce drew the title of his work.

91. J. Lacan, "Joyce-le-symptôme," *op. cit.*, p. 27.

92. An allusion to the "Geneva lecture on the symptom," where Lacan describes Joyce's relation with women as "his own unique song," *Analysis* 1 (1989), p. 27.

93. This word comes just before "who ails tongue coddeau," which is of course also "who ails from the gift of speech."

94. J. Lacan, "Joyce-le-symptôme," *op. cit.*, p. 27.

95. See J. Joyce, *Finnegans Wake, op. cit.*, p. 112.

96. *Ibid.*, p. 118. The function of the Name-of-the-Father is to fix the signifier to the signified, sound and sense through the materiality of a letter.

97. J. Lacan, "The Proposition of the 9th of October 1967," trans. R. Grigg, *Analysis* 6 (1995), p. 5.

98. See J.-A. Miller "Le sinthome, un mixte de symptôme et fantasme," *op. cit.*, p. 15.

99. J. Lacan, "The Proposition of the 9th of October 1967," *op. cit.*

Notes on Contributors

Frédéric Declercaq is a psychoanalyst of Freudian-Lacanian orientation. He is a Lecturer at the University of Ghent and the author of *Het Reële bij Lacan*. He can be contacted at *frederic.declercq @ping.be*.

Philip Dravers has a Ph.D. from the University of Oxford in Literature and Psychoanalysis, in which he explores the relation between fiction and the real in the theory of Jacques Lacan. His publications include "To Poe Logically Speaking" in *Topologically Speaking*, ed. E. Ragland and D. Milovanovic (Other Press, forthcoming); and "Making-do with Jouissance" in *Psychoanalytical Notebooks of the London Circle* 4 (2000). He can be contacted at *philipravers@compuserve.com*.

Bracha Lichtenberg Ettinger is a Visiting Professor in Psychoanalysis and Aesthetics at Leeds University, England.

Roberto Harari is a psychoanalyst in private practice in Buenos Aires. In 1977, he founded the psychoanalytic group Mayeutica, and he is the author of many books and articles, including most recently *Fantasme: fin de l'analyse* (Erës, 1999) and *How James Joyce Made His Name* (Other Press, 2002).

Dominiek Hoens is a Research Assistant at the Fund for Scentific Research in Flanders, Belgium. He has a Ph.D. from the University of Ghent, Department of Philosophy on the notion of affect in psychoanalytic theory. He can be contacted at *Dominiek.Hoens@rug.ac.be*.

Dany Nobus is a Lecturer in Psychology and Psychoanalytic Studies at Brunel University in West London. He is the author of *Jacques Lacan and the Freudian Practice of Psychoanalysis* (London and Philadelphia: Routledge, 2000), and editor of *Key Concepts of Lacanian Psychoanalysis* (New York: Other Press, 1999), along with numerous papers on the theory, practice, and history of psychoanalysis.

Ed Pluth has a Ph.D. from Duquesne University on Lacan's theory of the subject.

Luke Thurston is a Research Fellow in Languages and Literature at Robinson College, Cambridge. He is the translator of works by Jean Laplanche, André Green, and Roberto Harari, and has written many articles on psychoanalysis, literature, and critical theory. He is the author of *Impossible Joyce: Psychoanalysis and Modernism* (Cambridge University Press, forthcoming).

Paul Verhaeghe is a Professor at the University of Ghent, a member of the European School of Psychoanalysis, and a practicing psychoanalyst. His publications include *Love in a Time of Loneliness* (Other Press, 1999) and *Does the Woman Exist?* (Other Press, 1999).

Veronique Voruz is a Lecturer in Law at the University of Leicester, England. Her publications include "Psychosis and the Law: Legal Responsibility and Law of Symbolisation," *International Journal for the Semiotics of Law*, vol. 13–2 (2000), and "The Topology of the Subject of Law: The Nullibiquity of the Fictional Fifth" in *Topologically Speaking*, ed. E. Ragland and D. Milovanovic (Other Press, forthcoming). She is currently completing a Ph.D. at the University of London in Law and Psychoanalysis, taking psychoanalytic accounts of the law beyond the classical oedipal reading.

Index